LET THE GOOD TIMES ROLL

KENNEY JONES

THE AUTOBIOGRAPHY

BLINK

bringing you closer

Published by Blink Publishing
2.25, The Plaza,
535 Kings Road,
Chelsea Harbour,
London, SW10 0SZ

www.blinkpublishing.co.uk

facebook.com/blinkpublishing
twitter.com/blinkpublishing

Hardback – 978-1-911-600-09-1
Trade paperback – 978-1-911-600-67-1
Ebook – 978-1-911-600-68-8

A CIP catalogue of this book is available from the British Library.

Typeset by seagulls.net
Printed and bound by Clays Ltd, St. Ives Plc

1 3 5 7 9 10 8 6 4 2

Blink Publishing is an imprint of the Bonnier Publishing Group
www.bonnierpublishing.co.uk

To Jayne, for your love and support.

CONTENTS

CHAPTER 1

A RIGHT LITTLE HERBERT

'Nah. Never heard of him.'

That would have been the response to anyone in the 1950s walking down Havering Street in London's East End, where I grew up, asking where Kenny Jones lived. Back then I was known to my mates and everyone on the street as Kenny Ward.

I was the only child of Violet Elizabeth Jones and Samuel Thomas Jones, born on 16 September 1948. We lived at number 34 with my mum's parents, Jane and William Ward. That terraced house in Stepney had been the Ward family home for, well it seemed like forever, and although Kenneth Thomas Jones was my real name, no one ever thought of me as that. My grandparents were part of the furniture of Stepney, and very nearly ended up as part of the street itself.

My grandfather used to tell the story of a bomb dropping at the bottom of Havering Street during the Blitz, down by Commercial Road, while he and my nan were in bed. I don't know why there wasn't an air-raid siren, but obviously they woke up with the explosion. It was a very near miss. Not only did all the windows of their house shatter, but the blast was sufficiently strong also to blow in the bedroom window frame, which ended up hanging around their necks as they were sitting up, probably thinking this was it for them.

I saw something similar happen many years later to a very angry man in a hotel lobby in Honolulu, although with a picture rather than window frame. I thought it was a laugh; I'm sure my grandparents didn't find their experience at all amusing.

Our house in Havering Street was the centre of the whole family, the Joneses and the Wards. A happy home, full of love and affection. My dad's parents also lived close by, across the road, near Arbour Square nick, where I made my first public appearance. I'll get on to that in a moment.

Mum always told me that it was Nan and Granddad who brought me up because she was too ill. She was always telling me she was ill, and while it's true she didn't always keep the best of health, she lived to the age of 89. I think I'm right in saying that she was among the first women in England to undergo a pioneering colostomy procedure, a big deal back then. I was 16 at the time, and remember visiting her in hospital, telling her all about my hit record that had just come out. She was in the London Jewish Hospital, on Stepney Green, not that we are Jewish, but that, of course, didn't matter at all; people of all religions were cared for there. Mum was very well looked after.

The hospital had originally been built to help meet the needs of the large Jewish community who were very much part of the fabric of the East End, many working in the garment industry, known as the 'rag trade', and contributing to the vivid character of the streets on which I played and sometimes ran riot.

One Jewish lady in particularly stands out in my memory – or more precisely what she sold stands out. She ran a delicatessen on Cable Street, around the corner from us, where you could buy bread and dripping for a farthing. To serve you, she would tuck the loaf under her arm, dip her knife into the jar of dripping, slather it over the end of the bread, then slice off a massive doorstep. Brilliant.

Right opposite that deli was another source of wonderful treats – the local fish and chip shop. Not that we could afford the fish, but that didn't matter. For a penny you could walk out of that place with a bag of crackling – the scraps of batter that had fallen off the fish or saveloys of whatever was being cooked in the fryer. Better than boring old cod any day.

Before illness restricted Mum's working life, she was an engraver and cutter for T. & W. Ide, a glass factory just off Cable Street, very near my school. The section where she worked was fronted by a large, frosted window, embedded with wire mesh for security. This being the East End though, nothing was entirely safe. Some urchin had shot at it with an air rifle, leaving a convenient peep hole about the size of a sixpence, or a tanner as we knew it, for me to eyeball Mum and attract her attention with a shout of, 'Can I have half a crown?'

If she had anything in her purse she would quickly duck round to the side door and slip the coin to me. She was good like that. Then I'd trot off to school, deciding what to spend it on. I don't think it would have been cigarettes then, this was in Primary days, but I can't be sure.

Dad was a lorry driver. He'd learned to drive trucks in the army during the war, and after being demobbed he joined the firm J. Packers and Sons, based in Canning Town. In those days it was a motor and trailer, not an artic as is common now. Dad drove and his mate looked after the trailer. The lorry cab housed a big engine covering, which I loved to sit on because it was warm and exciting. They used to take me on trips, long distance sometimes, and even then, long before I'd ever thought of becoming a drummer, I had the best seat in the house, sitting between the two of them pretending to drive.

I got on well with Dad, I loved him to bits. He was quiet, loving and unassuming, but there was also a roguish element to him. I used to wonder what the hell was going on when, every now and again, he would come home, almost certainly after enjoying a few pints at the local, walk into the kitchen and throw a wad of cash into the air. It was such a sight. Notes back then were the size of a newspaper, and they used to float slowly and gently to the ground. I'm sure he was up to no good. That's probably how he managed to afford the various cars he bought over the years, including a fantastic Austin convertible which he loved. I loved it too, even though I once suffered a burn on my leg in that car. Mum and Dad were both smokers and one of them flicked a butt out when the top was down and it flew back in, landing on me, squeezed in the back. There were only ever a handful of cars parked on Havering Street while I was growing up, and one of them would be Dad's. Ask no questions, that was the neighbour-hood motto. Everyone understood that.

Flamboyant gestures were unusual for my father, who was by nature a shy man. Unless he'd been to the pub. Then a more theatrical side of his personality would nudge itself to the surface. I recall arriving home from school to find Dad a little worse for wear after an afternoon with his mates, during which he'd concocted a plan to play a trick on Mum. He was clearly very pleased with himself, sitting there with a smile as wide as the Thames.

'On you go, son,' he said, gesturing towards the kitchen. 'Take a look in the sink.'

I couldn't believe what I was seeing. Staring back at me was a pig's head. Wearing a flat cap – or a cheese-cutter as they were called in the East End.

This is going to be great.

Just after five o'clock, Mum arrived home from her work at the glass factory. 'Cup of tea, Sam?'

'Love one.'

Off she went to the kitchen, while Dad and I sat in the front room, desperately trying to suppress giggles as we waited for the big moment. Nothing. We could hear her putting groceries into the cupboard, taking out the biscuit tin, setting cups and saucers on the table, tidying up. Then at last, she went to fill the kettle. Crash! It clattered to the floor as Mum started screaming like mad. She thought it was a human; we thought it was hilarious.

Dad and I had a very similar sense of humour. We had a television at home (again, ask no questions), a massive thing with a tiny picture, it looked like an eyeball, and once when a cowboy show came on, Dad said to me, 'Have you noticed son, how the horses never shit?' 'Yeah Dad. I have.' 'Ah, but have you ever looked behind the set?' That made me laugh for ages.

Argentinean beef was a regular delivery for Dad, and sometimes (fairly often, in fact) during his round he would call in to home for a cup of tea and drop off some 'goods' for Mum. My father's brother, Uncle Jim, was a lorry driver as well. He delivered tea in big wooden chests. That was handy.

Although we didn't have much money, we didn't want for much. Growing up I lived off tea, Argentinean beef... and bananas when available on the markets. That's what it was like in the East End. Most people either worked as drivers, on the docks, or on stalls; bartering was a way of life.

The Kray twins, the gangsters, were distant cousins on Dad's side and I am sure I must have come across them as a kid, but I wouldn't have paid them any special attention; everyone around me was a rogue. Dad's driving mate, for instance, was father to Roy James, who went on to become one of the Great Train Robbers. My cousin Billy Boy, eldest son of my dad's sister Nel, and Uncle Bill, worked with the Krays. Billy Boy was a bit of a villain. I felt I was forever being dragged on busses and trains to Wormwood Scrubs to visit him when he was in the nick. It would never have occurred to Mum and Dad not to go see him; they were Billy Boy's favourite aunt and uncle after all. Nor did they hesitate for a second about whether to take me along, even if it was intimidating for a small lad to walk through those massive prison gates. We lived in a close-knit community, where family mattered. Values were different from those of today.

When I was in my early teens, Billy Boy met this woman and broke out of prison to marry her. We all attended the wedding in a church just off Cable Street. Of course we did, we wouldn't have dreamt of missing such a happy event.

Dad's family was Welsh, not that he spoke the language or anything. He was an East End boy through and through, but his father was born in Wales and all the family had Welsh names. As for me, I was named after my dad's best mate in the army, Kenneth. I always preferred Kenny. I only added the extra 'e' when I was 16 and starting out in the Small Faces. I'd just become a member of the Performing Rights Society (PRS), which looks after the interests of musicians and songwriters. I thought joining the PRS was great, like I'd really made it. Then I began to receive letters and royalty cheques for other people with similar names – turned out there were about five Ken Joneses, a few Kenneth Joneses, and number of Kenny Joneses. I contacted the PRS and suggested adding an 'e' in my name to make the difference. It stuck.

Our house on Havering Street is still there; the area hasn't suffered 'development' because the street is listed. I don't think it's because of me; it's classic architecture. Although they were talking about putting up one of those plaques, saying 'Kenney Jones lived here'. Underneath it they'd probably have added, 'So what?' Actually, there's now one in Carnaby Street for the Small Faces. It's green. That's important. It means I'm alive; it's blue if you're dead. For the Carnaby Street plaque, I suggested either turquoise or half-and-half blue and green, because at the time two of the band were dead. They didn't go for it.

I must confess, I like having that plaque. When they told me about it, I thought, 'Oh, good, just like Nelson'.

Havering Street felt like our own little village, with its own identity, a good identity. A lot of East End streets were like that. The people there supported each other, looked out for each other and occasionally knew a little more about each other than they might have liked.

We all had outside toilets, and everyone knew when old man Bainham, the grandfather of our next-door neighbours, had to go. Early morning you'd hear him in there, coughing his guts up, waking half the street.

I loved living in Havering Street with my parents. I felt comfortable and happy. I remained there well after I started enjoying success with the Small Faces, but once I did buy a place of my own, I didn't for a second miss that outside loo. The cold in winter made it a tortuous experience. Your bum would stick to the seat. Man, that was painful.

Strange to think that by the end of the 1960s, millions of people watching *Top of the Pops* and other music shows had seen Steve Marriott step into that same khazi, which featured in the 'Lazy Sunday' video we made. So much for privacy. Still, mustn't grumble.

Mum and Dad shared my huge affection for Havering Street. To the extent that it ended up costing me money. In the

1970s while I was with the Faces, I was living near the Robin Hood Gate, Richmond Park, in an area called Kingston Hill. Whenever Mum and Dad came to stay they would comment that it felt like having a house in the countryside, something they'd always dreamed of. For them, anything outside of the East End was rural.

'Well why don't you come and live with me, then? There's plenty of room.'

No. They said they wanted their own house. So, when I began to make decent money from touring, I bought them one close by – a terrace house at the bottom of Kingston Hill costing £11,500. It was right next to the shops, with a lovely garden and shed. Perfect. Not dissimilar to their place in Stepney, but within a minute's walk of Richmond Park and its open spaces. I decided to spring a surprise. I told them I'd bought it as an investment, and wanted them to come over and take a look, so I could talk them through the plans I had to renovate. They were enthusiastic and seemed to really like it. Time for the big reveal. I had a whole speech prepared. This was going to be great.

'The two of you have supported me all my life, made sacrifices and worked hard to give me every opportunity and chance you possibly could. Well now is the time when I give you something back, with my eternal gratitude and love. The house is yours.' Ta-da!

Their faces fell. 'You haven't, have you?' I wasn't sure how to take that. I think it was the sudden realisation that they would actually have to do something drastic in their lives, rather than just talk about it.

Back at my place they were quiet all afternoon. Eventually I asked, 'What's wrong? Don't you like the house?'

'Yes, but we don't know anyone up here.'

'You know me. And there's a pub opposite. What more could you want?'

A proper home, that was the answer. And they already had that. I hadn't thought it through. Sure, they liked talking about moving, a place in the country and all that, it was fun, but they didn't really want to do it. They were happy where they lived (we'd installed an inside toilet by then). I understood that.

I sold the house for ten grand, a loss of fifteen hundred quid.

We decided to look at buying their place. It was owned by a housing association, with Mum and Dad as sitting tenants, and when an opportunity arose to make the purchase I jumped at it. I knew we had to move fast if it was going to happen, but again I underestimated my parents' deep connection to the street. It wasn't merely the house they loved, it was the whole community. They weren't prepared to go it alone, they wanted to be part of a neighbours' group that was going to put forward a collective case for home ownership. That's the East End way, sticking together. Unfortunately, it all took too long to organise and the chance was lost. I was very sorry about that. It would have meant a lot to me for Mum and Dad to own their home. To this day I retain deep affection and close ties with Havering Street, visiting regularly. Mum and Dad would like that.

* * *

I enjoyed the first school I attended, Marion Richardson Primary, located just off Commercial Road. I first went there for nursery, where I used to fall asleep in the sandpit, before moving on to 'big' school, Primary 1. I stayed at Marion Richardson for a few years, and for a period I was quite happy, mainly because of the guy who taught maths, sums basically. I thought he was great, because for the first time in my life I found I was learning something. With his guidance and patience, I could add up. I remember him setting the class a question and me raising my hand, giving the correct answer. Unheard of. Maybe the only time it happened in my school life. Amazing.

With all the other subjects though, I struggled. I spent most classes standing in the corner of the room, with a dunce's hat on. Really, that did happen. Regularly. You can imagine how the other kids loved that – I had the piss taken out of me constantly. It doesn't take long for that to wear thin. Eventually Mum was called into a meeting with the headmistress, who declared, 'Mrs Jones, your son has a lazy brain.' How is that going to help any child?

Years later I learned that my problems at school resulted from dyslexia, not that we knew the word then, or anything about it. I think maths – and music – might be things I am okay at because I visualise numbers and notes in a different way from how I see letters. In many ways, I now view dyslexia as a gift, if you know how to handle it. Seeing the world differently can be a real advantage. You find ways around problems. You don't accept the first thing that's put in front of you. But it comes at a price, obviously.

As for learning to write, my mum taught me, by having me copy out swirly patterns she drew on a page, until I became accustomed to forming letters. If you look at my signature now, you can see where it comes from – Mum's patterns.

Other than the maths bloke, there was nothing for me at school. And when I was forced to change to a different teacher, it destroyed me. From then on, school was over, at least as far as any academic learning was concerned.

I've been back to Marion Richardson since, a few years ago, and had a lovely time. The headmaster contacted me, and asked whether I would like to have a look around. Delighted. I was interested to see the old place and it offered some good PR for them. I drove up from my home in Surrey and had planned on parking outside Mum's house on Havering Street, but ended up running late because of traffic. When I realised I wasn't going to have time to stop by to see Mum, I called the headmaster and asked whether there was any parking at the school.

'No problem at all,' he told me. 'Come in through the main gates and you can park in the playground.'

That was a moment for me. I got a hell of a kick out of driving my XKR convertible Jag into the same school grounds where more than 50 years previously I used to play tag and conkers with my mates, never imagining I could be a success at anything other than something decidedly dodgy. Mind you, thinking about it now, perhaps that exactly what happened.

From Marion Richardson, at around the age of 10 I moved for a brief period to Nicholas Gibson Primary, by Shadwell Park, where I did learn something important – how to be an entre- preneur. 'Kenny Jones, Milk and Biscuit Monitor', that was me, responsible for distributing free milk with an offer of a ha'penny biscuit to go with. Good deal, if that's what I'd charged. The thing was, there were kids there who didn't know the milk was free, or the price of the biscuit. For them I added commission, which I used to buy cigarettes that I would smoke at lunchtime in the park, just up the road from the famous Prospect of Whitby pub where Henry VIII moored his barges on the way to the Tower of London. I loved that area, they had a hangman's gallows and noose. What more could a boy wish for?

My little enterprise didn't last long. The headmistress sussed I was up to something and, though not quite able to pin anything on me, she took away my precious monitor's badge.

During my primary school days, I adored going to the Saturday morning pictures, often on my own, at the beautiful Art Deco Troxy cinema – it's a trendy venue for events now, and still beautiful.

When I was about seven years old, I saw the movie *Aladdin and His Lamp* there. I was mesmerised by the costumes, the genie, everything. The film transported me to a magical land and I was still there, in my head, as I wandered home, dreaming of meeting Aladdin for real. He was so brave and clever. I just knew we would be best friends. Then I looked up and there he was, walking directly towards me, all in white, with flapping trousers, turban and shiny gold shoes.

I could not believe what I was seeing. Aladdin. In the East End. Mouth gaping, I stood stock still, unable to say a word, watching as he walked past. Then I turned and bolted home. 'Mum, Mum!' I shrieked, bursting through the front door. 'I've just seen Aladdin. On Commercial Road!'

'Of course you have, love. Cup of tea?'

The man was most probably from the Sikh community – fairly new arrivals who were making their home in London following Indian Independence in 1947. I'd never seen anyone dressed like that before, not in real life. Not long after that encounter, families from India became an integral part of the neighbour-hood, but that first thrilling glimpse at such a young age made a lasting impression.

On a corner opposite the Troxy, across Pitsea Street, stood the shell of an old Victorian house that had been bombed during the war. Such sights were hardly unusual in London in the 1950s. Me and my mates used to play there often, after we'd been to the pictures, climbing all over the ruins. One morning a bunch of us were jumping up and down on the ground floor when one end gave way and we found ourselves somersaulting over each other down a makeshift ramp into the basement. There was dirt everywhere, in our eyes and hair, and we were all laughing and giggling. What an adventure.

We couldn't see a thing until the dust began to settle, and as the air cleared, sufficient for us to get a sense of our surroundings, we almost died of fright. Lying all around were bones, human bones – skeletons. Real skeletons. You have never seen six kids move as fast as we did then, scrambling up that dusty ramp, desperate to escape the basement of horrors. I swear bony hands were reaching out to grab us.

We made it to Commercial Road where we found a policeman. It must have taken the poor man 10 minutes to understand what these half-dozen filthy ragamuffins were trying to say as we coughed, shrieked and talked over each other. Eventually he understood. 'Leave it to me. Time you lot were off home to clean yourselves up.'

The local story around the family of that house was that they had been off on a boating holiday and the boat had blown up. That's what everyone used to say, and was why no one had gone looking for them in the rubble when the bomb hit.

You'd think an episode like that might have really spooked me but it didn't, not after the initial shock. I never had any nightmares about those skeletons, which was strange given that I've always been someone with an active imagination who regularly experiences vivid dreams. In my childhood bedroom was a little fireplace, and a recurring dream featured the tiny spacemen who lived in there and only crept out at night (honestly, they did). I can see them now, as real and as clear as you like. I guess perhaps I'd been reading a science-fiction comic or something. Whatever it was that initially sparked those dreams, they came from the subconscious, which is an amazing thing – I believe it tells you a lot about yourself. Mind you, quite what deep meaning was represented by those mini spacemen, I've no idea.

* * *

In the East End, most families didn't have enough money to go on 'proper' holidays. Abroad was unthinkable, there were no package deals back then. The only places you might consider were Margate, Brighton, maybe Camber Sands, or Canvey Island and Southend, which were nearest to us. But these were also expensive, especially for the big families that were common then. Even if you were lucky enough to have a car large enough to pack in multiple kids, petrol wasn't cheap and rail tickets cost a fortune.

For many in our neighbourhood, picking hops in Kent for local breweries offered the best solution, and it became an annual pilgrimage. You could earn money and have a bit of a holiday. My grandparents and their grandparents all went hop-picking and we happily followed suit. We'd go there for five weeks or so, for the late summer season. My first birthday was spent down in Kent, and every birthday after that, through to my twelfth. Then it stopped. Picking machines arrived, and before long an East End tradition was lost.

Around the end of August, Uncle Jim's tea chests would be stuffed full of anything we might need for our trip – sheets, clothes, pots, pans, and tins of food we'd been saving all year that we could heat up in little clay ovens or over an open fire. We didn't have suitcases, except a tiny one each for our toothbrushes, combs – toiletry things. All the hop-pickers in our street did the same and, once everyone was packed, we'd wait outside for the magic lorry to appear. That's what it felt like to me, because it would be transporting us to a wonderful new land.

The lorry was one of those with canvas tarpaulins down the sides, which the driver would yank open so we could load everything on board, then climb in ourselves, perching on the chests, laughing, excited, singing songs as we made our way to a little village in Kent called Tudeley. My favourite ditty was the one we sang about the music hall act 'Old Mother Riley'. I can't remember it all now, except the line that always had me rolling around that lorry in hysterics: 'When we go down hoping, knock on number one. See Old Mother Riley, with a finger up her bum.'

Home for those five or six weeks was a wooden stable with beds made from our sheets stuffed with straw. Dad would join us every weekend, Saturday and Sunday were days off from picking, driving down in his old Ford after his week's work to take us out on day trips around the county. Often he would bring some meat with him as a treat. Funnily enough, it was always Argentinean.

Hop-picking was hard work, for my mother and grandparents. Me, I mostly watched. The season started in the nearest fields, but as they were picked clean the workers would venture further and further out, into the land of discovery as I saw it. That's where I was happiest. While they were picking I'd go off exploring, sometimes with a couple of mates, but mostly on my own. The River Medway ran through the fields, providing an endless source of adventure and excitement as I dared myself to make longer and longer leaps from bank to bank, fishing for sticklebacks or searching for water rats. Playing by the riverside was really quite daring for me. I couldn't swim back then, I was terrified of the thought of immersing myself in water. Whenever Mum told me it was time for a bath, I'd run a mile.

If I fancied a change of scenery, then it was off to the orchards of young apple trees for an afternoon of scrumping. My favourites were the massive Cox's apples. Even though I was a London boy,

I knew how to identify them. If you could hear the pips rattle, that was a Cox. The taste was phenomenal. I also discovered the secret location – well, *I* didn't tell anyone – of the three wild pear trees that grew along the river. Bite into one of them and you were in heaven.

In time, I would help with a bit of picking myself, but only for so long. I'd make sure my hands were well and truly stained black from the hop juice, to show willing, and then I'd decide enough was enough, usually by morning tea break. 'I'm off now Mum. Bye! See you tonight.'

Those summers offered a glimpse of a life so different from home. For the rest of the year my world was one of bricks, motor vehicles and pungent smells. You could always find your way around the East End by following your nose. Walking to school blindfolded would have been no bother – keep the smell of coffee being unloaded from the docks at Wapping on your left, and the acrid smoke billowing from the paper mill chimneys on your right.

Kent was a magical playground and an education. I learned about life, people, enjoying your own company and nature. I developed a strong connection with the countryside. My life today is rural rather than urban, and that suits me.

Many years later, when I was in The Who, I had a vivid dream. I was flying over the Kent hops. I could go anywhere I wanted, like a bird. I swooped down, skimming along the Medway, past the banks where I had made my brave leaps, to the orchard, and then further along, to the pear trees. All was exactly as I remembered. I was happy.

No drugs involved, I promise.

* * *

Secondary education began at St George's-in-the-East, on Cable Street. That's when, age 11, I suddenly enjoyed a growth spurt. Honestly, I shot up. Almost overnight I was taller than all my school mates. Coinciding with this miraculous event, came the arrival of the first two Indian boys to join our class. They were horribly picked on from day one. Ours was a rough school.

I felt immediately sorry for both of them, but one in particular, who would have had a hard time looking after himself in a playground bust-up. He'd clearly broken one of his fingers at some stage, and it had been set at a right angle. I'd never seen anything like that before. He couldn't have made a fist if his life had depended on it. (To be fair, our school wasn't quite that bad.) I set myself the task of doing what I could to defend them and, given the new-found respect my sudden height had earned me, I was pretty successful. It was nice to feel tall, once.

I vividly recall one incident when they became involved in a big fight and I was in the thick of it, trying to protect them when a teacher arrived. There was a lot of wrestling, swinging of fists and lashing out of kicks – a melee of boys tumbling over one another, with the teacher doing his best to put a stop to it. He wasn't having much success, until he yelled out the words that have stuck with me to this day.

'You bent my spoon! You bent my spoon!'

Who on earth comes to break up a punch-up carrying a nice tea cup in a saucer? We all burst out laughing.

I learned absolutely nothing at St George's. Probably because I used to bunk off all the time. I'd cycle to school, park my bike by the building opposite, go to registration making sure the teacher marked me down as present, then, in the pandemonium of kids dispersing to their various classes, I'd wander back out, over the road and be on my way to Dempsey Street School. Now,

I wasn't going there because I thought it had a higher educational standard. No, it was where most of my mates went. Why shouldn't I?

It was easy to slip in and join them for the classes I enjoyed – art, woodwork, metalwork. I was alright at that stuff, good with my hands. And interested. At home I loved making things, like go-karts out of old prams. I once pinched the cover off my aunt's sewing machine and stuck it to the front of a kart so that it looked like a giant beetle. Brilliant. I don't think Aunt Rene ever forgave me.

I received decent grades from those Dempsey Street classes, which was more than I ever managed from St George's. Which is where I was a pupil. I only remember receiving one report from there. It read: 'Who is he? Does Kenneth Jones actually go to this school?'

When St George's folded into a far bigger school in Stepney Green, that was it for me. What little connection I had with education was permanently broken, the new place was massive and I felt completely out of touch with everyone, including my Indian mates, who for a while had barely left my side after that playground punch-up (on the occasional days I attended school).

There was a tall fence surrounding the new school, like you see on tennis courts, keeping all the kids prisoner. I found a way out. In one of the corners of the grounds you could leap onto the top of the fence, then slide down and away. I was the first to manage the escape, and very quickly copied. The fence ended up with a dent at the top, from all the kids making their bids for freedom.

Once over the fence I knew I had to leave the neighbourhood quickly because members of the school board would be patrolling the streets, searching for truants. If I'd been caught, Mum and Dad would have gone mad. To be safe, I'd leg it straight to Stepney Green underground station, and from there into the heart of London. To Soho.

What a place. I'd spend the days happily wandering around, absorbing what was going on in the new Italian cafes and becoming friendly with the street girls. I'm not a great reader, never have been, but one book I adore is David Niven's *The Moon's a Balloon*. I can relate very closely to the story of him as a young man following the prostitute and getting to know her. I'd see the girls most days I went up there, but nothing racy ever happened. Worst luck. They were friendly and fun to talk to, but to be honest, they went on a bit too much like my mum. 'What are you doing here? Kenny, you should be at school. Get back there.'

I remember once I was dying for a pee and had to pop into the public loos by the statue of Eros in Piccadilly Circus. As I entered, it seemed to me that the place was full of men in some sort of uniform all looking the same, like soldiers, only these weren't military blokes, they were smart City gents identically dressed in bowler hats and pinstriped suits. I guess that's where all the nobs hung out.

They were lined up, having a wee, with the only available space right in the middle of the row. Intimidating, but as I was desperate, I'd no choice. No one paid any attention to me, but even still, I wanted to get out of there as quickly as possible, so having finished my business, I swiftly yanked up my zip. Too fast. I caught myself rather nastily, screaming in high-pitched agony as the gents did their upmost to ignore me. In complete shame and embarrassment, I managed to hobble across to a free cubicle, where I very slowly and very gently pulled down my zip to release myself from my predicament.

That incident aside, I felt at home in Soho – I belonged there. Thinking about it now, it seems pre-ordained that as barely a teenager I was discovering an area of London that in a couple of years' time would be instrumental in shaping the rest of my life.

* * *

The boys I hung around with in Stepney were just a group of typical East End kids. A right bunch of Herberts. I spoke broad Cockney then. 'Awright mate, kna wot I mean.' That sort of thing. Wherever we went, we'd cause trouble. When the travelling fairground was in town we'd hang around there, deliberately bumping into people, nicking bikes, acting tough. One of our favourite haunts was the Victoria Park lido, South Hackney. We'd break in at night, just to muck around. Some of the guys used to go for a swim in the pool; not me, of course. Far too dangerous.

Another favourite pastime was to gather together as many of us as we could and go marching through the East End, knocking over the vending machines that were a feature of almost every street corner. We'd bust them open, take the money and fags, or chocolate bars, or whatever it was, and scarper. That was my crowd. It wasn't like we were in an organised gang or anything. We were just bored and looking for things to do. Little hooligans, really.

We stole a beat-up Lambretta, which we later found out belonged to an old boy we'd seen riding around, wearing one of those funny helmets, a bit like the early police helmets, which made your ears poke out. The scooter was in bad shape so we repaired it, fitting a new clutch, but then we went too far. We should never have gone for the full chrome treatment. It made it way too noticeable. Not a smart move. We drove it around for a couple of weeks and word got out that we'd pinched it.

We were near some school playing fields at Bethnal Green, when we got nicked. Not exactly a surprise, as we were only a stone's throw from Arbour Square police station, with local bobbies coming and going all the time. Pretty dumb. When the coppers pulled up, by chance I happened to be walking away from them, all innocent. I could have kept going, disappeared around the corner, but like an idiot I turned back towards my mates. It probably didn't matter though. They knew I was involved so I'd have got done anyway.

The police arrested us and banged us up in the station, where my dad had to come and collect me. It was on a Saturday afternoon. I know that, because Dad had been out in the pub at lunchtime. He came with one of his mates and the two of them were great. Being a bit merry, Dad came on more cocky than normal, all swagger, with a touch of slurring thrown in. 'Where the fucksh my son? What you shayin' he's done? He's done nothing.' Meanwhile his pal, Albert, tried to look menacing in the background. He most probably succeeded.

I was brought up from the cells and released on bail, but before I could go the duty officer insisted I sign a form stating that I had retrieved all the contents of my pockets, which had been confiscated when I was lifted. No thanks.

'I don't want 'em. I don't want 'em.'

'Listen lad, you've got to take them.'

'Please, no. Toss 'em.'

I probably had no more than thruppence on me at the time, which I wasn't too happy about abandoning, but if it meant the police not dumping the fags I'd been hoarding on to the counter, then it would be worth it. The thing was, Dad didn't know I smoked and I was certain he'd go mental if he found out. In those days, I used to take a couple of drags of my cigarette and then put it out for later. My pockets had been full of half-smoked dog-ends. That desk sergeant was deaf to my pleas and handed everything over, right in front of Dad.

'You pick them up son, you put them in your pocket.' I had no choice.

Dad was good, he didn't embarrass me there and then, but outside he grabbed hold of both my arms. 'If I ever catch you smoking, that'll be it.' Then he had me up against the wall. 'I don't give a shit what you do. Just don't get fucking caught.'

I had to appear in court, but luckily one of my mates, Raymond Rising, was a butcher's boy who delivered meat to the local magistrate. Raymond put in a word.

'Alright sir, here's your order. Oh, I hear you're seeing Kenny Jones later today. I just wanted to say, eh, he's a good boy. He's really not a bad 'un at all.' Apparently the magistrate wouldn't talk about it, but I think a seed had been planted.

My mother was too scared and angry with me to attend court, so her sister, Aunt Floss, came along, pretending to be Mum. It was madness, she could have been locked up herself, but somehow we got away with it. I think I was given a conditional discharge. I remember not feeling frightened at the time, but subconsciously I think it did begin to make me realise this was probably not the best road to set off down. Perhaps it was time to find something else to occupy my time.

* * *

It was around then, 1960/61, that me and my mates, and many other kids around London, invented Mods. The scene seemed to explode on to the streets almost overnight. To my 12-year-old eyes, Mods, or Modernists, originated in the East End, but I soon realised that wasn't quite true. Very quickly, during my expeditions into Soho, I found I couldn't go two feet without bumping into someone who looked like me – brown suede Hush Puppies or maybe dessert boots, white Levis rolled up to show off the darker inside seam (that was an important detail) or trousers hemmed three inches short by understanding mums, both designed to highlight the colourful socks we all wore, plus bright shirts, blue Pac-a-Macs, and in the early days short-back-and-sides haircuts – the Mod-look. The invasion had landed in almost every area of the capital at the same time, later extending throughout the country with the help of rock and pop music TV show *Ready Steady Go!* which hand-picked Mods for its audience.

Mods were born out of Rockers. Rockers would hate that, they don't want to admit any connection, but it's true. When Italians families started to settle in London after the war, they opened cafes, initially frequented by their teenager children, nipping from one hip location to the next on their Lambrettas, decked out head to foot in classic Italian styles – Cuban heels and sharp, shiny mohair suits, but with greaser hair, influenced by the American rock 'n' rollers pumping out of the cafe jukeboxes. As we began to gather at these cafes, we clocked the look and adopted the good stuff. Yes to the clothes, no to the hair. That's when the two groups, the Mods and the Rockers, split.

A lot of Mods also rejected the Rocker music. Not me. Those early Elvis singles, a constant in every cafe, together with Gene Vincent, Jerry Lee Lewis and Chuck Berry blew me away, so full of excitement and energy. What else was out there?

My hunger for new music was fed when I discovered the late-night shows on Radio Luxembourg, featuring more off-the-wall tracks. Hunched over the radio in my room, ignoring the bursts of static interference and fluctuating reception, during those formative years I fell in love with Muddy Waters, Howlin' Wolf, organist Jimmy McGriff, Booker T & the MGs and a little later Georgie Fame and Zoot Money, who is less well-known these days but wonderful, in a sort of Georgie Fame mould.

A little later, local dance clubs offered another opportunity to hear great music. At the weekends, we would queue for venues such as The Lotus in Forest Gate, which initially played dance records before it began hosting bands, and Ilford's Room at the Top and Palais. We were underage, of course, but no one seemed to care much. And anyway, if we did receive any hassle, we could always shoot over to the Poplar Civic, a community centre that ran a youth club with live performances. Music was fast becoming my entire life and I would happily take my hit wherever I could.

The classic early Mod look soon evolved because that was part of the deal, to be at the forefront of fashion. There were hardly any shops selling Mod-type clothes then, but that didn't matter, not to me and my mates. We had no money to pay retail prices anyway, certainly not while I was still officially at school. So we invented our own style, looking good on a shoestring.

The key was the existence of the East End rag trade, right there on our own patch, running along both sides of Commercial Road, up to Aldgate, into Petticoat Lane Market and around Spitalfields. These were mainly wholesale outlets, but the owners were always happy for us to hang around, picking up the best of the cast-offs for pennies to create our own look. Bell-bottom trousers, for instance, they were in for a short while, long before flares became the thing to wear. We'd slit a pair of jeans, from the knee to the hem, sew in a section of fabric, and a new style was born.

The army surplus stores that had sprung up after the war, places like Silvermans on Mile End Road, offered an additional source of inspiration. These sold both British and US military gear. That's where parka coats with the hoods originated. They first came over from the States, and the reason we adopted them into the Mod world was out of pure practicality. They were cheap, and they kept you warm on a scooter.

Although none of this was expensive, it wasn't free. I had to save up my meagre pocket money, plus handouts from aunts and uncles and the little I could make from doing odd jobs around the neighbourhood. One other source of income could prove quite lucrative, although it wasn't exactly regular.

Once or twice a year Dad and his mates would go on a day trip, or a beano, to somewhere like Margate. Timed right, these beanos were a godsend to a hard-up young Mod. The men would all meet in the pub to get tanked up beforehand. When the time came for them to head off, the local kids who were smart enough to sniff an opportunity would line up by the coach parked outside, knowing it was customary for the blokes to hand out coins before they boarded. A cheeky comment might get you a playful clip around the ear, and an extra shilling or half-crown if you were lucky. Well worth it.

As the Mod fashion changed, so did the hair styles. Not always for the better as far as I was concerned. Fine when backcombing arrived, so your hair stuck up a bit, but when it became even more bouffant than that, no thank you. I remember Mum and her sisters coming in with new hairdos, all swept back and piled on their heads. I asked what it was called. 'It's a cottage loaf.' I could see why. When the Mods started down that route, I thought, no chance, that's out the window for me. Who wants a barnet that looks like a loaf of fucking bread?

That developing Mod world I found myself a part of had a far greater impact on my life than school ever did, and at the age of 14 I knew I was done with formal education. Good riddance. I'd already learned everything I needed, and none of it had come from a classroom.

CHAPTER 2

BLINKIN' HECK

August 1961. Me and my mate are washing neighbours' cars for half a crown. We're having a laugh, mucking around. He's just thrown his sponge into my face. Between us, we've got more soap and water on ourselves than the motors. Then my mate looks across at me. He looks ridiculous, covered in suds, and out of the blue says, 'I think we should form a skiffle group.'

Eh?

I have no idea what he means. 'What's a skiffle group, then?'

'It's where three or four of you get together and one of you finds a tea chest and sticks a broom handle in one corner, attaches a piece of string from that to the other corner and you pluck it.'

We've got plenty of tea chests at home, but still, what's he on about? By now, though, I'm listening hard, my wet sponge dripping on my shoes.

'Then you get your mum's washboard and go into your gran's sewing box, find the thimbles, stick them on your fingers and start strumming.'

Okay, he's nuts.

'There's one on television tonight.'

This I must see.

We finish washing the car and I walk home. There's a weird feeling in the pit of my stomach, it's fizzing. I'm excited, although I don't know why. Six o'clock arrives and sure enough there's Lonnie Donegan and his skiffle group on the box, singing 'My Old Man's a Dustman' then 'Rock Island Line'. I can relate to the lyrics, and the music. He's playing the banjo. That's fucking great. That's for me.

Up to that moment, although I was fast getting into music the possibility of it being something I could be involved with had not entered my head. The only live playing I'd been exposed to was through Aunt Floss's husband, Davie Reed. And he could hardly play a note, except for a little bit of flute and piano. But he was very good at wearing a hat, sticking his chest out, and marching in a brass band while twirling and catching a mace. He was a maestro at that.

Uncle Davie's band was affiliated to the Catholic church in Limehouse, and took part in processions around the East End. I used to love watching him march proudly along the street, but what really caught my eye were the side drummers. I'd run alongside, banging away on imaginary drums. Then, when they'd passed, I'd race home, straight into Dad's shed. He was a bit of a carpenter, not a fine carpenter, mind you. He made fun stuff that kids in the neighbourhood could play with, dollhouses, garages, wooden Mickey Mouses, that sort of thing. In the shed, I'd upend the biscuit tin in which he kept his nails and screws and bits and pieces, scattering them all over the floor, grab a couple of pieces of fire wood and off I'd go, banging away, having fun, trying to sound as much like those drummers as possible. That was the limit of my ambition.

Lonnie Donegan changed all that.

Me and the boys used to hang around Bethnal Green, causing trouble no doubt, and I remembered seeing a pawn shop there, opposite the hospital and next door to the tube station. In its window, I could picture a banjo. It had been hanging there for months. Everything was coming together.

The next day my mate and I legged it to Bethnal Green. We had no money with us. Did we need it? Did pawn shops take money? No idea. It didn't matter. I only cared about getting my hands on that banjo. We arrived out of breath and panting hard. My heart was racing, but not from running. This was it. This was the beginning of something big. Only, it wasn't. The banjo had gone.

Inside, we confronted the man behind the counter, kicking up a right storm.

'Where's the banjo? It was in the window, where is it?'

'Calm down,' the bloke said. 'What's wrong with you?'

'I want the banjo.'

'Well I'm sorry, but you can't have it.'

'Why? It's not fair!'

'The owner, he came back and paid for it. He's picked it up.'

I didn't have a clue what he was on about. All I knew was that the banjo had gone and my dreams had been shattered. We trooped out.

All along Commercial Road my face was tripping me up and I didn't say a word. Eventually my mate, who was clearly very perceptive, put his hand on my shoulder. 'Kenny,' he said, 'you're upset, aren't you?'

'Yeah, yeah I am.' My bottom lip was trembling now. I'd been so desperate for that banjo, and having missed out on it, it felt like the end of the world.

Being an only child I was used to getting my way. Most of the time. Even though we didn't have much money (so there were limits, lots of things out of reach) if I wanted something and it was possible, I tended to get it. If I didn't, I'd pull a face, make a fuss.

'Listen,' continued my mate. 'I've got a friend who has a drum kit. Shall I ask him to bring it over?'

My mate was as good as his word. That afternoon, a drum kit arrived at 34 Havering Street.

It was a wonderful, sunny day, all the windows were open when this bloke turned up with a bass drum, floor tom-toms and two drumsticks, one of which was broken. We tried to fix it using the glue from Dad's shed. 'The tube says wait an hour for the glue to set.' Fuck that.

I smashed those drums with one and a half sticks for three hours, until Mum arrived home from work. She said she'd been walking down the road wondering why all the neighbours, on both sides, were out on the street. Before long, she understood. There was a God-awful racket coming from somewhere. And as she drew nearer to her house, she realised exactly where that 'somewhere' was. To say she was unimpressed would be an understatement. My mate, and his mate, and the drums, were swiftly hooked out of there. Me too – I was hooked.

Now I had a problem. How the hell could I get hold of some drums? I eventually solved that all on my own. With a little help from my cousin Roy.

Roy was like a brother to me, we adopted each other. He was the only child of my mum's sister, Rene (who, a few years on, would feature in a Small Faces song, but that's for later). Being three years older, Roy's teenage years came a little before the original Mods arrived. His style was more like a sharp-suited spiv. Needless to say, I thought he was fabulous. It annoyed me when he wouldn't let me go everywhere with him. He did let me clean his shoes though, one of my odd jobs to earn a little extra money. Thanks Roy. We are still incredibly close and see a lot of each other.

By now I was 13 years old, and all I could think about was drums. Drums. Drums. Drums. I'd been going on and on to Roy for absolutely ages, until he finally cracked. 'Well, why the hell don't you do something about it. There's a music shop over in Manor Park. The J60 Music Bar. Go. Take a look. And shut up.'

Two bus journeys later I walked into Aladdin's Cave. I couldn't believe it. Everywhere, musical instruments. Wandering around, eyes the size of, well cymbals, I came across this second-hand white drum kit. The label said it had been owned by an old geezer (not the exact words). I continued to look around, but that kit kept drawing me back. It was an Olympic set, the cheaper Premier range, with original calf skins. I sat behind it. It was good quality, as far as I could tell. Two cymbals, high hat, bass drum and pedal, piccolo snare drum, tom-tom and floor tom-toms. A small kit, just want I wanted. Only one problem, it cost £64 13s 6d. I didn't have that sort of cash. Nothing like it. I spoke to the shop assistant, who said that I'd have to put it on HP. 'What's that?' The only HP I knew was brown sauce.

'Hire purchase. You pay weekly.'

'Oh right. Great. Put it on that, then.'

'You know you still need a deposit?'

'How much?'

'Ten pounds.'

Tricky. 'Okay, I'll go and get it.'

I headed home. Mum was still at work, but her purse was there on the mantelpiece. I sat looking and looking at that purse.

It was winking at me, I swear it. Eventually I had a peek inside. Ten pounds. I'd love to say I hesitated but I didn't.

Back at J60 I handed over the deposit and the bloke said he could deliver the kit later that day, at around 6 pm. Then came the zinger.

'You're too young to sign the HP forms. One of your parents will have to do it.'

'Oh, that'll be fine. Tonight, when you come round,' I breezily replied. Hoping.

It got to six o'clock. All afternoon I'd been terrified. We'd had our dinner and I was upstairs in my bedroom. Waiting. I heard the knock on the door and I could picture the startled look on Dad's face. No one came to the door in the East End after six. Once the man of the house was home, that was it. Unless it was bad news. Or the police.

From the top of the stairs I watched Dad open the door. There in front of him was the sales guy, holding a big bass drum. Dad's mouth fell open.

'Where do you want it, Sir?'

'It's okay Dad,' I called down. 'No problem. It's all fine.'

In the background, I could hear Mum: 'Who's that Sam? Who's at the door?'

Dad looked at the bloke again. 'Eh, put it in the front room, just down the hallway there.'

I came down and gave the guy a hand. Dad just stood there, saying nothing, clueless to what was going on. He frowned at me. 'It's okay Dad, I've just bought this drum kit. Great, isn't it?'

When the kit was set up in the front room, the guy asked, 'Can you play?'

'No, not really. But I did have a bash a few weeks ago.'

'Right. Okay, let me show you something.'

He produced some brushes and started on the snare drum, giving it a cool, easy touch that grabbed me instantly. *What the hell are they? I thought. I only know one and a half sticks.*

Then he said I should have a go. All the time Mum and Dad watched silently, throwing daggers with their eyes.

I sat behind the kit, and he showed me how to hold the brushes. I looked at them in my hands, then at the snare drum, glanced across to Mum and Dad, back to the guy, then I shut my eyes and started playing.

The sound, it was just like he showed me. And I was doing it.

According to Mum and Dad, the biggest smile ever lit up my face at that moment. Dad said he'd never seen me look so happy. He signed the form.

After the bloke left, I got hell. Especially for the tenner I pinched.

Then for the rest of the evening they kept repeating, 'I just hope this isn't a five-minute wonder, son.'

When I started to drive everyone nuts practising, I'm sure they began to wish it had been.

Initially the kit lived in the front room, and for the next three months or so I was at it every day. I used to get up at six in the morning and play until I was dragged off to school. If I hadn't spent the day in Soho, at lunchtime I'd run home for an hour, then wherever I'd been, I was always back playing at four, with a brief break for dinner, and continued until I was shut down at around seven. Mum and Dad weren't too happy about this, obviously.

Nor were the neighbours. When the complaints started to pile in, we moved the kit to the basement. Less publicly noisy, but still disruptive as this was Dad's television room. Between us, we made it work. Then after I'd had the first hit single, well everyone on the street was so proud of me. It was lovely.

The only records we had in the house when I first started to play were three 78s – Michael Holliday's 'The Story of My Life', the *Rawhide* theme tune, Rowdy Yates and all that, and a version of 'Twelfth Street Rag'. I learned drums to those three records. At first, I used to play them on this old, clapped-out machine we had, which produced a terrible sound, but once Mum and Dad were convinced I was taking this seriously they bought me a proper record player with a lid, a little Dansette. The records sounded great then.

The best one was 'Twelfth Street Rag' because instead of the traditional 4-4 time that you find in a lot of rock 'n' roll music, that record had 8- and 12-bar sequences, which meant that by playing along I was unconsciously introducing a swing feel into my 4-4 drumming. It's perhaps the greatest thing that ever happened to me in a music sense, that first introduction to jazz. I've loved the music ever since.

The drummers who properly made it from that era, oldies like me, Charlie Watts or Ringo for instance, we all play with a swing. We deliver a 4-beat in a different way to most modern drummers. We're not stiff and on top of it; it's a looser style, because we learned from jazz. We understood that, 'It don't mean a thing if it ain't got no swing'. As far as I'm concerned, that's one hundred per cent true. Those days in the front room with Dad's 78s never left me.

Alongside those three records, in the very early days of my drumming I found further inspiration from what today may seem an unlikely source – the wonderful Edmundo Ros and his Orchestra, who introduced infectious Latin American band music to Havering Street. My parents and I used to watch him on Saturday night variety programmes such as *The Billy Cotton Band Show*, transported to exotic new worlds through rumba and samba rhythms.

From the moment I had my own drums, though, it was the percussionists who fully captured my imagination. I had no idea of the range of sounds it was possible to produce – not only from a kit that I recognised (sort of, mine was very basic in comparison) but also from the congas and bongos that I had never seen before. It was classic Latin percussion, spiced with Ros's individual twist, to produce a real mix of styles and rhythms. Edmundo Ros and his Orchestra opened my eyes to the versatility that drums offered. Just like Dad's 78s, those Saturday evenings in front of the TV have never left me.

I was still very much an enthusiastic novice when I heard about a 'drum clinic' taking place in a basement theatre called Cavern in the Town, just off Leicester Square. I learned of this odd-sounding event from the guys who ran a sheet music shop over in Shoreditch that I had started visiting once I discovered drumming. I couldn't read the music, but that didn't matter. I loved hanging around there, the atmosphere, the music they played, US jazz tracks that were a revelation to me and which I absorbed while studying the photographs on the sheet music. 'Who's that? Is he the best drummer in the world?' I would ask. The staff were great, patient with this urchin who spent no money, happy to explain who was who, and what they did that made them special. Buddy Rich was number one they all said (they knew their stuff – I still agree with that today), with Joe Morello a very close second. Kenny Clare, they reliably informed me, was the only drummer in Britain who came close to matching either of them.

I took in every word, and when I was told I could witness both Kenny Clare and Joe Morello, world-class superstars, giving demonstrations and engaging in amazing drumming battles in this thing called a drum clinic, I couldn't contain my excitement. This I had to see.

To the 14-year-old me, Cavern in the Town sounded impossibly glamorous. My excitement was out of control as I walked down those steps into an auditorium packed with seasoned drummers rubbing alongside kids just like me. It was also noisy as hell and Kenny and Joe hadn't even taken to the stage. I loved it instantly. Then I loved it even more.

Sitting there, waiting for the show to begin, fidgeting with anticipation, I suddenly went rigid. I could not believe what I was seeing. Walking down the sloping aisle between the rows of seats, only yards from me, was one of my heroes. Brian Bennett, the drummer with my favourite band, The Shadows, was in the same room as me! And man, did he look good – immaculate in a blue mohair suit, slim-cut trousers, and smoking the longest cigarette I've ever seen. So cool.

I loved The Shadows. I came across them listening to DJ Brian Matthew on the BBC's Light Programme, *Saturday Club* and Sunday morning's *Easy Beat*. While Radio Luxembourg offered a gateway to many US musicians, those BBC shows focussed more on UK chart hits. That's where I first heard Ray Charles and Del Shannon, both of whom I thought were brilliant. Del Shannon's 'Runaway' was one of my very favourites at the time. My heart, however, lay with The Shadows, initially playing with Cliff Richard and then, even better, in their own right. I thought Tony Meehan, their original drummer, was the best thing ever. Until he left, replaced by Brian Bennett. I remember catching the new line-up on TV during an edition of *Thank Your Lucky Stars* on a Saturday evening at the beginning of October 1961. Wow. Tony was a great drummer, but Brian took it to a new level. Not only that, but where the other members of the band looked a bit like Rockers, there was no question that Brian was a Mod. Just like me.

If someone in that drum clinic audience had at that point turned to me and said, 'Hey kid, in five years' time you'll be playing that bloke's drums,' well, I'd have more likely believed that my tiny spacemen friends had formed a band and were top of the charts. But that imaginary bloke would have been speaking the truth.

I came across the kit by chance. In 1966, I was standing in a queue at Drum City in Shaftesbury Avenue, waiting to pay for some bits and pieces I'd picked up, when I heard a distinctive voice up ahead of me. 'Got any maracas?' It could only be Mick Jagger. When I reached the counter, Mick was still hanging around, and didn't look too happy when one of the guys working there spotted me. 'Oh, Kenney, I've been told to give you this.' It was a 26-inch Paiste Cymbal. They apparently wanted me to start using them. No problem, it was a fantastic cymbal, although I'd never seen one so big in my life and I struggled to carry it. As the bloke handed it to me, I glanced over at Mick, who was staring at the salesman. If looks could kill. I knew exactly what Mick was thinking. *Why's he getting something free, and I'm not?*

It was while Mick and I were standing there having a laugh about the size of the cymbal, that I noticed a black drum kit stacked up on the far side of the shop. It looked good. Very good. Much better than the Ludwig Silver Glitter I was currently playing. When I asked where it had come from, well, my heart skipped a beat. Brian Bennett had brought it in to sell. This I had to try out. I set it up, sat down, played for five minutes and fell in love. I wasn't about to lose what to me was a once-in-a-lifetime opportunity. I handed over the money there and then and played those drums for years to come, on many Small Faces hits, through to the first Faces album.

Kenny Clare took to the stage first at the clinic, demonstrating his techniques. It bore zero resemblance to anything that was happening in my house. Then he introduced Joe.

'A lot of people ask me,' said Joe, by way of a lead-in to his segment of the show, 'what a drum clinic is. And I always tell them, it's a hospital for sick drummers.' I thought that was hilarious. There I was, in a room full of very ill people, all just as poorly as me.

Joe started playing one-handed rolls, incredibly fast. *That's impossible*. I watched and I watched and I watched, mesmerised, but could not work out how he was doing it. His hand was a blur.

Back home I spent hours practising, over many months. I even tried using iron sticks on a drum pad so that when I went back to the wooden sticks, they would feel lighter. I couldn't get it. I did everything I could think of to relax my left wrist like Joe seemed to, but still I never reached a quarter of the speed he managed that day. I was correct all along, I eventually realised. It is fucking impossible.

It took me years before I cracked it. It looked as though Joe was playing at blinding speed with an up and down movement, but really you can only move that fast if you play in a back and forth motion, as if you're holding paintbrush. That's the secret. Even then, once I'd discovered how it's done, by which time I was widely regarded as a pretty good drummer in my own right, I never fully mastered it. Not like Joe Morello.

Knowing how he did it was enough. I decided not to mess with my playing; my rolls would remain a two-handed affair. All that effort and practice did not go to waste, however. I ended up being able to do much more with my left hand than I ever imagined possible. I became more fluid, which has proved to be a powerful weapon in my drumming armoury.

Other people picked up on this. Kenny Clare did himself, when the Small Faces performed live on *Ready Steady Go!* The show featured a house band with Kenny Clare as resident drummer.

Kenny had a lazy eye, and it wasn't always obvious in which direction he was looking. We were playing our set and across the studio I didn't think for a second he was paying any attention to me. I was wrong. The following week, while we were rehearsing in a studio, our lead singer Steve Marriott appeared with the latest copy of one of the big music papers, *Melody Maker* I think. There on the front page was a picture of me, trailing an article inside by Kenny Clare. I grabbed the paper out of Steve's hands. 'Kenney Jones is one of the best drummers I've seen for a long time. Lovely left hand. Great technique.' Kenny Clare, praising little me? Astonishing. I kept going on and on about it for weeks.

The other aspect of the drum clinic that made a lasting impression on me was how both Kenny Clare and Joe Morello played their bass drums, using the toe-heel timing technique. They didn't just thrash away, stamping on the pedal to create noise. For them, the bass was a precision instrument. That made me think.

It's about understanding the action of the pedal, how much power to give, when to back off, when to speed up, when to slow down, and from there learning to play triplets in between everything else that the bass drum must provide. That was a challenge, given that triplets – three notes played together quickly in a different tempo from the regular beat of the song – are normally performed on a snare drum. They are not generally known as a bass drum technique. Certainly not back then.

Learning triplets with one pedal took time, a lot of time. Practice. Practice. Practice. You're trying to replicate on demand those strange moments that everyone experiences, when the nerves in your foot start to tap uncontrollably. You want to harness that movement, control it, and deliver it with power. Eventually, I perfected it, although with the Small Faces I only used the technique sparingly. There was no reason to overcomplicate those songs. They didn't need, and wouldn't benefit, from embellishments. I still enjoy playing triplets during sound checks, just for fun, because people often don't believe I can do it. But it's true – and I've only got one pedal.

I didn't go to another drum clinic for a long time. The experience had so blown me away that I knew nothing else could compare and I didn't want to be disappointed. I have been to a couple over the past 20 years – I've particularly enjoyed Chad Smith from the Red Hot Chili Peppers for instance – but nothing since has been quite so exciting, memorable or meaningful as that first one.

I have been asked many times to take a clinic myself, but I've always declined, for one reason – many of the things I do just don't have a name and can't be described. Yes, I can explain how to execute a paradiddle bang on, or mummy-daddy rolls, but other techniques, I wouldn't know where to start. Perhaps people might come away with something if they could sit next to me, watching closely, but that doesn't work in the clinic environment. I do, however, give lessons every now and again, hoping to pass on what I've learned over the years.

What's my number one tip? Easy. Learn how to hold your drumsticks correctly. Unless you master that fundamental, everything else will go out the window. It's not between two fingers or in a fist. You grip the stick lightly between your thumb and index finger at the point of balance, the centre of gravity, with your other fingers underneath, acting as brakes when you are playing.

Also, make sure your sticks are the correct size. I usually take an inch or so off the standard 2B sticks. Phil Collins does the same. If I use longer sticks, once I've found the centre of gravity, the ends tend to catch in my cuffs or sleeves. Even more than that practical aspect, your sticks must feel right – the length, the weight, the balance. For me, if a stick is too long, I don't relax into playing – it inhibits my style. Shorter sticks allow me to drum with a martial arts motion – a chop or flick, rather than a stiff-armed bang. I'm known as quite a loud drummer, but I don't bash my drums, I play them. I never dent a skin. If you just thump away, you deaden the natural tone of the drum; it sounds like power, but it isn't. People often say that it must be great being a drummer because you can release your anger when playing. Nonsense. If you did that, you would merely be thrashing. I never play when I am angry, and I never take anything out on my drums.

Finally on sticks, make sure they are straight. I'm very fortunate now, my sticks are custom made for me by Vic Firth. Before then, when I was buying mass-produced brands, I made sure to roll each one along a table, to check it was both smooth and straight. Sometimes I'd end up going through 25 sticks before I was satisfied. It's worth taking that time, I promise. Mind you, in my early days of playing, insisting on that level of perfectionism was a pain in the ass. Sticks used to break all the time – you'd need half a dozen at each concert to be safe. That's meant a lot of rolling sticks along a table. Today, thank goodness, a stick is more likely to wear out than break.

Two further pieces of advice to pass on. The first was given to me by a drummer named Roy, who I met in the British Prince pub when I was starting out. He asked me if I was right- or left-handed. When I said right, he advised me to try to do as much as I possibly could with my left hand – unlock doors, light cigarettes, put my change in the 'wrong' pocket, things like that – so both hands would eventually become equally as effective.

The second nugget comes from Booker T & the MGs' Al Jackson. He once said that every drummer should know his place. What he meant is that the drummer is there for a reason, to keep time, to create the movement of the song. He or she is not there to show off, to be too flashy. Basically, don't over-play. If you get too busy, you will end up doing the same things over and over again, throwing it all in there. One of the most common mistakes is to keep repeating the same fill. Sure, there may be some songs that require repeats, but ideally you should try to make each of your fills slightly different. I think that's one of the reasons that the Small Faces 1968 album *Ogdens' Nut Gone Flake* works so well. It's a variation on similarity. There's a consistent feel to each track, but they are all different.

While I'm thinking about drum techniques and tips, there's one note of caution worth mentioning. For a long time, I could never work out why at the end of a gig my snare drums would be splattered with blood and I'd have cuts all over my pinky. The adrenalin rush and frenzied concentration of playing live had masked the culprit. Eventually, I worked out whodunnit – I was smashing my hand into my high-hat, with its razor blade edge. It's a dangerous business, drumming. Be warned.

* * *

Having acquired my new drum kit on HP, I then had to pay for it. And at £2 19s 11d a month, that was asking a lot of a young lad. Initially, Mum and Dad helped me out and I contributed what I could. After I left school, however, it was all down to me. A mate of mine got me part-time work at Speciality Foods in Steel's Lane, a couple of minutes from home. Turned out to be an appropriately named location.

One of my jobs at Speciality Foods was being a lorry-driver's mate. I'd get up at four in the morning, often in the freezing cold, and walk to Cable Street to meet the driver, Jimmy Tonks, in his small artic, so we could be first in the queue at the docks. There we would pick up barrels of pickled vegetables – cauliflower, broccoli, onions, gherkins, etc. – that were coming off the boats. We'd roll them up planks into the flatbed truck and, once loaded, deliver them to the Speciality Foods factory. It would be about 7 am by then.

There, the barrels were smashed open with a wooden mallet and, honestly, invariably a two-inch layer of dead flies would be floating on the top. These were scooped on to the floor without a flicker from anyone, except me. I shuddered in disgust every time. I've never touched piccalilli since.

Next the various pickled vegetables, no doubt with the odd fly, were mixed together in gallon-sized glass jars, four to a crate, heavy as hell. Sometimes there would also be rollmop herring and other pickled and preserved fish. Speciality Foods was a big operation. We then loaded the crates onto a different truck, and off we went, delivering around the West End to fancy restaurants and hotels.

One of the stops on our rounds was a well-known nightclub in Jermyn Street – Dolly's. There I would bump the crates down the stairs in a wheelbarrow and into the kitchen. We made a lot of deliveries to Dolly's, and I got to know the staff. That's how I learned about the secret panels that had been installed in the alcoves, probably for gangsters to hide in or escape from. Years later, when Dolly's became a regular haunt, I loved playing tricks on people by hiding in those secret spots. No one ever worked out how I managed to disappear into thin air.

Another of my jobs at Speciality Foods was occasionally to sweep the factory floor at the end of the working day. No one else seemed very keen on this, but I volunteered whenever possible. Why? Because as last person there, they gave me the keys. I'd have the run of the place. Whenever the opportunity arose, I was sure to remind Mum that if she was planning on heading up to

Watney Street market, five minutes further along Commercial Road, she should bring an extra couple of shopping bags. She knew why. She'd walk back home along Steel's Lane, past the factory, where I had been keeping an eye out for her. We were slick. Mum would stop for a moment at the gates, and I'd stuff boxes of sardine tins, big ones for the trade, into her bags. Poor Mum then had to stumble home, her arms almost pulled out of her sockets. She was tough though, everyone was in the neighbourhood. You did what you had to do.

I sold the tins to family and friends for half a crown. A good deal for them and a fair bit of cash for me, which went on my drums and housekeeping. Dad loved those sardines; me, I very quickly grew sick of them.

We queued up for our weekly wages at 4 pm on a Friday. The amount varied depending on the number of hours I'd done, but it was usually around the four pounds and four shillings mark. The foreman handed over the wages, which were carefully counted out in front of you by one of the two brothers who owned the factory. Every time I stood at that window, waiting for my money, looking at the boss, I couldn't help bursting out laughing. And it wasn't only because he dressed like the Penguin from my Batman comics. Although that was very funny.

Every Friday, the same thing. Me at the counter laughing. Eventually the owner had enough, and asked Jimmy Tonks what I found so amusing. Good for Jimmy, he didn't tell him a thing, although he knew full well why I was so happy. Some weeks I was nicking up to 20 quids' worth of stuff. I reckon I was working hard enough to earn that just on labour. And, anyway, I knew the owners were also on the fix. From time to time we delivered crates of pickles to their houses, and there was no way they were being put through the books. It all evened out, that's how I looked on it. Still, I probably do owe them a royalty, as they paid for the drums. They aren't going to get it, though.

It's how we survived in those days.

* * *

After those three or four months of sitting in the front room playing along to Dad's records, plus that one visit to the drum clinic, I'd decided I had learned how to play. Now it was time to start a band.

I think it might have been my cousin Roy who introduced me to a guy who had a Burns guitar. He played mainly Shadows songs. That worked. Now that I was earning I'd recently bought the *Out of The Shadows* album, the band's first release featuring Brian Bennett. It was about time I added to Dad's limited vinyl collection. I played it constantly, in particular the instrumental track 'Little "B"', following Brian's drumming as accurately as I possibly could.

In respect of my new bandmate's musical repertoire, we were an excellent fit. What wasn't so good was his jet-black hair and Rocker's cut. As a Mod, that pissed me off royally. Still, I was in a band. That's all that mattered.

We rehearsed our Shadows covers, together with some Bert Weedon numbers, in the basement of a rectory in Poplar, to the east of Havering Street. It was a hassle transporting my drums there. I couldn't take the full kit, just the bare essentials, packed into shopping bags – snare drum, cymbals, foot pedal and high hat. Three stands. I made sure always to be at the front of the bus queue, so that I could dump everything in the luggage area. Otherwise I wouldn't have been able to get on. And I had to be smart getting off, everything in one go, making sure I didn't leave anything behind. The bus wouldn't have waited for two trips.

The church the rectory was attached to ran a youth club. That was my first-ever gig. I think we called ourselves The Side-walkers. It's a very long time ago now, and I can't be a hundred per cent sure, but it makes sense, when you think of the step-over routines Hank Marvin and the boys used to perform when they were playing.

To celebrate I bought a pair of trendy hobnail boots. They were bright red and called 'Tough', part of the Mod look at the time. 'I'm having these! Perfect for the gig.' Only thing was, I had never actually tried to play drums in them. Turned out they were far too big and heavy to work the pedal properly. We were so bad, we must have driven every one of the 11 people watching us to despair.

We stuck it out for a few months, playing tiny halls and occasionally tucked away in the corner of a pub. The fact that we were clearly never going to go anywhere really didn't matter. I was staying out of trouble, that's what mattered. By the time I had packed in school, my mates who once had been nothing more than little Herberts were now becoming involved in gangs; rascals turning into ruffians and worse. I know I would have been drawn into that world had it not been for the drums. It's not too strong a statement to say they saved my life, or at the very least my liberty. No question.

The Sidewalkers picked up a bass player, and we improved. A bit. I was playing better, no doubt about that, but I knew I somehow had to find a way to take the next big step.

Then I heard about a jazz band with a Friday night residency at a pub called the British Prince in Bromley Street, across Commercial Road. Apparently, the drummer, Roy, was a bit special. Time to check him out.

Summer 1963. I'm sitting at a small table on my own in the British Prince. The band are good, the drummer especially, with a real swing. He's the singer as well. I've been coming here for the past few Fridays, closely studying him. Tonight, during one of the breaks, he comes over. He doesn't look too thrilled. I'm guessing maybe he's become unnerved by this kid sitting near the front of the stage, eyes focussed directly on him. What the hell is he going to say?

'Why do you keep staring at me. And blinking?'

Was I? 'Oh. Sorry. I didn't know. I think it must be because you are always blinking. I'm just copying you. You see, I play drums as well.' I'd noticed that tic he had, when he concentrates, but I hadn't realised I'd adopted it myself. This is embarrassing. He's a good bloke though, alright about it.

'Right. That's okay. But, you know, try to stop, eh. It's distracting.'

Next week I'm back, eyes wide open. I'm totally into the music, when during the set my new friend suddenly announces that for the next song he's stepping aside for a guest drummer.

How exciting. I look around. Who is it going to be? Then he's pointing at me. 'And here he is.'

What the ...

This isn't being chucked in the deep end of the pool; this is the ocean.

I sit behind this massive kit, much bigger than mine, much better, with the bloke's Reslo microphone sticking up between my legs. What do I do now? The other three guys in the band look at me. I swear to God, they are ten feet tall. Giants. Then they start to count in the song and the world shifts into slow motion. I can't move. I'm in total shock.

'One ... two ... one ... two ... three ... four.'

I start to play. Snap! The world comes alive again, and I am in heaven. I am the driver who has to make the song fly. And utterly unbelievably, the band start following me. Amazing.

I come off stage shaking, adrenalin pumping, and sit down in my seat. I am trying to take in what just happened.

'That was great. Really good. Are you excited?' Someone is sitting next to me. The barman. I hadn't noticed.

'Yeah, yeah, I am.'

'Are you in a band?'

'No, but I am going to form one. I want to.'

Things have suddenly changed. Shadows covers aren't going to do it for me anymore. My two band mates are out the window. They are no longer part of me. Anyway, they're Rockers. I don't think many fans will mourn our passing.

The barman nods. 'My brother's a guitarist. Well, he's learning, like you. Just now he can't play much, but shall I bring him down next week to say hello?'

'Sure. Why not.'

'Great, I'll tell him. My name's Stan by the way, Stan Lane.'

CHAPTER 3

JUST A NOISE

I arrived at the British Prince around 5.30 pm, eager to meet Stan the Barman's brother. The band weren't due on for an hour or so. At around quarter past six, the pub door opened and in walked a skinny rake, maybe a couple of years older than me, with a Beatles haircut, the first I'd seen apart from the Fab Four. He was wearing a smart grey suit and tie, with a very tight knot. His white, starched collar stuck out stiff and sharp. It could have been classified a dangerous weapon. Every time he moved his head, the collar stayed still. He looked fantastic.

'Hey, you must be Kenny. I'm Ronnie Lane, Stan's brother.'

From those very first words, Ronnie and I got on like a house on fire. We fitted together – same sense of humour and musical interests. Ronnie lived in the Manor Park area of the East End, upstairs in a big old Victorian place on Romford Road, not far from the J60 music shop. Within days of our meeting I was lugging my drums on to the bus and heading over there to practise.

For the first couple of weeks it was just the two of us, until one evening Ronnie mentioned that he'd met someone who was forming a band. He'd asked Ronnie to join.

Okay. But what about us?

'Kenny, they're also looking for a drummer. There's auditions tomorrow. Bring your kit. You'll be great.'

I didn't really like the sound of this, I wasn't convinced I was ready to audition. But I went anyway. There was one bloke there already, a brash, show-off drummer. He'd obviously had lessons, which immediately put me right off him, and was giving it all the fancy twirls. Shame he couldn't play a beat to save his life. When my turn came, I played well, better than Mr Fancy Pants that's for sure, and the band seemed to appreciate what I could do. Things were looking good; until they decided to go with the Twirler.

When they announced their decision, Ronnie was not impressed. 'Well, fucking stuff the lot of you,' he shouted, giving them the V for added effect. We stalked out as fast as, well, as fast as two blokes carrying a drum kit, guitar and amp can.

Now we both *really* wanted to be in a band. Ronnie put some feelers out and caught up with a mate of his from school, Ron Chimes, who we all called Ben, after the Big Ben clock tower I think. 'Ben' owned a Vox organ and we built a band around that, calling ourselves The Outcasts. Ben enlisted a friend, Steve Taylor, to join Ronnie on guitar, and a little later Ronnie persuaded another mate, Alan Hunt, to come on bass. Alan was a little older than the rest of us, with a day job driving a van, which in the evenings doubled as the group's transport. That made a big difference, allowing us to jump at opportunities that otherwise would have been impossible. Life rapidly began to change for the better.

One of the opportunities we took advantage of brought me back to the British Prince. The jazz band was moving on, and we were offered the chance to step into their residency spot. We didn't blink.

We played Friday or Saturday nights, mainly covers, 20 quid for the weekend, 15 split between us and a fiver into the kitty for petrol and sandwiches. With the British Prince residency, plus town hall and youth club gigs in between, I might pocket up to 15 or 20 quid a week. Good money, usually spent badly on fags for my mates, but I did manage to keep some of it back for house-keeping and finally paying off the HP on my first kit.

Regular gigs, regular paid gigs, at the age of 15 – this was everything I'd wished for since picking up those one and a half sticks. I was living the dream. Then three months into the residency, at the end of a Saturday session, this.

'Kenny, listen. I'm really sorry but, you see, me and the boys, we've been talking and it's just that, well, we've all decided, we don't think, you know, that you're getting it. We're all there, tight, improving each week, but you, well, we're leaving you behind. Kenny, we've decided. Unless you improve, quickly, we're gonna find a new drummer, someone who can keep up with us. You understand, don't you?'

No I do not.

It was Ronnie talking. My mate Ronnie. Clearly he'd been elected to do the deed. I didn't say a word. I didn't trust myself. I felt the tears behind my eyes, trying to force themselves out. Not in front of the band. They were huddled across the other side of the little dance floor. Watching. Guilty as hell.

On the way home, no one spoke. At Havering Street I unpacked my kit, slammed the van door shut, and watched them drive off. To success? *Fuck, it's all but over for me. And it hasn't even started. What now?*

The next day, cousin Roy popped in for a cuppa.

'Kenny, how's the life of a rock 'n' roll star?'

'They want me out the band.' It's all I could manage.

'What you talking about? Tell me.'

I told him.

Once again, I was close to tears, but despite myself, Roy's response made me smile. 'That's bullshit. None of you are good enough! You're all still learning. It's just a fucking noise.'

Roy knew how much the band meant to me, how much I'd put into it, into my drumming. The following Friday he came down to the British Prince, and had a go at Ronnie during the break, getting right in his face.

'What's this about Kenny, Ron? You don't want him anymore? That's what I'm hearing. Tell me different.'

'Well, Roy, you see, it's nothing personal, but we just don't think he's good enough yet.'

'Listen Ron, to be perfectly honest, none of you are exactly musicians are you. Let's face it, you've only got a couple of chords, and that's it. You're all the same. Crap. Don't pick out Kenny as if he's the only problem. Give it more time. See what happens. Okay, Ron?'

Ronnie was never comfortable with confrontation. He started to nod, vigorously. 'Yeah, yeah, fine. I get it. No problem. No quick decision.'

Until then, Ronnie and Roy had been getting on great, but after Roy's intervention their relationship changed. Roy was in and out of our music careers for many years afterwards, helping out in a variety of roles, but whenever he was around, Ronnie always kept his distance. He was apprehensive of Roy. I don't think Ronnie ever really forgave Roy for what he said that night.

Me, I forgave Ronnie, because deep down I understood. He was thinking of the band and at that stage I probably wasn't good enough. The thing is, when a drummer makes a mistake it's like dropping a dustbin down the stairs. It crashes through the song. But when a guitarist or bass player drops a note, no one really notices. That's what Ronnie and the others were getting at. I wasn't yet at a level to glue the music together. Ronnie was speaking the truth and his words had a huge impact on me. I started practising even more, virtually every moment I possibly could, and quickly my playing took off, overtaking the others. I'd needed the push, the extra drive. I never heard talk of another drummer again.

Before too long, however, we were talking about a new band. The Outcasts had come to their natural end. The British Prince residency had been fantastic, playing Shadows, Chuck Berry, Jerry Lee Lewis covers, great material like that, and it had paid well, but after a few months they were looking for something new, fresh. So were we. The time had come to expand the repertoire. Rhythm and blues was featuring more in our lives, certainly for Ronnie and me. Muddy Waters and Howlin' Wolf had led to people like BB King and John Lee Hooker. At the same time, Tamla Motown songs were beginning to hit the airwaves, in the shape of The Miracles and then Martha Reeves & The Vandellas, while soul was beginning to make a big impression in the shape of Solomon Burke and pretty much anything we heard on the Stax label, in particular our favourite, Booker T & the MGs. When both Ronnie and I first heard the track 'Green Onions' we were blown away. That was the direction of travel for us. These were exciting days in music, a heady mix of styles and influences, and we wanted to reflect it all in what we played.

Ronnie in particular voiced his need for change. He felt his playing wasn't strong enough to carry the band. We needed a better guitarist. He also no longer wanted the lead singer role. We needed a vocalist. We spread the word.

The live music scene in the early 1960s had exploded; groups formed, disbanded, re-formed, merged, all the time. Fluid. The Outcasts breaking up, morphing into something new, The

LET THE GOOD TIMES ROLL

Pioneers, was no big deal. Ben and Steve left and in came George Cambridge on vocals and Terry 'Noggsy' Newman on lead guitar, with Ronnie concentrating on rhythm. Noggsy was a hell of a guitarist, better than Ronnie, just as he'd wanted, and a great laugh. He loved Bo Diddley and Little Richard, and suddenly we were into their songs as well, further branching out.

The Marquee Club in Wardour Street, Soho, was another source of inspiration. They had recently moved to their new premises and we'd all go along to see whoever was playing, wishing we could be up on that stage. Ronnie and I saw The Who there, at the start of their long Tuesday-night residency towards the end of 1964. I was already a fan, even though I hadn't previously seen them play. Walking around town over that summer I used to see these posters, advertising Who gigs, featuring their lead guitarist swinging his arm wildly in the air. I was fascinated by that image, and the concert itself certainly lived up to it. Afterwards Ronnie and I headed home, talking very little, both occupied with the same thought. *We've got to make that happen for The Pioneers*. By then, however, although we didn't know it, the band's days were numbered.

For the year or so that The Pioneers were together, we were serious. Alan Hunt had his own sky-blue van by then, and he stencilled our name down the side. In that band wagon we toured the East End, playing pubs and town halls, sometimes up to the other side of the North Circular, maybe even West London, but not too far west. That wouldn't have suited us. I remember when I first heard more about The Who, or The High Numbers as they were then, around mid-1964, and how they came from Shepherd's Bush. I thought that meant they must be well-to-do; everything outside the East End was posh. Then one day I met them ...

* * *

By summer 1964 I knew I needed a proper job. How did I know? Mum and Dad told me, that's how. In fact, they insisted. I'd been working on and off at Speciality Foods for a while by then, and making some money from gigs, but that wasn't sufficient. 'You need a full-time job, son. Just in case.'

By then I had my eye on a new set of drums. I'd be sorry to say goodbye to the Olympic, it had been ideal starting out, but in truth it wasn't really a proper kit. Buying one of those though, costs money. So a job, why not?

When I first met Ronnie Lane he told me he was working as a plumber's plumber's mate. We had a right laugh about it. I'd tell him he was talking nonsense, that there was no such thing, and he'd insist that, 'I'm not just a plumber's mate, you know. I'm a plumber's plumber's mate. Much more important.' Yeah, right Ronnie. Big head.

Anyway, he wasn't plumbing plumbing for long before he was offered a fantastic job, testing amps at the Selmer's Electronics factory in Theobalds Road, central London. Vox amps held the top spot on the market for quality, but Selmer's came a close second. If Ronnie had to have a job, this was the one.

Ronnie worked in a sound-proof room at the end of the assembly line. When all the components had been fitted into the shells, the completed amp would be wheeled into Ronnie's room, where he would plug in a guitar or bass and try it out, playing anything he wanted. 'Green Onions' naturally became a standard. In effect, he was being paid to practise.

This sounded like my sort of place, and when Ronnie mentioned there was a position going at Selmer's I jumped at it. He omitted to mention it was on the assembly line, fitting the reverb units. Still, I needed a job.

In a storage room at one end of the factory, the empty units were piled as high as a house, a wall of simulated leather shells, which would then move down the line to be made up. That's when I discovered a new word – 'shellac' – the liquid I dipped the wingnuts into when fitting the reverb units. Perhaps not the most exciting job in the world, but Ronnie and I had a lot of fun there.

My boss on the assembly line was a Polish guy called Felix. I felt he was a terrible slave driver, although he wasn't really, he was just doing his job. Which was usually more than I could say about myself. Or Ronnie. Basically, we didn't want to work, and just took the piss the whole time. Ronnie would always know which amps I'd been working on when they arrived in his room and would regularly reject them for no reason, claiming they were not up to Selmer quality. Felix would go mad, have a right go at me, and I'd have a go back at him. It wasn't a happy working relationship.

I loved winding up Felix. When he wasn't on my back, he spent the rest of his day marching up and down the line making sure everyone was doing exactly what they should be doing. I'd clock when he reached the point furthest from me, then wander off for a stroll and a laugh with the other blokes in the factory, until Felix had completed his round and was heading back towards my section. I made sure he saw me, that was the whole point. 'Jones, Jones, get back to your work!' he'd scream, and break into a run to try and catch me as I scarpered round to Ronnie's room.

In there, we'd cut a hole in the wall through to the adjoining room, where the amp shells were stored. Ronnie always made sure this escape hatch was hidden behind the amp he was testing, so that when I appeared he could quickly pull that amp to one side, allowing me to dive through into the cubby hole we'd created in that second room, behind stacks of damaged amps and odd bits of wood. Ronnie would then quickly slide the amp back into place.

Moments later, when Felix burst through the door he'd see Ronnie casually sitting on the amp, playing away, doing his job. Cool as you like.

'Everything alright Felix?'

Bemused, Felix had to walk out, shaking his head, muttering to himself as he headed back to the assembly line. Where he would see me, diligently working away. That drove him nuts.

That secret cubby hole acted as a den for Ronnie and me. We'd skive off in there, to play cards and smoke. We could access it either through Ronnie's sound-proof room, or from that storage room, via a second hole we'd cut in one of the damaged amps protecting our secret. That's how I was able to scamper back my work station without being seen.

We played out this routine on numerous occasions, con-founding Felix every time. He never sussed how we did it. Once, Ronnie told me, Felix grew so annoyed at my disappearance that he searched everywhere in the room he could think of. Including the pockets of Ronnie's coat. *Come on Felix, I know I am not the tallest guy, but ...* We knew we were safe though, Felix wouldn't dream of touching the amp Ronnie was testing. That was valuable company property, not to be messed with.

Big surprise. I didn't last more than a few months at Selmer's.

It was long enough, however, to afford my new set of drums. Two new sets, in fact. I'd needed an upgrade from the Olympic, but ended up with a downgrade with the next kit.

Trixon drums were the new thing – innovative shapes, imported from Germany. And if it's new and innovative, it must be better, right? Wrong. The bass drum was shaped like a cone. That's unusual. I like that. That'll be great. No, it won't. Fucking awful. But, unbelievably, that bass drum was better than the snare. When I hit that, all the lugs that you use to tighten the skin snapped. They were die-cast.

I quickly blew that kit off, trading it in for a proper upgrade, a Ludwig Silver Glitter. This was the real thing. Miles better quality, much louder, great cymbals, and capable of being set up just as I wanted it. Now I was ready.

* * *

The Pioneers came crashing to a halt at the beginning of 1965, days after Ronnie told me he no longer wanted to play guitar, even though he loved his maroon Gretsch, just like George Harrison's. His dad had helped him buy it, but having caught the bass bug at Selmer's he decided that suited him better. As he told his father, 'I'll always find work as a bass player. Everyone else dreams of being the lead.'

'Okay Ronnie,' I said to him when he broke the news, 'if that's what you want, great. Let's go down J60, see what they've got.'

It's Saturday morning and Ronnie meets me off the bus in Manor Park. He lives five minutes away from the music shop and we walk over together. Ronnie tells me he has his heart set on a Harmony bass, but he's not sure he can afford one.

'Well let's just see Ronnie. Maybe we can get a deal.'

As we're looking around, this Flash Harry swaggers over, a young guy, cocky.

'Awright? Need help?'

Ronnie gives the bloke a nod, shakes his hand. He seems to know him vaguely, like they've met before. I also recognise his face, it stirs a memory, but I can't place it. Maybe he plays in a group that has been on the same bill as The Pioneers? Perhaps that's where Ronnie knows him from. There's something about his attitude though, I've seen it before.

'Hi,' Ronnie says, 'I want to try out a bass. I've been playing guitar for a couple of years, but I'm not getting anywhere, you know. I want a bass.'

'Okay mate, I've got just the thing. Come and try this one.'

The two of them go off to check out the stack of basses, but I can't help them with that, so I make a beeline for the drum section. I can hear them talking over the other side of the shop.

'Nah, you don't want that one. It's fuckin' horrible. Try this.' I see Ronnie glance at the price tag and grimace.

My attention is pulled back to the drums. There's a belter of a kit set up on display. I've got to have a go.

I'm playing away, some rolls and little fills I've been working on, trying not to be too loud, the shop's busy after all, when Ronnie and the bloke come over. Ronnie's carrying a Harmony, and wearing maybe the biggest smile ever on his face. He's smitten.

'Mind if we join in, to see how the bass sounds?'

'Yeah, great.'

The sales guy plugs in Ronnie's bass and a guitar for himself and we start. Right away, it's magic. We gel. We've got a blues riff going on. We're getting into it, cranking it up. We've forgotten where we are.

'Oi! You three! For God's sake give it a rest, will you! I'm trying to serve someone.'

It's the J60's guvnor. He's not happy.

'Alright, alright. We get the message. Keep your hair on.' Our new guitar friend doesn't seem too concerned. 'We was just trying out his bass. He's thinking of buying it.'

'Well either buy it or get the hell out of here.'

We stop, and the guvnor leaves us to it.

'So what'd you think?'

Ronnie looks down at the bass and sighs. 'This is it. But I can't afford it. It'll have to be that first one.'

'Nah. Don't worry about that. Leave it to me.'

Half an hour later we're back in the shop with Ronnie's dad Stan, who needs to sign the hire purchase forms as guarantor. As Mr Lane is filling out the paperwork, which miraculously now lists the Harmony at the price of the first bass Ronnie looked at, the three of us get chatting.

'So you two in a band, or what?'

'Yeah, yeah, we are,' I tell him. 'The Pioneers.'

He shrugs. 'Not sure. I've maybe heard of you.'

'Well we're playing tonight, if you fancy it. Bermondsey, just over Tower Bridge. It's a regular gig. Where'd you live?'

'Flat in Ilford.'

'Easy, we'll pick you up on the way.'

He shrugs again. 'Why not?'

'Great. I'm Kenny by the way. This is Ronnie.'

'Pleased to meet you Kenny and Ronnie. I just work here Saturdays. I'm Steve Marriott.'

He says his name in a significant way, like it should mean something. It doesn't, not to me.

As usual, I was the last stop on Alan's pick-up. We had to pack everyone else in first, then cram my drums around them. It was like the old joke: how do you fit a five-piece band into the back of a small Bedford van? With difficulty.

As soon as I opened the rear doors to hand in my kit, Steve was sitting there right in front of me. Again, I had that flash –

I know you. It came to me halfway across Tower Bridge, heading to the gig at the Earl of Derby pub on Grange Road.

'From the Troxy! Of course. He's that right little geezer in the Peter Seller's film *Heavens Above!*, that's it.' I blurted it out. Steve looked across at me, with that crooked smile I would come to love, and raised his eyebrows – course you know me – we all burst out laughing.

There was something more, that I held back. Too embarrassing. I whispered it to Ronnie later that evening, as we were setting up the gear.

'I've been dreaming about Steve. Well, you, me and Steve. It's happened loads of times. I could never make out the faces, but now I've met him, I know it's the three of us. We're in a band. On TV.'

Right from when I was teaching myself how to play drums, driving the whole street nuts, then through The Outcasts and into The Pioneers, I always said that we were going to be on television. Up until that moment of recognising Marriott in my dream, I'm not sure I really believed it. After that, I knew for sure.

Halfway through the gig, Ronnie introduced Steve to the stage. We knew he was a singer because we'd been talking about it in the van. I remembered then that I'd also seen him perform on stage, in a band called The Moments. To be fair, it was the equipment rather than his face that stuck in my mind. He had a Reslo mic hanging above him from a goose neck stand. I'd never seen anything like that before. Then out came this fucking amazing voice. That I also remembered.

Not being a shy bloke, when Ronnie called him up, Steve leapt on stage, straight over to the piano tucked away to the side, and started playing and singing. The crowd went crazy. We were giving it James Brown, Wilson Pickett. The place was rocking.

Then Steve got carried away. First, he's up on the piano, singing, movin' and groovin', then inevitably he's onto the keys, dancing up and down, smashing them up. Not surprising, the pub landlord got the hump. He let us finish the set before he threw us out, and with us, our Saturday night residency. Me, Steve and Ronnie thought the whole thing was hilarious but the other boys were incredibly pissed off that we'd screwed up a good little earner. They looked down their noses at us and drove off in the van.

I called my dad from the telephone box across the road and, as we sat on the kerb waiting for him to rescue us, amps, guitars and drums piled around, we looked at each other and burst out laughing again.

Lifelong friendships forged in laughter. I'll take that any day.

* * *

The three us became inseparable. A couple of days later we were in Steve's flat, sitting in the front room, listening to his record collection. He had albums by all the artists Ronnie and I were into. It was amazing, as if we were meant to be together. He put on album after album, introducing us to tracks we never heard on the radio. On that afternoon, and on many days thereafter, Steve offered an advance course in music. We'd be listening to Ray Charles, for instance, and I'd say how fantastic I thought his voice was. 'Absolutely,' Steve would reply. 'One of the greatest ever. But also listen to those backing singers. See how they complement Ray's vocals. How they hold the track together.' It was an education in how the best songs were constructed. As we talked about the music, I knew I wanted to be in a band that could create that quality of sound.

There was a piano in the room, proudly displaying framed family photos, a typical domestic scene, until occasionally

Steve would sit there and start playing some of the music we'd been listening to. Then, with Ronnie and me accompanying him on whatever was lying around, tins or books, slapping our thighs, making noises, we transported ourselves to smoke-filled, basement clubs in Memphis and Detroit. Something was happening, something special. We knew it.

When it came to knowing the happening places in London, Steve had a lot more street-smarts than either Ronnie or me. By 1965 he'd already spent a year playing the Artful Dodger in Lionel Bart's stage show *Oliver!*. Steve had stayed in touch with Lionel and later introduced him to the band. I was pleased he did. Lionel was a lovely man and I enjoyed his company. Having made a success of his role as the Dodger, Steve was then accepted into the Italia Conti acting school, which proved to be his intro-duction to the trendy haunts of London's West End. With Steve as our guide, Ronnie and I soon became well acquainted with places like the 100 Club on Oxford Street, where you could listen to wonderful jazz and R&B, and the hip La Gioconda coffee bar in Denmark Street. It was there, over frothy coffee – they didn't have much of that in the East End – we began to talk about forming a band.

That talk grew serious when, a few weeks after meeting Steve, Ronnie and I were sacked from Selmer's. What little interest either of us had in working for a living had soon disappeared with all the talk of a new group and we began to turn up at the factory later and later each morning until they'd had enough. Not unfair, and not unwelcome. We were both out on the same morning and immediately headed west. La Gioconda. Steve had already been given the elbow from the J60 – his boss hadn't appreciated the unauthorised discount to Ronnie – and we knew that's where he'd be.

He looked up as we walked through the door and smiled. We were going to make a go of it.

Until then it had been talk; now it was time to make plans. We realised we needed two things: a keyboard player for sure, but more than that, a place to rehearse.

Steve provided the solution to the latter. 'I've got a mate, Jimmy Langwith, I met him in J60, his old man runs the Ruskin Arms, up Manor Park. They've got a little ballroom out the back. Loads of bands play there. It's made for us. I'll ask him.'

Steve was right, the room at the Ruskin Arms did prove an ideal place to rehearse. Thank God. We needed it.

Ronnie Lane grew to become one of the best bass players in the business, but in those very early days of the band, his experience amounted to a matter of weeks. He had a lot of learning to cram in, even though it was clear he had the gift. Those couple of years on lead guitar helped, I think. He hadn't been a great guitarist, proficient yes, but not much more, but having made the move to bass he immediately found it a damn sight easier, and with that came confidence. With the hours of practice the Ruskin Arms offered, his natural talent quickly blossomed.

Steve's presence also helped Ronnie. To start with, Steve was a decent guitarist even then, who became better and better as the weeks, months and, eventually, years passed. Even if he didn't always recognise that himself. His ability spurred us both on no question, but perhaps more important, especially during those initial sessions, was his attitude. He took being in a band far more seriously than the other guys we'd been playing with and that determination to improve his performances and expand his musical range had a significant impact on Ronnie and me. Steve's inherent drive pushed us onto another level. And it was fun, that was critical. The three us got along famously, we were excited, having a laugh, enjoying each other's company, looking forward to hanging out, talking and making music.

As for my playing then, well, Steve said years later that he thought I was a rotten drummer at the beginning, and that I would probably say so myself. *No, I would not.* Following the kick up the arse I received by almost being dumped from The Outcasts, I had been so intent on improving that during the Ruskin Arms days I was as good a musician as the other two, and over the years, for a variety of reasons, I believe I overtook them. I think Steve would probably say so himself. Perhaps.

Jimmy Langwith (or Jimmy Winston as he liked to be known), Steve's mate from the J60, would occasionally hang out during the rehearsals, sometimes playing with us. He was into his guitar then, but as Steve had that covered we never thought of him in any other way than a decent bloke, a bit older, who'd helped us out with the room.

Then he bought a Vox organ. Now he became a regular at the rehearsals, part of the furniture even. Jimmy and his keyboards.

Before long, Steve had a word with Ronnie and me. 'Jimmy wants to join the band. We need an organ player. What'd think?'

'But he doesn't know how to play the organ.'

'I know, but I can help him there. Show him a few simple chords, get him started.'

'But ... '

'His brother owns a van. He's offered to drive us around.'

Jimmy was in.

The van turned out to be an old police vehicle, known as a Black Maria or Meat Wagon, which was just about large enough for us all to squeeze in, plus instruments and amps. There was also the bonus of a functioning bell. We had a lot of laughs ringing that as we drove past old ladies.

The van had been designed with a metal divider separating driver and front passengers from the rear section, no doubt for safety reasons. Set into this panel was a sliding section with wire mesh, allowing the officers to check on their 'guests'. Security rather than comfort had been the priority. There was no covering or insulation on the floor, along the windowless sides or on the roof, which was a pain as that was covered in rust. Every time you jumped over the amps to get out, your barnet would be dusted in flakes. Definitely not the Mod look. In the back, the only sign that the primary function of the van had been to transport people, was the two low, hard benches running from the rear doors to the dividing panel.

With only the four of us, plus an occasional mate helping out, the space was fine – three in front and one or two wedged in the back with the gear. Before too long, however, modifications were required when touring outside of London necessitated the recruitment of a couple of roadies. Additional seats were needed, a problem solved with the installation of an old sofa behind the driver's panel. With that in place, whoever was in the back would pile in first, the equipment crammed in after. The only way of escape was when the lucky sods up front dragged out an amp or two, allowing you to squeeze by.

None of it bothered us. We were a band on the road. That's all we cared about.

We started to pick up gigs, nothing special initially, just the usual pubs and clubs around the area. One in particular sticks out during this early 1965 period, when for the first time we became a five piece. Almost.

We'd grown friendly with one of the regulars at Gioconda, a short Mod like us, cottage-loaf hairdo, the lot. He was a song-writer and guitarist, into protest songs about banning the bomb and all that. A folk Mod, I guess, and great fun to be around. We got on incredibly well, even though we weren't really into his style of music.

We spent hours together in that cafe, swapping records, talking about artists we'd discovered, dreaming of a different life. We became close. He'd tell us about the songs he'd been writing and one afternoon asked whether he could play some with us. No problem, we said, we've got a gig in Romford tonight. You're welcome to come along, provided you help us load and unload the van.

At the gig, as the interval approached, he was sitting down at the front, trying to catch Steve's eye, all expectant. 'Now?' 'Not quite yet.' 'Now?' 'Nearly.'

Eventually Steve gave him the nod. 'Now.' Thrilled, he climbed up on stage, guitar in hand, ready to go, and we buggered off for a beer! He didn't mind, he was happy to play to the crowd on his own. After that gig he played with us on several occasions, in Ilford and other places. He was good, very good, even if his songs weren't exactly our cup of tea. I thought of him as the unofficial fifth member of the band, and if he hadn't primarily been a singer I'm convinced he would have joined. But Marriott didn't want another vocalist, fair enough, and there was also that conflict in terms of the material.

For all the right reasons, it never happened, but we continued to support him in whatever he was doing, going to his gigs, talking up his talent as we began to make it. We were mates and we wanted him to succeed. Not that I think we were responsible for his career taking off. It was just a matter of time. David Jones was destined to become a star – as David Bowie he proved that.

There was a strong bond between us and David, our lives were intertwined, kids imagining similar futures, encouraging each other to step out on the road. To know he's now gone is hard to believe.

* * *

Now that we were a 'band', Steve, Ronnie, Jimmy and I decided we needed our own place. The idea was to create an environment to foster creativity. You know. Oh, and to smoke weed away from our parents.

Jimmy organised a flat in Stratford, and we moved in. Well, Steve, Ronnie and Jimmy moved in, I didn't fancy it. I was only 16 and enjoyed home. Mum and Dad never gave me any hassle, I could be as much of a jack-the-lad as I wanted, and still sleep in my own bed. Where it was quiet.

Taking on that flat felt like a big step, like we were growing up. Even though I wasn't living there I used to go over every day to watch television and listen to records late into the night. And get stoned. It was impossible not to. The room where we hung out was dense with bluish smoke as the boys rolled and passed around spliff after spliff. Occasionally I would join them, but I never really got into it. Smoking a joint just made me first feel woozy, then hungry. While the others were lolling around, laughing and giggling, talking nonsense, I'd be in the little kitchen, raiding the cupboards for every tin available and mixing the lot in a giant pot on the stove. It wasn't exactly Mum's home cooking, but I'd eat the lot.

During that early run of gigs, we hadn't settled on what we were going to be called. We performed under a variety of guises, usually daft names made up by Steve on the spot. Until one evening, after playing at a youth centre, I think, we found ourselves in the flat of a posh bird called Annabelle, one of Steve's Italia Conti crowd. Nothing like us.

No doubt there were a few smokes being shared, and drinks, as we lay around in the front room, not doing much, listening to music, when suddenly Annabelle sat up and stared across at us. 'You know what,' she exclaimed, 'you all have little faces, you're all small, you should be the Small Faces!'

We looked at each other, our eyes lit up, then we burst out laughing. What a ridiculous name. Give us a break, love. Only a right bunch of Herberts would call themselves the Small Faces.

CHAPTER 4

CAVIAR AND BROWN SAUCE

We were that right bunch of Herberts. Having mercilessly taken the mickey out of calling ourselves 'Small Faces' for a few weeks, the name then stuck. We ended up loving it.

With our musical horizons expanding, we decided to do the same geographically. A tour was required, if we could find anyone to book us. Gigging around London – the East End mainly – had generated a strong local following and we felt we were starting to come together as a unit. Now the time had arrived to experiment with new audiences and explore different scenes.

I'm not sure who landed our first northern club gigs. It may have been a friend of Steve's, a guy we called Terry the Egg, our roadie for a while, but I can't be certain. All I do know is that in May 1965 we had a couple of venues booked, in Manchester and Sheffield, and off we went. It was crazy really. The sensible thing would have been to hold off until we gained more experience. We only knew a handful of songs for goodness sake; basically we were largely untried, untested and unprepared. What's stopping us? Nothing. That was the attitude: we don't care, it'll be a laugh and we'll learn. That was important to us. From the very beginning, we never wanted

71

to settle into a cosy comfort zone. We were always looking to push ourselves.

The first ever Small Faces tour was not a glamourous affair.

We were on our way to Knutsford in Cheshire, driving up the M1, and I was incredibly excited. Sitting in the back of the van, bouncing up and down on our newly installed sofa, I kept pestering Jimmy in the driver's seat to let me have a go.

'Leave off. You haven't passed your test.'

'Come on Jimmy, I've been driving Dad's lorry for years. Give me a go.'

Eventually he relented and there I was tearing up the motorway, having a rare old time, until it started to piss down. This wasn't so much fun. The wipers, or more accurately, the wiper, was hopeless. A single, short blade, in the middle of the windscreen, slowly stuttering back and forth. I couldn't see a bloody thing, added to which we were getting buffeted around by increasingly strong winds. This was rock 'n' roll alright, just not how I'd imagined it. Then the bloody wiper blew right off, disappearing into the distance behind us.

I pulled on to the hard shoulder. Somehow this was all my fault and I was bundled out into the pouring rain to retrieve the wiper. Luckily it had bounced off the main carriageway and we were able to re-attach it with some gaffer tape. I wasn't allowed to drive again.

A few hours later, just south of Knutsford, where we planned to stay overnight in a B&B, the van broke down. For a while we'd been hearing a disturbing rattling noise, but thankfully Jimmy had managed to nurse our ailing vehicle to a garage before it gave up the ghost. The mechanics had a look under the bonnet and after a period of tutting and shaking of heads, they announced there was a problem with the engine. No kidding. Worse, they didn't stock the necessary part. Great.

Jimmy called his brother who worked in the car trade in Loughton. He'd been driving us around London, but couldn't get time off work for the tour. Once again, though, he helped out. He located a nearby auto parts supplier who had what we needed in stock and Jimmy headed back south on the train to pick it up. The rest of us slept in the van.

In the middle of the night Ronnie needed a piss, waking Steve and me as he shuffled out into the pitch dark. We heard his footsteps walking towards the garage. Then suddenly a big yell. That doesn't sound good. We waited a moment, wondering what the hell was going on. When Ronnie didn't reappear, we went looking. He wasn't hard to find, lying on his back at the bottom of the mechanics' inspection pit, pissing himself. With laughter, thank God.

In the morning we were starving. And virtually penniless. Having bought my new drums, twice, again on HP, I was very conscious of keeping enough money back to make the payments, which meant I carried around very little cash. None of us did, and what little we had we'd pooled together to pay for Jimmy's train ticket. We had thruppence to our name.

We asked the guys in the garage where we'd find the nearest place to buy something to eat.

'There's bakery just down the road. About three miles.'

'Fuck that, it's too far.' Steve and Ronnie were not up for it at all. 'You go if you want Ken, we're staying put.' What else was I going to do all day?

I was knackered by the time I found the bakers. I stood limply by the window, gazing at the cakes and pastries, my mouth watering. A little boy lost. The woman behind the counter kept glancing at me, suspicious. I must have looked quite a sight. Dishevelled and unwashed, with a glazed, forlorn look. I decided to buy the biggest thing they had, to be split three ways. My eyes came to rest on this huge rock cake. 'That'll do.' Except it cost fourpence.

Almost crying because I didn't have enough money, I approached the counter. 'Excuse me,' I said, pointing at the rock cake, 'have you got a thruppenny one of those? That's all I've got and we're so hungry.' Her expression softened. I went for it, giving the whole sob story of the van breaking down, the garage not stocking the part, having to kip there overnight and poor Ronnie falling into the pit, although in my version, he'd suffered a nasty bump on his head. For a second I was worried I might have over-egged it, but no, she took pity on me.

'You poor things. Of course you can have it for thruppence. Good luck to you, dear. And I hope your friend is out of hospital when you get back.'

The return walk was murder, looking at the rock cake, fighting temptation. I knew if I even nibbled a crumb, I wouldn't be able to stop. Marriott wouldn't have had any such qualms. I knew that. Neither would Ronnie. In my hands, breakfast made it back safe and sound, much to Ronnie and Steve's astonishment and delight.

Jimmy appeared that evening and managed to fit the part himself. We were on our way again, arriving at our B&B a day late, well after dark, and straight into another horror story – for me at least. Having signed in, my room was pointed out to me, and being so wiped out from lack of sleep the night before I didn't even bother to turn on the lights. In the gloom, I made out two beds, falling into the nearest. I didn't give the other one a moment's thought. Until I heard very heavy breathing, incomprehensible mumbles and worst of all, loud snoring. Another dreadful night's sleep, this time thanks to a bloke I didn't know. Boy, was I pissed off.

Eventually morning arrived, and I was first up for a long-overdue wash. Standing there under the dribble of water pretending to be a shower, I looked down at my feet. I was standing in a pool of reddish-brown water. What the ... ? Ah, the roof of the van. This was too good an opportunity to miss. Time to wake the boys. I grabbed a towel, wrapped it round my waist, and was out into the corridor, hair wet and dripping on my shoulders. 'Help! Help! Ronnie! Steve! Help me!' I screamed, running up and down. 'I've gone rusty!' That got them up.

The fact we had any sort of shower that morning was a treat. Often during our early touring days, we'd drive through the night to get to the next town or city, or if we did have accommodation, the shower regularly didn't work and there'd be no time for a bath. On those occasions, when we really needed to wash, we would head straight for the local swimming baths. For a few pence we'd have a swim and a shower. It was on one of those visits that Terry the Egg picked up a second nickname when he took a running jump into the pool, and instead of swimming, lay there floating. He became 'Amphibious Egg'. Well, it made us laugh.

Our first gig was that evening, at a basement club in central Manchester, the Twisted Wheel on Brazennose Street. This was a significant venue in the Northern Soul scene – a hot, sweaty, loud magnet for R&B fans and bands. It couldn't have been a more appropriate opening night. This was exactly the reason we'd decided to pile into our van and head north. Did we have an audience outside London? Would we relate to them? Recognise them? After that session, we knew the answers. Yes. We could see ourselves out there in the crowd, dancing, kissing, smoking, posing. Fabulous.

It's been written that we didn't play the Twisted Wheel on that tour, that we had to audition the day before and failed. I know that's not what happened. We played. We rocked the place.

Next stop, the following night, a working man's club in Sheffield. Not quite so fabulous.

Looking out on the crowd, we didn't see a trace of ourselves. This audience was after an evening of old-style music hall entertainment; what we were offering, they didn't get. We were giving it Muddy Waters' 'You Need Love'; they were crying out for Pat Boone. Still, they heard us out, giving us a chance. They were nice, decent people and, once again, unlike what's been claimed elsewhere, we were not thrown out of that club. We completed the set, to an admittedly muted reception.

We didn't have a gig booked for the next day, but knowing Sheffield was a kind of happening place we decide to stick around and see what we could find. We were more than happy to go knocking on doors, asking to play. We just didn't know where. Wandering around the city centre, we met this girl – well, Steve probably did – and started chatting to her.

'We're a band. Anywhere good we should be playing around here?'

'Yeah sure, the Mojo, up in Pitsmoor. Check it out. It's cool.'

That afternoon we headed to the north of the city and knocked on the door of the King Mojo Club. The owner himself answered, a bloke called Peter Stringfellow. We told him we wanted to play and that we'd do it for nothing. He looked at us, up and down, like he was assessing, then nodded and invited us in. He sat us down, fed us and said he'd sort out a spot for that night. We brought the house down.

As we were packing up, Peter came over. 'You were great, boys.'

I'm sure Peter never gave us another thought after we walked out of his club that night. We were another band passing through, nothing more. But we never forgot what he did for us. He gave us a chance, believed in us, and a few months later, with a hit single to our name, we bumped into him again on our *Ready Steady Go!* debut. He was warming up the audience and when he'd done his bit we re-introduced ourselves and thanked him.

As a band, we ended up great mates with Peter and played at his club on three or four more occasions. The Mojo was a hugely popular venue and a great place to perform. We made a lot of friends up there in Sheffield.

* * *

Back in London, another of Steve's contacts stepped into the picture, an Irish promoter who booked bands at some of the capital's best clubs and theatres, like the Cavern in the Town, a venue I already knew from the drum clinic. Steve had a word. 'Okay, you're on tonight,' his mate told him. 'Let's see how you do. We'll talk after.'

The club was bouncing throughout our set and the manager knew it. 'The next five Saturdays are yours.'

A week later, 5 June 1965, we appeared on the bill as the Small Faces for the first time.

We were standing at the bar afterwards, on a high, when a bloke approached us. 'Hello boys. Good show tonight. I've been hearing a lot about you. That's why I came down. To take a look, you know.'

We carried on giggling amongst ourselves, too excited after the performance to pay much attention to this stiff.

'Let me introduce myself. The name's Pat Meehan. I work alongside Don Arden. You've heard of him, right?'

The giggling stopped. Now this was interesting. We'd heard of Don Arden. Who hadn't? Big-time London agent.

The bloke pulled a card out of his inside jacket pocket and handed it over.

'Come up to the office tomorrow, boys. Mr Arden would like a word.'

Don Arden's office was in Carnaby Street, above the John Stephens clothes store. Of course it was. He was more than smart enough to recognise the importance of being at the centre of what was fast becoming the heart of London's youth culture. That was one of the many positive things about Don. He understood his market, the kids he was selling to.

Don was sitting behind his desk when we were shown in. Dressed in a smart suit and tie with a trim beard, he appeared a large man, even though he wasn't particularly tall. There was an aura about him, a presence, a whiff even of the underworld.

As I grew to know Don, I recognised this as a front he enjoyed cultivating. He had begun operating in the golden era of Frank Sinatra and the Rat Pack, when it seemed chic to be associated with gangsters. Don fancied the idea of giving off some of that glamourous sheen. In truth, however, Don's show-business background lay in the variety circuit. He'd been a comic singer of all things, who used to impersonate the tenor Enrico Caruso. He had some talent, but eventually recognised he wasn't going to make it as a performer and moved into management.

Having shaken our hands, Don wasted no time.

'Boys, you've got a good reputation and I can offer you a deal. How does that sound?'

Great.

'Here's the thing, in this business it's either a percentage or a wage. Up to you. What d'ya want?'

This was all going too fast. Steve spoke up. 'Mr Arden, we appreciate you seeing us. We appreciate you offering us a deal. But we've got to think it through. Do you mind if we step outside for a moment?'

'Be my guest, lads. Take your time.'

Down on Carnaby Street, smoking furiously, we huddled together and agreed what we wanted.

'Mr Arden,' Steve said, back in the office. 'We've decided. We want a wage *and* a percentage.'

Raised eyebrows. Tight lips. 'Agreed. We can draw up the ... '

'Just a couple more things. We're going to need to kit ourselves out, you know, suits, shirts, boots. Got to look the part. We'll need help with that.'

Eyebrows further raised. Eventually, 'Fine, I can arrange access to my accounts in the best shops on the street. Now, if that's it ... '

'One last thing, Mr Arden. Our parents. We're living at home, they help us out. Food, laundry, all that. Lets us focus on the music. They should get something, don't you think? It's only fair.' Mostly this was true. There was still the Stratford flat, but it was a dump, and the boys were spending less time there.

I began to think Don Arden might hurt himself. His lips were so pinched, they'd turned white. 'Okay, I'll add in an allowance. Now that really is it. Right?'

We nodded.

'Fine, the contracts will be ready in a couple of days. I'll give you a call. Welcome aboard boys.'

We thought we'd done a good deal. We were pleased with ourselves. On paper it wasn't too bad. The going royalty rate at that time was probably around 2.5 per cent and we negotiated

1.5 per cent, plus 20 quid a week wages each, eventually rising to 60. Good money, as a basic.

The wages end of the deal was fine, we received the money regularly, pretty much, plus the parents' allowance, which continued until the end of the year when Don arranged a flat for us. I know Mum and Dad were pleased with their payments. It was like an extra wage coming in.

Having some cash in my pocket made a big difference to my look. Carnaby Street was great, but it wasn't anything like what people imagine it to be, trendy clothes shops lining both sides, selling the latest fashions. Not then anyway, not when we signed with Don. Sure, it was heading in that direction, but 'Swinging London' was still a little under a year away. Instead, I would look out of Don's office window and see Shire horses pulling brewer's drays, wagons piled high with barrels of beer for delivery to the local pubs. I had to cast my sartorial eye further afield.

My cousin Roy offered his advice, directing me towards his tailor, Leach's, in Rathbone Market, for made-to-measure suits (blue, slim-fit, seven inches around the hem, no wider) and to Whitechapel for handmade shoes by Terry de Havilland, who later shot to fame when he opened his Cobblers to the World shop on the King's Road in 1972. Now I really was beginning to look the part.

Not that we forgot about our Carnaby Street shopping accounts. Not at all. We made good use of them. Even then there was Toppers, with their multicoloured leather and suede boots and shoes, and the super-trendy Lord John and John Stephens. In those first few months with Arden, I was stockpiling 10 bright shirts, two off-the-peg suits and a few pairs of shoes every week. As much as I could carry on the bus. All on Don's account. I thought.

The problems lay buried in the royalties, and when these came to the surface 18 months later, our relationship turned sour. One and a half per cent of nothing, that's how it worked out. Unbeknown to us, everything we did, everything Don as our manager 'paid for', was charged back against the record sales – travel, accommodation, promotion, the lot. 'How can I give you a percentage, boys, when you've already spent the money?' That was his line. And it was bullshit.

In the end, Don Arden screwed us. There's no other way to put it. And yet I've still got a lot of affection for him. He became like a father figure. We all liked him. He had faith in the band and he guided us. He worked hard on our behalf, he thought big, he put huge promotions together in Britain and throughout Europe. I like to believe we would have made it anyway because of the talent within the band, but history shows it was Don Arden who gave us our break.

He used every trick he knew to make us a success, and quickly. Probably because he didn't think we'd last much more than a year. Even still, there's no denying he created a hell of a launchpad. Our TV and radio exposure was second to none. Arden was brilliant at securing those appearances. So yes, he screwed us, but he also made us. The others wouldn't have agreed with that, but I'm more pragmatic. I keep an open mind and try to see the bigger picture.

It's like when I said to the boys we should invest in ourselves, in our future, by agreeing to have our music used on adverts, even at the height of our fame. We could have been more savvy with our finances, agreeing licensing deals where we received payment, not the label, to secure independence in the years ahead. That would have given us freedom to make the music we wanted to make, on our terms. They weren't having it. They saw it as selling out, degrading the songs. That was a mistake.

So, Don, I thank you, I do. I just wish you hadn't been such a lying bastard when it came to the money.

On 10 June 1965 we signed the contract Don put in front of us. A three-year deal with his company Contemporary Records. The paperwork out of the way, Don announced he had already set up our first professional gig. We didn't realise it at the time, but we were about to be granted a glimpse into the future.

Don Arden introduced us to a friend of his, Ron King, owner of the booking agency Galaxy Entertainments. I only discovered later that Don owned a slice of the Galaxy action. Like Arden, Ron King was a larger-than-life character. He travelled around in a chauffeur-driven Rolls-Royce, shadowed by a Land Rover, stuffed with four heavies. Ron and Don – no surprise they were thick as thieves.

The gig was in Romford, at Wykeham Hall, a venue owned by King. We turned up as instructed to discover we were one of about a dozen bands on the bill. Okay, fine, we'll do our thing, get paid and be on our way. We did our thing, we didn't get paid.

'Lads, lads, it's an audition. Didn't you know? You don't get paid for an audition. But if the crowd here vote you their favourite, you can come back next week, top of the bill and 15 quid richer.' Needless to say, each audience member had paid an admission price.

Nice deal, Don. For someone.

Arden did not hang around. Days after we signed with Contemporary, he negotiated a record deal with Decca. Brilliant work. Although, not particularly tricky. Turned out Arden's company and Decca had a formal understanding, no doubt involving some form of retainer or suchlike, about signing the bands on Contemporary's books.

Nice deal, Don. For someone.

Despite what may or may not have been going on behind the scenes, Decca was the right label for us at the time. They were focussed on turning out hits, and that was the direction Don was guiding us towards. Within a month of signing with Contemporary, within six months of first meeting Steve Marriott, with me still only 16 years old, we were in a studio, being instructed that our A-side tracks had to be of radio length. Nothing over two and a half minutes. Ideally less. Anything longer would have to be cut down to size. Yes, we would be given some leeway on the B-sides to produce the more authentic, edgier R&B feel that represented the Small Faces as we saw ourselves, but essentially we were there to make hits. That was made clear. Arden knew it was the only way to bring success. I have nothing but praise for him in that respect. It was a necessary evil and he made us.

Over the previous weeks, Steve had been playing around with a riff inspired by Solomon Burke's classic, 'Everybody Needs Somebody to Love'. Ronnie then joined in, and between them they worked it up into something we all liked. Arden agreed, but it needed the edges sanded down and, of course, lyrics.

Don approached the songwriting duo of Ian Samwell and Brian Potter. We were happy with the choice. We needed a single fast and had nothing appropriate other than Steve and Ronnie's piece to put forward. These two were highly regarded. Samwell had written Cliff Richard's 'Move It'. That was pedigree enough for us.

They came back with 'Whatcha Gonna Do About It'. There were elements of Steve and Ronnie in there, but this was a Samwell–Potter composition. We loved it. It had a great groove, was soulful and each one of us was given a starring moment. That was quite something for our first single, a huge vote of confidence in us as individual musicians and as a group.

The single was released on 6 August 1965.

The following evening, we were playing the Kingston Jazz Cellar. We set up in the afternoon, which, at five thirty, gave us time to pile around to the flat of a girl we knew locally. We wanted to watch TV, *Lucky Stars – Summer Spin* specifically. We made it just in time and switched on the set.

The world had gone mad. Just the week before we'd been up in Birmingham, recording the show. This was primetime, and we were entirely unknown. Don worked wonders to get us on that show. Joe Brown & The Bruvvers were top of the bill. They were brilliant. Very encouraging to us. Then there was Sonny and Cher – also great. They were performing their soon-to-be number-one hit 'I Got You Babe' and it was clear they were going to be huge stars. They had that undefinable quality that marks out certain performers from the rest. At the same time they were very down-to-earth, not the least bit full of themselves. In fact, they were more interested in us, repeatedly saying how much they enjoyed our sound, and even asking for some records and photos to take back to the US, so they could spread the word.

It had been a crazy whirlwind, and now we were in Kingston about to watch the broadcast. Sure enough, there I was on TV! Literally a dream come true. I got the shock of my life. I hid under the table.

Exposure was one thing, but success required airplay, and the route to that was to make it on to the charts. Don worked wonders once again.

We knew he was buying up multiple copies of our single. How? Because he asked us to do it as well. We only got involved to a limited degree – if I was passing a record shop in the East End I might buy five. I soon stopped even doing that. I was nervous. We'd been on television and I didn't want to risk being recognised. Instead, I asked family and friends to do what they could to help.

Our purchasing was small fry, however: Arden was involved on an industrial scale. Teams of people bought in bulk at the key stores relaying sales information to the chart compiler. It was a scam, and it didn't worry me in the least. Instead it opened my eyes to the workings of the music industry – just as dodgy as life in the East End. Everyone there was a rogue, just like Don Arden. If there's a deal to be made, make it. Don't ask questions.

Arden was following the largely accepted practice that management companies and labels regularly engaged in to launch bands. He wanted us to have a shot at a hit, and was taking no chances. He was doing what was necessary. Break into the charts, radio follows, then it's a hit or not, based on merit.

'Whatcha Gonna Do About It' entered the charts on 2 September. Hearing it on the radio for the first time was the biggest kick, the song coming on out of the blue. Fucking hell.

The madness continued. On my seventeenth birthday, we made our *Top of the Pops* debut. Turning up at the Wood Lane studio in London for rehearsal – even though we were miming – we were so nervous. We watched the other studio bands – The Hollies, The Silkie, Manfred Mann – go through their songs, then it was the actual recording. This being our first appearance, Steve was invited to introduced the band. A recording exists, and it's strange to listen to his voice. He'd had training, after all, and was usually so assured, confident. That evening, though, under those lights, on the biggest music show on television, Steve sounds like a young boy – high-pitched and nervous. This is what he said. As usual with Steve, it has to be taken with a pinch of salt.

'This is James our organist, and Kenney our drummer. And this is Plonk [Ronnie's nickname]. Our bass. We've been together nearly 11 weeks. We met in a pub in the East End. Sort of, over a beer. It [Whatcha] has been out about three weeks, and was written by our recording manager, Ian Samwell. I think he did a good job on it.'

The single climbed as high as number 14, and stayed in the charts for 12 weeks. We had our hit. Arden, however, was only beginning.

The follow-up single to 'Whatcha Gonna Do About It' had been agreed – it would be Steve and Ronnie's 'I've Got Mine'. We thought it was perfect: commercial, with a nice feel, which we were convinced would appeal to the fans of 'Whatcha'. Most importantly, it was ours. A sure-fire hit.

Especially given Don's promotional plans. Alongside the usual TV and radio appearances, he somehow landed us a part in an upcoming film, *Dateline Diamonds*. Sure, the plot's thin, revolving around a smuggling operation between London and Amsterdam via a pirate radio ship (the real-life Radio London), and the cast perhaps not A-list (the most recognisable actor is probably Kenneth Cope, better known to some as Marty from *Randall and Hopkirk (Deceased)*, plus Kiki Dee, and Kenny Everett), but who cares. We were in the movies.

To be honest, the best thing about that film was the tagline: 'The hottest rocks in Britain are being smuggled by the hottest rockers in Britain'. Genius.

We played an up-and-coming band called the Small Faces, popular in Britain, recently returned from a successful tour of America (ironic) whose manager gets involved in some dodgy dealings (ironic). Three of our songs are played in the film, plus an on-screen performance of 'I've Got Mine', the intention being for the single and film release to coincide. A good idea of Don's.

The only problem was that the film was significantly delayed, eventually hitting cinema screens on 3 April 1966, five months after our single had sunk without a trace. It didn't even chart. I still don't understand why. I love that song. Maybe if the film had come out when originally planned ... but no, I doubt it would have made much difference. Whatever magical mix of originality and familiarity hits songs seem to require, it wasn't there. I can't explain. It was too good to disappear completely, however, and in 1968 we resurrected the backing track as the basis for the title instrumental on our *Ogdens' Nut Gone Flake* album. A happy ending.

I'm not sure *Dateline Diamonds* fared much better than our single. Today I think it's probably best known as the first film to feature a Ford Transit van. Now that's a proper claim to fame.

* * *

Looking back now at the handful of clips from *Dateline Diamonds* in which we appear, one thing strikes me: Jimmy Winston. He doesn't quite fit. It's not his fault, but he looks older and taller than the rest of the band.

In the weeks prior to filming our *Dateline Diamonds* segments, it became clear that over and above the differences in height and age, there were two fundamental problems with Jimmy. First, during our gigs and TV appearances, it was evident he was trying to upstage Steve. Marriott was our frontman, the lead singer, but instead of leaving him to it, sticking to his role in the group like the rest of us, Jimmy would be jumping around behind his keyboards, trying to do a Mod dance, as if to say, 'Notice me, notice me!' That wasn't the band we wanted at all. We weren't show-offs, craving the limelight. All we were interested in was making music. We saw ourselves as serious musicians. Jimmy seemed to have a different agenda. He became distracting, and the audience and Don Arden noticed it.

Then there was his playing. To be fair, Jimmy never really claimed to be a keyboard player. His instrument was the guitar, on which he was certainly competent and could be inventive. I remember him experimenting with his Rickenbacker, plugging it into a Leslie amp to create a Hammond organ sound. That was innovative, but it wasn't what we required. We needed keyboards, and frankly Jimmy wasn't quite up to the job. Steve had to teach him the organ part on 'Whatcha Gonna Do About It', a basic one-handed section, and he wasn't comfortable with that.

Don Arden was aware of all this, and wasn't happy. Then when we began moaning, that was it for Jimmy. At the beginning of November 1965, Don called Jimmy to his office and told him he was out. That same day Arden telephoned Jimmy's replacement: Ian McLagan.

Ronnie first brought Mac to our attention. Backstage at a gig in Stockport he was passing the time leafing through a copy of the music magazine *Beat Instrumental* and came across a review of a gig by a band called Boz People, which spoke in glowing terms of their keyboard player Ian McLagan. They even had a photo of him, and he looked great.

Ronnie mentioned Mac's name to Arden, we were having our doubts about Jimmy by then, and Don sent Pat Meehan off to investigate.

We met Mac on the same day Don phoned him. Arden asked us to come to the Carnaby Street office as he wanted to explain his plans for the band. We didn't know Mac had arrived earlier and agreed terms, and was still there. We were sitting with Don, nodding along, agreeing with him, when he stood up and opened the door to the other office.

'Boys, meet Ian.'

There he was, standing in front of us. Two thoughts flashed through my mind. First, he didn't appear anything like his photo. Not surprising, when we discovered the photo was of Boz Burrell, Boz People's lead singer, miscaptioned as Mac.

My second thought was simple: *Good*.

Mac looked like one of us, and from what we'd read, we knew he could play. In a muddle of smiles and laughter we were hugging him, lifting him off the floor, spinning him around. *This is it*.

I later learned from Mac that totally by chance he'd quit Boz People the day before, and when he received the call from Don he didn't even know which band he was being asked to join. It could have been The Animals or The Nashville Teens, both of whom were signed to Contemporary. Thank God it was us.

There was immediate work to be done. The following night we were booked to appear on Radio Luxembourg, on a show broadcast live from the Lyceum in central London. Mac had to learn how to mime Jimmy's guitar piece on 'I've Got Mine'. Yes, our new keyboard player's debut performance with the Small Faces was miming guitar on a live broadcast.

Jimmy turned up backstage at the theatre, banging on the dressing room door. He was angry and upset. Mac stayed back – this had nothing to do with him – while the three of us tried to placate Jimmy. He was very emotional.

'What's all this about?' 'You can't do this to me.' 'I don't understand.' 'Why?'

It was a difficult situation for everyone, mostly Jimmy, of course. Then he started to cry, and somehow I was elected to steer him into another room and talk to him. What could I say? 'It's nothing personal. Just one of those things that hasn't worked out. It's a collective decision. It's right for the band and for you ...'

I gave it all that. I felt sorry for Jimmy, definitely. It was tough on him. But I didn't feel guilty. It was the correct decision.

Jimmy eventually left quietly. It was years before I saw him again.

Unfortunately, some difficult issues arose later when Jimmy's brother Frank claimed we'd agreed to pay him a percentage of our earnings for five years in return for the use of his van. We ended up in court in 1969. The case was dismissed.

I met up with Jimmy in 2007 at the unveiling of the plaque in Carnaby Street, at the location of Don Arden's offices. Jimmy's name is there. He's part of the band's history. We said hello, shook hands. I felt awkward. We've met since, at a commemoration event at the Ruskin Arms. Things are okay now. It all happened a long time ago, for both of us.

The day after the Lyceum, we had a gig booked in Swindon. We drove over in the afternoon, to allow time for a rehearsal. That would be the first time that Ronnie, Steve and I properly played with Mac.

I couldn't believe it, I was in heaven. I'd always felt there was something missing in the band for me as a drummer, and suddenly here was this Hammond organ providing solid foundations on which I could build. That was it, from that moment we were a creative unit.

It almost didn't happen. We nearly lost Mac that evening, before he'd even played with the band on stage. After the rehearsal, prior to the gig, we were relaxing in a hotel and, as Mac and I were sharing a room, I decided to get to know him better. I proceeded to tell him all about every single aunt, uncle, cousin, niece and nephew I had, their names, where they lived, what they were like, probably their favourite colours. I nearly bored him to death.

The difference Mac made to the Small Faces was immense. Musically he affected the whole band, but none more so than me. I was able to tune into his playing, which brought us together. Mac and his Hammond organ had been the missing instrument. Now with him standing alongside, we could produce the sound we'd always wanted. The Small Faces sound.

In a lot of the music we'd been listening to, at Steve's flat, in the Stratford fleapit, anywhere, the Hammond organ was always prominent. That was the vibe we were looking for, the platform from which to create our own music. Now with Mac, I could play my jazzy movements because he was with me. It released me, and we started to swing. Previously, when covering Jimmy McGriff or Booker T & the MGs' tracks for instance, we'd sounded flat; not any longer.

Mac's arrival also freed Steve and Ronnie.

Until then, Steve had been forcing two instruments into one. When he was playing rhythm, the song would be filled out. Nice and chunky, with a Chuck Berry style of riff. Then he'd come to the lead solo and the rhythm would stop, the song suddenly sounding thin, just me and Ronnie behind Steve. With the rhythm gone, there was a massive hole. It still sounded decent, we made good records before Mac, but something was definitely missing.

Now Steve could relax, no longer worried about keeping the rhythm going. Mac had taken over that role, filling the hole, leaving Steve to concentrate on singing and anything else he wanted to do with his guitar.

The pressure also came off Ronnie, giving him the space to develop his own style of bass, which I could also tune into.

With Mac, the band felt complete. On the drive back from Swindon we spent the whole trip talking nothing but music. Of course. And specifically Booker T & the MGs. Of course.

By unanimous agreement, they were a brilliant band. What really struck me, though, as the conversation grew increasingly animated, was that Steve felt guitarist Steve Cropper was the stand-out musician, while Mac claimed it was Hammond organist Booker T himself. Ronnie had a double vote, original bassist Lewie Steinberg and his recent replacement Donald 'Duck' Dunn. Me, I went for Al Jackson on drums. Of course. We loved the band as a complete entity, and also its separate parts. That was something we aspired to emulate – to be a whole and to be individuals. Now that Mac was on board, it felt possible.

As we relaxed into our instruments, we started to move to a different level, with a clear path ahead, as far as we were concerned, forged by bands we admired. The Beatles, Hollies, Shadows, and Stones had all achieved huge chart success while maintaining their integrity by producing great music. That was the model we were aiming for: hits, but on our terms. There were bands out there that we liked as people, and respected for carving out successful careers in the pop music explosion that was happening all around, groups such as Freddie and the Dreamers, Herman's Hermits, and the Dave Clark Five (vocalist and keyboard player Mick Smith was a great mate of mine, with a fantastic voice), but we didn't want to follow in their footsteps. We understood what they were doing, we weren't knocking them, but those songs, popular certainly, but light and gimmicky, they weren't for us. We were going to be taken far more seriously.

* * *

The beginning of 1966 brought the first of many European tours. As our popularity grew, we seemed to be constantly in and out of London Airport, flying off to this country, driving through the night to the next. Perform, sleep, travel. Perform, sleep, travel.

Only when back home again could I take stock of where we'd been. Holland, Belgium and Germany on that first trip.

This was not luxury living. The planes were usually old Caravelles or Tridents, which stank to hell, the engines pumping toxic fumes into the cabin. Once we even flew to Belgium in an ancient Dakota out of the RAF base at Brize Norton. When that thing took off, at an incredibly steep angle, full power, the noise was deafening and I don't just mean the engines. Absolutely everything on that plane rattled. My cousin Roy was with us on that trip, as drum roadie, and we started madly chewing gum so we could stick it behind the panels, under the flooring, on the seats – anywhere to stop the vibrations. That became a habit for us, even on some commercial flights, where the vibrating around the windows could almost be as bad.

One of my favourite cities was Berlin. I loved that place, there was a buzz, as though the residents were determined to make the most of every day, but I didn't enjoy getting there.

In the 1960s you flew into the city through the Berlin Air Corridor, over East German airspace. The flight path was narrow and planes were required to approach Berlin at a restricted height, relatively low. Fine in decent weather, but if it was stormy, you weren't permitted to fly above the turbulence. You had to plough through the clouds. You'd be bounced around so much it felt like you were in a pinball machine. I hated that. Especially if I was sitting next to Steve. He was even more nervous of flying than I was, and would grab my leg in a vice grip whenever we hit an air pocket. Ronnie was totally different. He was the laid-back philosopher. 'If it is going to happen,' he'd say in his slow drawl, 'it is going to happen. Don't worry about it.'

Berlin airport was relatively close to the city centre, so when arriving there, instead of hanging around and travelling in with the rest of the crew in the vans as normal, we'd jump straight into a taxi. Same on the way back. That wasn't always a good thing.

I clearly remember being in a cab, heading towards the airport, passing war-damaged churches and buildings, with Marriott going, 'Fucking hell, we missed that one. Oh shit, we should have flattened that one.' Our driver, who understood enough English, did not see the funny side. On the short section of autobahn, near the airport, he pulled over, started shouting, then chucked us out. I didn't know a lot of German, but I think it's safe to say he was pissed off. I didn't blame him.

Four blokes trying to hitch a lift on a German motorway with cars passing at 100 mph, is not easy. Fortunately our crew weren't too far behind and spotted us. They had a lot of fun at our expense after that.

Marriott was always doing daft stuff like that. On another occasion in Berlin, years later, at a big club he decided to introduce us as Nazi war criminals. I was Hermann Goering. That also didn't go down well. The bottles came flying. Thank God I had my cymbals for protection.

That wasn't the only time I used them as a shield in Germany. We played the Star-Club in Hamburg, made famous by the Beatles, and just before we came on a group of German sailors staggered in. Hard as nails and each carrying a crate of big, heavy beer bottles. They walked to the middle of the dance floor, made a pile of the crates and stood watching us, drinking heavily, as we played. Midway through the set, the first bottle crashed on to the stage. By the end it was bedlam, but we weren't about to stop the show and ask, 'Hey chaps, would you mind awfully not doing that?' We just dodged and carried on.

When we weren't screwing things up, we went down very well in Germany. I was extremely nervous that first time, worried that

CAVIAR AND BROWN SAUCE

the people there would hate us because of the war. I couldn't have been more wrong.

The first surprise was that we already had a decent fanbase before we'd even played a note there, built up through TV, radio and magazines. Our fantastic reception came as a complete shock, but then as we looked out on the crowd, we could see the fans were the same age as us, teenagers, wearing our style of clothing. It felt as though we had somehow acted as an influence. That hit us all, that we had managed to make a connection across the sea. We loved those German fans and they loved us. The hatred I worried about was non-existent. That was a real eye-opener. I'm still very proud that we were amongst the first teenagers to go to Germany after the war and make friends.

Copenhagen in May 1967 proved to be another eye-opener.

We arrived at the hotel just in time to check in and dash to a fancy restaurant before it closed for lunch. The place was so posh that the head waiter had a silver wine tasting dish hanging from a chain around his neck. I'd never seen one before but Marriott, of course, knew what it was for. So in true rock 'n' roll style I asked to taste my milk in it. Had to be sure it came from a good cow.

We were starving, and virtually the only diners there. The lunchtime crowd had largely finished their meals and left. The waiter handed out the menus, which were in Danish, so of course we couldn't read them. Not that it really mattered – we were creatures of habit. As the waiter took the order all I could hear was 'steak and chips' 'steak and chips', 'steak et frites'. Marriott's voice, that last order. He loved showing off.

It came to my turn but I kept thinking, 'I can't face steak and chips again'. So I shut my eyes, pointed at the menu and raised it up so the waiter could see what I wanted. 'One of those please. Ta very much.'

The waiter looked at me with an odd expression, shrugged his shoulders and wrote down the order.

The food arrived and the boys got stuck right in. Mine appeared last: a bowl of black stuff, sitting on a bed of ice, alongside two smaller dishes of what looked like chopped egg and chopped onion, plus a basket of rolls.

Oh no. I've fucked up. What the hell?

Ronnie glanced up from his plate and started laughing, quickly followed by Mac and Steve.

'Enjoying your fish eggs, Ken?' said Steve. 'Big caviar fan are you?' Smart arse.

They went back to their steaks while I sat looking at my plate. Panicking. I could see the waiter standing over by the kitchen doors, looking at me. Then out of nowhere, our early trips up and down the M1 came back to me. With no money to our names, we used to stop off at the Watford Gap Blue Boar service station to nick bread rolls and sachets of sauce for lunch. Tasty. I caught our waiter's attention and he came over to the table.

'Sir?'

'Erm, do you have any, erm, brown sauce, please?' He looked at me. 'You know, HP?' Still nothing. 'Daddy's Sauce?', I tried, hopefully. I knew that was a brand in some European countries.

'Of course, Sir.' He said, his face sceptical.

It came out in a little silver gravy boat, which was not what I was expecting, so I dipped in my finger, to make sure it was what I wanted. Phew.

Then, just as I was picking up a bread roll to cut in half for my sandwich, out of the corner of my eye I noticed the waiter standing by the kitchen doors again, with a second head now poking out. The chef, by the look of things.

I smeared a roll in caviar and feigned to pour on the sauce. The waiter visibly stiffened. I put down the sauce. He seemed to relax. The chef then stepped out into the restaurant, and a third poking head took his place. I was gathering quite an audience. Again, I feigned to pour the sauce on to the caviar – again they froze in horror. I was enjoying myself, but I was also starving. It was time to go for it: a caviar, brown sauce, egg and onion sarnie. Delicious. The staff disappeared into the kitchen, presumably to cry in private.

It was many years later before I finally overcame my shyness and worked up the courage to try caviar properly. I thought I'd better find out what it really tastes like. Delicious. I'm happy to admit that brown sauce adds very little to the dish.

A few months later we found ourselves in Paris, recording a segment for the French TV pop show *Discorama*. On this occasion, it was us who were doing the disapproving.

The production crew were the most disorganised I'd ever come across. As we mimed our track, the cameras kept bumping into us as the operators tried to shoot from weird angles, while random people were constantly wandering behind us, in shot. We were there far too long for a simple video, growing increasingly pissed off with, 'One more take', 'One more take'. Eventually we'd had enough. If this was broadcast, we'd look like idiots on screen. We told the producer we needed a break, to collect our thoughts, then sneaked into the control booth, nicked the tape, and legged it down the road to a bar, where we collapsed in a heap of laughter.

'Oh Là Là.' As the Faces later sang. Almost.

* * *

Even to this day I still can't properly get to grips with how quickly it all happened.

At the age of 15 I was out of school, working in a pickling factory, a child. By 16 I was in a band with a hit record, an adult. I was earning as much as my dad. Not that I ever thought about money then. As long as I had a few quid in my pocket, that's all that mattered. That's where Arden was so clever. He gave us just enough to feel we had plenty of cash to spend.

One of the trendy hang-outs then was the Golden Egg restaurant on Oxford Street. I used to take my East End mates there. We'd order a bottle of wine, but none of us were very interested in drinking it. We'd be talking so much, we'd end up leaving most of it. I would pay the bill, because I had the money. I was the grown up. At 16.

What I missed out on was being a boy in my late teens. That's part of the reason why my family today do understand me, and at the same time don't understand me. On the one hand I'm the responsible dad, and on the other I'm still looking to be that boy. The 17-year-old is still alive and kicking in me, trying to get out at last. He really is. (Although now I'm getting older I've moved his age up to 18.)

Perhaps I did grow up quicker than was good for me, but they were great days. Each of us found his instrument and music independently before coming together in the band. We were friends, we weren't thinking of becoming rich or famous. That wasn't the driving force. For me, I just loved my drums and wanted to play with other people. Money and fame never entered my mind. I'm sure the others felt the same.

Thinking back on those touring days, travelling up and down Britain and across Europe, it's the friendship, the camaraderie, that sits most prominently in my memory. Four young blokes footloose and carefree, mates who were always watching each other's back, going out of their way to support each other, both musically and personally. We rarely squabbled, and if we did always found a quick solution. It was a laugh, a great experience and adventure. I used to be terribly homesick, but it was impossible to stay down for long. Being with Steve, Ronnie and Mac was too much fun. The four of us were taking on the world, that's what it felt like then. A very powerful emotion.

CHAPTER 5

ALL IN THE MIND'S EYE

December 1965, IBC recording studios, Portland Place, London. Following the commercial failure of 'I've Got Mine', Don Arden is taking no chances. He's brought in the songwriting duo Kenny Lynch and Mort Shuman. Our next single has to work, or the momentum built up with 'Whatcha Gonna Do About It' will be lost.

We all like Kenny. He's a decent bloke and a great laugh to be around. He's from the East End and used to sing in a pub called Kate Odders, around the corner from Havering Street. We have a lot in common and we've hit it off. It's fun working with him in the studio. He's even found a way to write himself into the recording, suggesting that the song would be improved by the addition of a falsetto on backing vocals. 'I can do that for you,' he offered. Naturally you can, Kenny. Steve's not bothered. We all want a hit.

Kenny and Mort have delivered a song called 'Sha-La-La-La-Lee'. Understandably, Steve and Ronnie aren't too thrilled by having their writing credentials questioned, but they're being professional, getting on with things. Mac's not too happy either. He's worked with Kenny Lynch in the past on keyboards as a member of Kenny's backing band during a summer season of seaside resorts. They get on well, but I think Mac sees recording this as a step backwards. In truth, it's a good song. Catchy as hell, with enough drive to power it along. It's one of those tracks I know will be even better live, with a rawer sound. Here, though, it's all about cutting the single.

Later I'll be overdubbing some cowbells on to the recording, which should be a laugh, but right now, it's the drum track. I'm getting into it, trying out a few flash fills, when Kenny suddenly interrupts over the control-room mic.

'That's great what you're doing there Kenney, great. Only thing is, don't play anything you can't mime.'

I hated having to mime. I'd much rather have played live, even though it was nerve-wracking.

Television shows insisted on bands miming so they didn't have to worry about mixing sound in the studio to ensure what was being played closely resembled the actual record. That's what the viewers wanted to hear, ran the argument, so much simpler just to play the single itself.

They gave me plastic cymbals and rubber pads on the drums, although in the early days of *Top of the Pops* they didn't even have those. I had to pretend to play, trying to look convincing while concentrating on pulling the sticks up short at the last moment. That was horrible. I could hear the single playing in the background, and worse, the unplugged guitars twanging. It was all very distracting. I'm a perfectionist, and when I look at footage of myself miming, missing the beats, I see imperfection. Most viewers wouldn't have realised we weren't properly playing, and must have been looking at me thinking, 'What's going on? He's all over the place.'

ALL IN THE MIND'S EYE

The situation changed in 1966, shortly after the BBC moved the recording of *TOTP* from Manchester to London. The Musicians' Union was kicking up a storm, insisting that bands play live, which would allow them to charge a performance fee. The BBC tried to accommodate the union's demands, but it only lasted for a short period of time. By the mid-60s many hit singles featured a lot of over-dubbing and multi-track recording, which was impossible to reproduce live in a studio. Too many acts were sounding nothing like the single the audience at home expected; a compromise was reached. A mad compromise.

From 1967, groups were instructed to go into a studio a couple of days before filming *TOTP* to re-record their song. That would be the version played, with the band miming their instruments and the vocals often live. Crazy. Inevitably what happened was each group dutifully turned up at the studio, hung around, had a few beers, some laughs, maybe a smoke or two, and didn't record a note. When the union official arrived to pick up the 'new' recording, the sound engineer would hand him a tape of the original backing track, very slightly remixed. Everyone did that, for years.

Of the four of us, thanks to his training as an actor, Marriott was the expert when it came to TV miming. If you look at footage of him, he's invariably looking away from the camera during the intro, seconds before the vocal cuts in. He gives the impression that he's smiling at the rest of us, relaxed and enjoying himself. In fact, what he's doing is making sure he doesn't miss his cue. Once he's picked up the words, he turns back to camera looking like he's been singing all along.

Top of the Pops was the number one music show on television, but our favourite was ITV's *Ready Steady Go!*, 'where the weekend started'. We loved appearing on that, mainly because

103

the performances were live. It's a shame that declining viewing figures led to its cancellation at the end of 1966, after little more than three years. We featured on *RSG!* on seven occasions, I think, from September 1965 to November 1966, and over those shows we were fortunate to appear alongside some great artists, and some outstanding ones, including Dusty Springfield, Wilson Pickett and Tom Jones.

Our old friends Sonny and Cher would certainly classify as outstanding artists, and we were delighted to come across them again at an *RSG!* appearance in August 1966. Their valiant attempts to help break us in the US hadn't quite paid off, but we didn't hold that against them. It was lovely to catch up, and there was a special treat for me when the show's musical director asked if I would mind playing tambourine with the studio band to accompany Sonny and Cher's 'Little Man'. I was thrilled to do so, although I did wonder if the request and the title of the song were related ...

Perhaps the most memorable group we met, however, was on our last appearance – The Four Tops. They seemed to share our East End humour, no doubt helped by the fact that we ended up smoking several large spliffs with them. I don't think they knew much about us as a group, and as they were the final act on the show they weren't paying attention when Steve started to sing '(Tell Me) Have You Ever Seen Me'. They told us after that they couldn't believe their eyes or ears when they looked over to discover the singer with such a big, soulful voice was a little white guy. Steve took that as a huge compliment.

That was one of the best things about those music shows, the opportunity to hang out for a while with other bands. I'll never forget sitting down with Graham Nash of The Hollies in the tiny little bar halfway down the stairs in the BBC's Wood Lane studios after recording *TOTP*.

'You alright Graham? You look a bit glum.'

'Ah, well. I've just told the band I'm leaving. I'm going to live in the States. I've met these two American guys and we're going to see if we can do something together. I'm excited, but at the same time, really scared.'

'Anyone I know?'

'Maybe. David Crosby and Stephen Stills?'

I'd heard of them, but didn't know them. 'Listen Graham, they're good guys aren't they?'

He nodded.

'Well then. You'll be alright.' He was.

One of the few downsides of all those early TV appearances was that when we started to play more live concerts, we were rumbled. I can't remember exactly where we were, but it wasn't long after our *Lucky Stars* debut and the first *RSG!*, sometime around September 1965. We'd had our first hit and were gathering quite a following, mainly screaming girls. That suited me just fine at the time. Bill Corbett was driving us (he'd also been the Beatles' chauffeur) and as we leapt from the car, shrieking madness all around, police holding back the girls, I heard one fan yelling at her pal, 'Eugh! Ain't they small!' Total deflation.

Everybody appears bigger on television. Even us.

Seeing all those screaming girls was a strange sensation. Up to then I'd had a couple of girlfriends, all very casual, nothing serious, and then suddenly there I was, an object of mass adoration. I'd dreamt about that of course, hundreds of girls apparently lusting after me. Was it everything I'd hoped? No. It was the numbers, they were intimidating. I didn't see girls I might possibly get to know and then go out with. These weren't groups of real individuals. Instead, what I experienced during this period was an overwhelming, solid wall of screams and raw emotion that hit me slap, bang in the face. I found that hard to get my head around.

Meeting girls on a one-to-one basis, to ask on a date, therefore became a priority. In clubs that wasn't going to be too big an ask – there clearly seemed to be plenty of girls out there who were keen on getting to know me much, much better. But where could I take them? Back to Havering Street? No thanks.

Turning 17 in September 1965 offered a solution. I just had to pass my driving test as soon as possible. I did view driving partly as another important milestone in growing up, but mainly I wanted to pass so I could actually start enjoying the benefits of fame, ideally at some of the lovely secluded spots in Epping Forest where privacy was guaranteed. I'd just about saved enough money to buy myself a little car, but what good was that without a licence?

I had no intention of hanging around. Our success could wither in an instant, and I didn't want to miss out. I knew how to drive, Dad had taught me years before, as soon as my feet could reach the pedals. During those hop-picking summers, when Dad came down at the weekends he'd take me out in the fields and let me drive his car. Then from the age of about 11, whenever Dad wasn't around but his lorry and trailer were outside, I used to jump in and take it for a run around the block. That was exciting, although I had to be careful reversing. It was so much harder with the trailer than if I'd been in an artic. So I had the ability, all I required was a couple of lessons on how to pass the test. After that, the keys to freedom would be mine.

Sure enough, two or three weeks after my seventeenth birthday, with lessons under my belt, I booked in at a test centre in Stratford. When I mentioned this to a mate the day before, he smiled, 'You'll be alright then Kenney. Don't worry – they're all bent up there. You can bribe 'em.'

'What do you mean?'

'I'm telling you. They'll make a beeline for anything. Like that gold ring you've got there. Make sure you wear that and make sure the examiner sees it.'

Now, I was confident I'd pass without any assistance, but why take chances? Throughout the test, like a right prat, I made sure the bloke couldn't miss my ring by unsubtly tapping my finger on the steering wheel when stationary and generally drawing attention to it at every opportunity. Sure enough, as I pulled the Ford Anglia into the centre and he was writing up my pass or fail he kept glancing at my hand. 'That's nice,' he said. I nodded. 'Yes, that's very nice. I like that.' I nodded again, not committing to anything until he'd signed the form, which I could see was a pass. Then, as he went to hand it to me, he stopped midway. 'Yeah,' he said, 'I do like that ring, Mr Jones.'

'Thanks,' I said, grabbing the piece of paper, 'it is nice, isn't it?' and jumped out of the car. Still wearing the ring.

* * *

Don Arden arranged for us to move into a four-storey, four-bedroom house in Pimlico, 22 Westmoreland Terrace. We felt we needed a place to hang out together, be more creative and write songs. On a practical level, it made sense. We were all living back home with our parents by then, which for me worked fine, I'd never left, but the others found it difficult. Being high as kites from adrenalin and various uppers when they got back late at night from gigs made creeping quietly into their boyhood bedrooms without disturbing the household a near impossibility. For Mac in particular the situation was untenable. He lived miles across town, so instead of trekking there on his own, he would regularly crash with one of us. Far from ideal for anyone.

Steve, Ronnie and Mac jumped at the opportunity, while I remained at home. I knew there was not a hope in hell of a decent night's sleep there, plus by then I was the proud owner of a driving licence and Mini and the digs were a five-minute drive from Havering Street. I spent most days there with the boys, having a laugh, playing music, then happily disappeared home when evenings inevitably segued into drunken, weed-fuelled, noisy all-nighters. That wasn't for me. I had to escape the blaring record player and amps and find some peace. I loved music, still do, but it has never consumed me.

I remember George Harrison saying something similar years later, at a Christmas party at Ringo Starr's new house, near where I now live in Surrey. Ringo had removed all his furniture from the huge living area and set up round tables of 10. I was sitting with Eric Clapton, while George was at another table across the room. Midway through the evening, George wandered over to say hello. Eric was sitting next to me, George standing on my other side, chatting generally.

Suddenly Eric became very animated about a tape that George had sent him: 'I got that tape. I got that tape. What did you think of the third track? I think we could do something with that. Maybe change it a bit. What d'ya think, George? What d'ya think?'

Eric kept at it, until a clearly startled George quietly inter-rupted, 'Eric, there are things in life other than fucking music'. That put a smile on my face. That's an attitude I relate to. There are times when you just have to step out of the bubble.

During our 18 months or so at Westmoreland Terrace, before girlfriends and wives came along and the boys found places of their own, the house became a magnet for the Swinging London scene, an experimental lab for the new adventure we were all on. The address also became well known to fans, and we regularly discovered extremely personal messages scrawled in lipstick on our cars and front door.

You never knew who you might bump into there. *The Avengers* actress Honor Blackman lived one door down. We got to know her well, and of course fancied her rotten, even though in our eyes she was the same age as our mums. She would have just turned 40. Or it might be Mick Jagger, Paul McCartney, John Lennon or Georgie Fame, having a smoke, trying out new songs, or, very occasionally, quietly watching television.

My room was taken up by a mate of Steve's, Mick O'Sullivan. Mick didn't play any instruments – except when stoned, tunelessly blowing into a bloody harmonica – and he wasn't a roadie, he wasn't paid. He was what you might term a 'friend' of the band. Every group has one, someone everyone knows, who helps out, hangs around, runs errands, is generally useful and makes things happen. As Steve sang in 'Here Come the Nice', his song about Mick, 'He knows what I want, he's got what I need, he's always there if I need some speed'. For uppers, downers, weed and later LSD, Mick was the man. 'Here come the nice (he'll make you feel so good).' He sure did.

Mick was part of our lives for some time. He was a great laugh, a good personality, and was always ready for a beer, especially if you were paying. He also co-wrote 'Green Circles' with Steve and Ronnie in 1967 – no mean achievement given they were wild on acid during that period. It's a track I've always particularly liked, as it gave me the opportunity to introduce some new techniques. Rather than dropping tabs, which everyone else seemed to be doing that year, I'd started working on sessions with big bands and brought that experience into the studio. There's a strong orchestral dynamic to the drums on 'Green Circles', which I love.

Ronnie Lane tried to kill himself at Westmoreland Terrace.

This was after we'd been on a package tour, arranged by Don Arden. These tours involved various bands travelling and playing together at venues throughout the country. Typically, each group had a 20-minute slot, usually playing to two packed-out houses per night. Lucrative, for Don.

Those tours were great, as we got to spend time with the likes of The Hollies, Dave Berry and Roy Orbison. I also found the tours useful for keeping a watchful eye on rival drummers, to see if there was anything new I could learn. My favourite was The Hollies' Bobby Elliott. He had a unique style, as every drummer should, but not every drummer does. I became a big fan of Bobby's and absorbed a huge amount from him, from being in close proximity during rehearsals and sound checks.

Bobby was the only person I'd ever seen who played with his left hand low and his right high on the cymbals, which he set flat. I had mine at an angle, playing the top and a lot on the bell. He'd also perfected a fabulous technique I'd never seen before. When playing his tom-toms, he would bring his right hand up, flicking the flat cymbal from underneath, then in a wide arc he came over to the left-side cymbal, crashing down on top of it. Fucking brilliant.

Poor Ronnie's problem arose from a package tour featuring Lou Christie, who had a hit in early 1966 with 'Lightnin' Strikes'. Ronnie got to know Christie's girlfriend very well, basically nicking her off him. They went out together for a while, then she dumped Ronnie. Devastation.

Not long after, I arrived early one morning at Westmoreland Terrace, let myself in and went downstairs to make a cup of tea. There was Ronnie, on his knees, arse in the air, head in the gas oven. I tapped him on the shoulder.

'Ronnie, what you doing?'

'I'm killing meself.'

'Oh, right. Well you'd better turn on the gas first.'

As I started to laugh, Ronnie twisted his head in the oven to look at me, and burst out laughing himself. The girl was never mentioned again.

* * *

Don Arden had made the correct call by bringing in Kenny Lynch and Mort Shuman. 'Sha-La-La-La-Lee' proved to be a big hit, reaching number three in the singles chart in March 1966, the same month we made our debut at London's Marquee Club. The contrast between that single and that gig in many ways sums up the story of the Small Faces. It's what would eventually lead to the break-up of the band.

Prior to the Marquee appearance, we'd been up and down the country promoting our new pop release at concerts from Redhill to Southport, Kidderminster to Oldham, Grimsby to Shrewsbury, Southampton to Buxton, appearing in front of mainly hysterical teenage girls, screaming so loud no one could possibly hear a note. People say Steve was the big heartthrob. Well, maybe, but I secretly suspect the reaction was largely down to the fact that I had recently discovered hair tongs. To my mind, it was my now longer, straighter locks that were driving the girls crazy. Or perhaps it was Marriott.

Whoever the fans were screaming for, we weren't complaining, not then. We were pop stars, carried away on the drug of adoration. We were enjoying ourselves.

That level of success also resulted in an upgrading of our accommodation while on the road. Gone were the grim B&Bs with dribbling showers; now it was hotels, usually with a room each. Occasionally, though, if the hotel was busy we had to share. While certainly an improvement on loud-snoring strangers, an overnight stay with Marriott was no bed of roses. He'd be so hyper after a gig, stalking around, talking incessantly, asking if I'd mind him bringing a girl back ('Yes Steve, I would'), that it drove me nuts. I tried to avoid sharing with him whenever possible.

Ronnie was a far better roommate. Instead of pacing, he spent his time slowly wandering around, shirt hanging out, wondering where he'd put something. At the time I found his forgetfulness amusing. I didn't know I was catching the first glimpses of Ronnie's desperate future.

'Sha-La-La-La-Lee' is a great song, no doubt about that, and was a significant factor in our gigs selling out. But it is a great *pop* song, confirming in the eyes of the record-buying public that the Small Faces were a teeny-bop band. That wasn't how we thought of ourselves; that's not who we wanted to be. Mac in particular found that label incredibly frustrating. If any press coverage likened us to a band he thought of in that category, like the Dave Clark Five for instance, he blew his fuse. The rest of us would be annoyed, we didn't like it, but we'd let it slide, at least in those early days. Not Mac.

The Marquee gig on 22 March is a more accurate representation of the Small Faces we saw when we looked in the mirror. The audience that night was not screaming girls. They were young, certainly, but they were kids who were into the music, not the image. They were critical, not easy to please. You had to be good musicians to make it at the Marquee.

Our set-list focussed on R&B and blues, such as Booker T & the MGs' 'Plum Nellie', the classic blues track 'Baby, Please Don't Go' and our version of Muddy Waters' 'You Need Love'. We did play these at other concerts, but it wasn't what the crowd wanted to hear. In contrast, this was exactly what the Marquee audience demanded. That gave us the freedom to be ourselves. We held nothing back.

By good fortune, part of the concert was filmed for a couple of European TV stations. Watching again, it's a sweaty, energetic, frantic performance – long intros, drum solos, Steve and Ronnie thrashing their instruments to breaking point with big, sweeping strokes, creating what we called their Cuba-Latin feel. Then there's Steve's giving everything he has on the vocals; a wailing, rocking, soulful blend of magic. That's the Small Faces that inspired Jimmy Page and Robert Plant. They came to gigs and freely admit they nicked our feel and our riffs when they formed Led Zeppelin.

If the Marquee was a highlight of our 1966 concerts, the final night in Boston, Lincolnshire, of the 'Swinging '66' package tour was definitely a lowlight. For me, certainly.

We were playing our set, well into the music even though the audience's screams all but drowned us out, when a heavy glass ashtray came sailing over the balcony, smack, on my head. The scar is still visible today. It didn't knock me out, but was I dazed. I tried to carry on, not realising the extent of the injury, even though Ronnie and Steve were looking at me in horror. Sweat dripped down my forehead, making it difficult to see. I wiped it away. I caught sight of a hand sticky with blood. Dizziness overwhelmed me and I slumped backwards on my stool, unable to continue. The roadies rushed on in time to save me from falling. As they carried me off stage, I caught a glimpse of Steve and Ronnie at the front of the stage, yelling into their mics, 'Alright, who did it! We're going to have you, you bastard!'

I was taken to hospital in an ambulance, stitched up and played the next night at the South Pier Theatre, Blackpool.

From what I was told, it was a jealous boyfriend annoyed because the girls were screaming at us. I don't think it was aimed at me specifically. Although, given those hair tongs, it might have been ...

* * *

By the mid-1960s, I'd found my escape from music, a passion that offered opportunities for time alone, to clear my head, to find a different, simpler perspective on life. Horse riding.

It was Marriott's fault. We were meant to be rehearsing at the Ruskin Arms one glorious sunny day, before we were the Small Faces. Once we'd gathered, ready to go, Steve suddenly announced. 'It's too hot to play. I've fixed us up with some riding lessons at Epping Forest. Let's fuck off there for the day.' Sure, why not?

At the stables – Pine Lodge, Lippitts Hill – the boys were mucking around, having a laugh, falling off their horses, pretending to be cowboys shooting each other, all that. For me it was different. The moment I sat in that saddle I felt at home. A weird sensation, given I'd never ridden before. After that first visit, I went back the next day and the next and the next. I became good friends with the lady who owned the stables, Bobby Stone. Over the years she taught me a hell of a lot about riding.

With the first real money I earned with the Small Faces, I bought a horse from the stables, a Welsh dun called Pedro who was afraid of traffic. They didn't mention that as I was handing over the cash.

My love of horse riding has led me into polo and show jumping, and it continues to this day. What is it that has so captivated me over these years? Well, I've found that whatever my stage of life, when the pressures of relationships, career, family, money and simply everyday living mount up; when they are no longer a challenge but have become a burden, weighing me down, clouding my judgement, I go riding and all those concerns and stresses disappear. The horse is my psychiatrist, relieving the tension, allowing me freedom to think clearly. I stop being a person with worries. I become a man on a horse.

The boys did not share my interest, but they knew how important riding had become to me, and were very supportive. On one of our first tours, not long after I'd bought Pedro, while we were staying at the Manchester Airport Hotel, they decided to have a whip-round and bought me a saddle. For no reason other than they wanted me to be happy.

They were good like that, the boys.

On another occasion, we were driving down the M1 when one of them claimed he heard a worrying noise from the engine. We pulled on to the hard shoulder and stepped out. As we were milling around, pretending we knew anything about cars, Ronnie suddenly looked uncomfortable and pointed down the ditch by the side of the road. 'Eh, boys, what the hell's that?'

There was certainly something strange there, sinister even, stuffed into a large brown paper bag. Our imaginations went into overdrive. An arm? A leg? What do we do? Someone should go and take a look. I was volunteered.

I took a moment to steel myself, then scrambled down to investigate. I prodded it with a stick; it didn't feel like a body part. Steeling myself, I ripped open the bag. A brand new bass drum pedal. A present for me. One of them had thrown it down there while I was distracted by the fictitious car problem.

That's what we were like as a group at our best, a band of brothers looking out for each other. We enjoyed being together, we enjoyed playing together. We couldn't wait to make music. When we started out we were teenagers, without a care in the world, just mates growing up, on a voyage of discovery. Over time things changed, of course. Nothing stays the same. Growing up, becomes grown up. Kids become young men, with girlfriends, wives, mortgages, children, responsibilities. Pressures build as people try to cope with living their own lives.

That all seemed a million miles away when we started out touring and making records. We were only trying to please ourselves, and if anyone else liked what we were doing, great. What mattered most was that we were happy, the four of us. I believe that's what made the Small Faces successful – the purity in our playing, born out of unselfishness. For such a long time there was no tension; that only reared its head at the end.

Those close bonds of friendship had a major impact on our music, creating an in-built telepathy, on stage and in the studio. We clicked. I haven't experienced anything like that since. I didn't tell Steve, Mac or Ronnie what to play, and they didn't tell me. We knew. We never analysed how this happened, we just went with it, this amazing feeling.

People have often said to me that it must have been great having Ronnie's bass playing to work with, and it was – he had a very effective but simple style and we gelled, both personally and musically. On stage Ronnie and I were locked in tight together – he followed me naturally. I had complete confidence in his ability. I knew the bass would always be covered. That was a huge release, allowing me the freedom to play to the lead guitar and vocals. That's what I listened to. Steve was such a visual singer and I understood how to follow his subconscious movements, knowing whether he wanted the song to slow down, be quieter or speed up. I could read the signs and back-off/come-on, as necessary. For instance, if he started to sing on tip-toes, or raised an arm, he was looking for the volume to increase. Similar with his guitar playing. I was tuned into that. I could hear where he was going, and then complement it.

When Steve and Ronnie, and a little later Mac, were writing the songs, they wouldn't think about the drum sections. They didn't need to; they trusted me, as I trusted them. That was the band in a nutshell – gaining in confidence and ability by believing in, and learning from, each other. I'd be there listening to them playing their guitars and singing, absorbing it, working out what would work, where I might introduce a new fill or swing element to complement their creativity. I've seen articles suggesting that in those days I became one of the best rock drummers in the industry. I don't recognise that description. I don't hear rock 'n' roll. I hear the Small Faces, four mates combining to create something new.

Song development was an on-going process. My nickname for a long time was 'Shut up Kenney'. That's what they used to shout at me when we were in the studio and they grew fed up with how hard I was working on the drum sections. The name stuck for a while, until at one rehearsal I uncharacteristically blew my stack. While they tuned up, I was playing flat out, concentrating, looking for additional fills to enhance what we'd produced so far. We all knew the song by that point, but I wanted to nail certain parts before we performed or recorded it. The three of them thought I was deliberately being annoying, and once again told me to give it a rest. I lost it. 'I'm not playing for the fucking sake of it. I am looking for a fucking part I want to add to the fucking track!'

'Oh, okay Kenney. You're right. Sorry.'

* * *

Our first US tour was pencilled in for autumn 1966. None of us had been before, and with so many of the artists we admired originating from those shores, it was an exciting prospect. Two years earlier, the Beatles had launched the 'British Invasion', sweeping through America to huge acclaim, and returning a year later to play a series of massive concerts in front of tens of thousands of hysterical fans. America had fallen head-over-heels in love with British bands. With us riding high in the UK and across Europe, we could take that momentum across the Atlantic. There was nothing preventing us from replicating the success of the Beatles.

We insisted that the follow up to 'Sha-La-La-La-Lee' had to be one of our songs and a comfortable compromise was reached with Don Arden. We had seen, and enjoyed, the success of the Lynch–Shuman hit, and understood the need to produce a commercial track. However, for the band to feel we were travelling down a route that we were mapping out ourselves, the next single had to incorporate elements of the music we wanted to make. Steve and Ronnie's 'Hey Girl' was the perfect blend, popular, accessible, with an R&B edge. The fans responded as we'd hoped and the single reached number 10 in the charts.

Steve's confidence had been dented by the failure of 'I've Got Mine', but he was now in full creative flow, as we witnessed one afternoon at the Station Hotel in Leeds. We had just checked in and Ronnie, Mac and I were hanging around in the corridor deciding what to do before our gig, wondering where Steve had got to. Suddenly the door to his room burst open. 'I've got it! I've got it! It's finally fucking come to me. The next hit!' He came running down the corridor, acoustic guitar in hand. 'Listen to this.' He started to play a melody, with half-formed lyrics. It wasn't complete, but the potential was obvious. We all chipped in to produce the final version, Ronnie working his magic on Steve's building blocks, while I suggested an opening drum fill based on the classic intro to Wilson Pickett's 'In the Midnight Hour'.

'All or Nothing' became our first UK number one, although on *Top of the Pops* we were jointly listed in the top spot with the Beatles' 'Yellow Submarine'. On the show's chart rundown, the

BBC solved this slight difficulty by pairing up our faces with the Beatles, half and half. I was matched with Ringo, naturally.

Next stop, the United States of America.

It never happened. Ever.

I believe that initially Don Arden was genuinely keen for us to tour the States. He had a personal incentive: he wanted to be seen across the Atlantic as a big-time manager of a big-time band. I think he was excited at the prospect, until reality came knocking.

First there was the money. It would require a major financial outlay on his part – shipping costs, initially to send over us and our gear, then to move the whole set-up vast distances between cities. Hugely expensive. He'd also have been required to employ local roadies, again at considerable cost. Plus, as we were unknown over there, some venues were likely to demand a deposit before they'd book us.

The fact we were not a name in the States created an additional problem for Don. Any chance of success would have required employing a local agent, and that would have meant Don giving up some control of his prize asset. That would have made him very uncomfortable indeed.

The potential international music mogul reined himself in.

This is how Don sold the tour to us: 'I'm all for it boys, it'll be great, but just before I sign the deal, I want to make sure you're all happy with a 12-week tour; eating, sleeping, travelling in a tour bus, across that big, big country; playing venues as the support band to audiences who've never heard of you and don't care, and being paid very little. Okay?'

In truth, I wasn't too unhappy when the talk quietly fizzled out. When initially mooted, I'd viewed the prospect of touring the US as a sort of pilgrimage to the land of the music that had so inspired us, but as time passed I began to have second thoughts.

I was homesick when we played in Scotland for goodness sake! Do I regret now that we didn't take the chance? Yes, I do. It pisses me off because I'm certain we'd have made it and the American public would have embraced us.

Four years later, with the Faces, I saw exactly how we could have been successful. We were also unknown when we set out on our first US tour in March 1970. We played small clubs and venues to begin with – college campuses, youth centres – creating a word-of-mouth following. That's how things worked in the States, how bands built reputations before most fans had been to a concert.

If you played a gig in New York one evening, say, and it went well, and you were then scheduled to play Boston the following night, by the time you arrived the buzz had travelled ahead. Excitement was already building around the next gig, and that momentum carried forward to the next and the next, growing stronger each time. That's what made it for the Faces, people talking about us. I'm certain the same thing would have happened with the Small Faces.

There could have been another opportunity to crack the US market, when in January 1968 'Itchycoo Park' made it into the Top 20 of the Billboard charts. That should have given us the platform we needed.

Unfortunately, a couple of mouths previously, Mac had been busted at Heathrow airport carrying a lump of cannabis. He pleaded guilty and was fined 50 quid. No big deal at the time, except for the fact that under US immigration law, such a conviction prohibited entry into the States. Our last chance of conquering America went up in a puff of bluish smoke.

* * *

The first nail into the coffin in which our relationship with Don Arden would be buried was heard being hammered down as we

1: Butter wouldn't melt in my mouth. Not sure about the Rocker quiff, though.

2: Dad on babysitting duty at Havering Street.

3: Fastest draw in the East End! Dad and I loved watching the cowboy shows on TV.

4: Me and my cousin Roy in Shadwell Park.

5: Helping my grandparents, Jane and William Ward, with hop-picking.

6: My lovely mum and me.

7: A rare photo. Me at school.

1: The start of it all. My first drum kit.

2: Mum knitted that jumper!

3: The Outcasts, with me at the back and Ronnie Lane in the middle.

4: Ronnie, me, Jimmy and Steve on the set of *Dateline Diamonds*, ever so casually draped across the new Ford Transit van.

5: Just back from a ride in Hyde Park and requiring assistance from Ronnie.

6: Mean and moody backstage. We couldn't keep that up for long!

7: One of Don Arden's Carnaby Street accounts about to take another pounding…

8: *Ready Steady Go!* Literally a dream come true, playing in a band on TV.

9: Keeping up with the fan mail in Westmoreland Terrace.

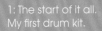

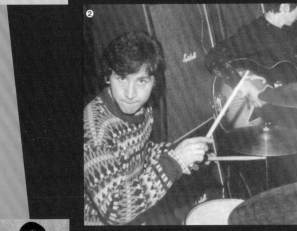

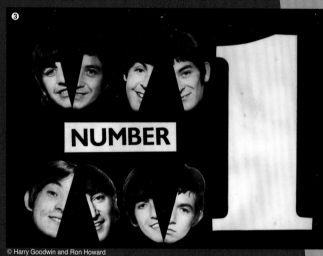

1: At Brand's Hatch. Keeping cool in the shades.

2: Outside Lord John clothes shop in Carnaby Street. Don Arden (far left) keeping a watchful eye on us, while trying to dodge the police.

3: The *Top of the Pops* solution when they listed 'All or Nothing' joint top spot with the Beatles' 'Yellow Submarine'.

4: Appearing in 1966 on *Top of the Pops*, the biggest music show on British television.

5: At Sydney airport with Andrew Oldham in January 1968, at the start of what proved to be a controversial tour.

6: The world's first circular album sleeve.

7: Rick Wills, Steve, Mac and me in the 1970s incarnation of the Small Faces. Not our best idea.

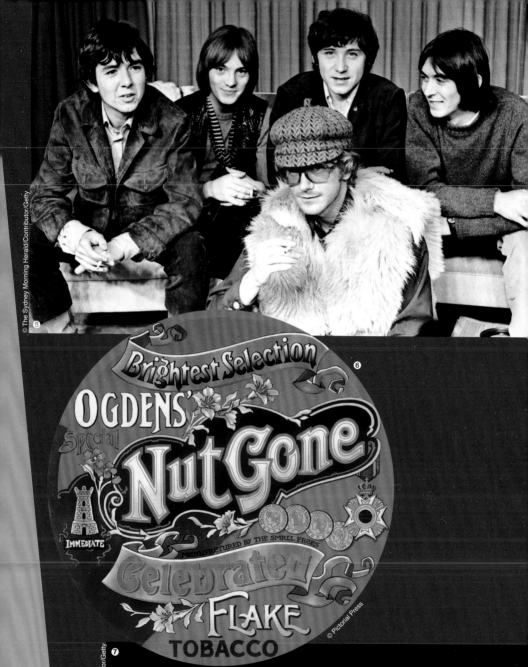

Brightest Selection

OGDENS'

Special

Nut Gone

IMMEDIATE

MANUFACTURED BY THE SMALL FACES

Celebrated

FLAKE

TOBACCO

Good times with the
Faces. Teaming up
with Rod and Woody
was just the antidote
Ronnie, Mac and
myself required after
the Small Faces split.
When Ronnie Lane left
in 1973, Tetsu Yamauchi
(bottom photo, left)
joined us on bass.

BRENDAN BEIRNE/REX/Shutterstock

1: Wembley Stadium, 5 July 1986, prior to joining Rod on stage for the first time since the Faces split. Ronnie Lane's MS had taken its toll. Bill Wyman, second right, stepped in on bass, with Ronnie sticking to vocals. A hugely emotional night.

2: Second Faces reunion, at the Brit Awards on 16 February 1993. Ronnie was too ill to attend. Bill Wyman once again kindly took up his bass.

3: Performing together again in public for the first time in over 20 years. Woody, Rod and me in 2015 at the Hurtwood Park Polo Club Rock 'n' Horsepower event in support of Prostate Cancer UK.

Mick Hutson/Contributor/Getty

Graham Prentice/Alamy Stock Photo

drove from Newcastle to London in November 1966, following the completion of yet another package tour. Steve's ex, the actress Adrienne Posta, was being interviewed on the radio. Bored, we tuned in. The interview was unremarkable, until at the end the DJ announced he was going to play the new single from the Small Faces.

The what?

We knew nothing about this.

A bad situation deteriorated. The track was Steve's composition 'My Mind's Eye'. We liked the song. We didn't like the version we were hearing. It had been taken from a demo Steve handed into Arden before we set out on the tour, to give Don an idea of what we'd been working on. It was raw, it wasn't ready, and it wasn't right.

It was all downhill from there.

Over the previous months, we'd become increasingly concerned that we weren't receiving the royalties we earned. We'd had hit singles, been top of the charts, plus a number-three album, but where was the money? Like good boys, each of us had raised these concerns with our parents, who collectively decided to investigate. They set up a meeting with Arden.

Nervously, they sat in Don's office and politely enquired, 'Mr Arden, we are here really to put our minds at rest. You see, we've been wondering, given their success, why the boys aren't receiving more money. We hope you can explain.'

'Of course, of course. Happy to.' Mum and Dad later told me that Don seemed very open, friendly and decent at this point. Then the punch landed. 'The reason they don't have any money, is that they have spent it all. You see, they are all on drugs.'

That shocked our parents and, as Don no doubt anticipated, completely changed the dynamics of the meeting. None of them wanted to know about the money any more, all they cared about was that, 'my boy is on drugs'.

Mum and Dad were in a terrible state when they arrived home. When I asked what was wrong and they reported Arden's claim, I was angry and outraged. Clearly by 'on drugs', Don had been inferring – and this is how our parents took it – that we were hard-drug users: heroin.

'No Mum, he's lying to you. Yes, we hang around drugs some-times, they're part of the scene now, but we are not on drugs. You know I couldn't. It would affect my drumming.'

Now, the truth was, yes we were having a few smokes, plus the odd leaper and downer – although only uppers for me, to keep me going through the relentless string of double and sometimes triple gigs a night. And, sure, the boys were beginning to experiment with acid for creativity, thanks to the Beatles' influence, but not me. Well, apart from when they spiked my drink in the studio.

I didn't have a fucking clue what was happening. I kept saying, 'Look at my left hand! Look at my left hand!' I thought I was drumming like Joe Morello with his incredibly fast rolls, something I'd been trying to master for years. And now, finally, I had it! Except in reality, my hand was moving in slow motion. So near to Joe, and yet ...

All that aside, we were not on the drugs Arden was alluding to, and that was not where the money had gone. He was trying to put the blame on us and, in so doing, he frightened our parents. Completely unacceptable.

By the end of the year, we had moved out of Westmoreland Terrace and severed our ties with Contemporary Records and Don Arden.

CHAPTER 6

THAT'S WHAT
WE DID THERE

Escaping Don Arden's financially crippling embrace marked the beginning of a game of managerial musical chairs. This was largely down to the fact that we had not in fact escaped Contemporary Records. 'Escape' gives the impression we broke free; in truth Don sold us.

Six months before the split, Don had vigorously defended his claim, fending off advances from legendary Bee Gees' manager, Robert Stigwood. Steve and Ronnie had a preliminary meeting with one of Stigwood's employees and somehow Don got wind of this. The story goes he then marched into Stigwood's office with a couple of heavies as back-up, dangled Stigwood out of a window and threatened to let go unless he backed off. Funnily enough, it worked.

By December 1966, however, I suspect Don was happy to cut the ties. Perhaps concluding our best days were behind us, he decided to cash in, allowing us to believe we were making all the moves. When we formally announced we were off, he didn't attempt to stand in our way or make the situation any more awkward. We took this as a sign of resignation on his part. A more accurate description might have been that he was relieved.

We approached Harold Davison, a well-regarded promoter. Harold agreed to take us on, for an across-the-board 10 per cent commission, appointing Tito Burns as our manager. Great, a new deal, a financial clean slate, exciting days ahead. Not quite.

Don Arden's long shadow soon darkened our optimism. When news of our new representation broke, Don slapped a bill for £20,000 on the Harold Davison Agency, money we apparently owed Contemporary. Naturally, Harold passed that debt directly on to us.

The bright new dawn was looking decidedly familiar.

We didn't last long with Harold and Tito, they were primarily booking agents rather than managers. Yes, they were good at arranging gigs – they set us up with a 30-date package tour featuring Roy Orbison in spring 1967 – but were less concerned with managing or developing a long-term plan to build us in Europe and break us in the States.

We next tried Robert Wace, the Kinks' manager, but that didn't work out as he couldn't devote the time we required. Chris Blackwell of Island Records was also considered, but again time issues prevented that marriage.

Managerially in limbo, one thing we had to sort out ourselves, and quickly, was a new recording contract. Continuing with our current label was not an option, Decca and Arden were hand in hand. We'd been hearing great things about a new kid on the block, an exciting, innovative independent label called Immediate Records, run by Rolling Stones' manager Andrew Loog Oldham and his partner Tony Calder. Through Mick Jagger we engineered a meeting with Andrew at Ronnie's flat in Earls Court.

We hit it off immediately. Andrew spoke our language, understood our music and saw where we were coming from. He said he loved the band and recognised that for musicians to be creative they had to be given freedom. He offered unlimited studio time, during which he encouraged experimentation, trying new techniques and discovering new sounds. In effect, he was saying, 'Free yourselves, and let's see what happens'. An almost unheard-of attitude in those days.

We were sold on Andrew and his ideas from that first meeting. On 10 February 1967, we officially signed to Immediate. I was proud to be part of the label. I saw it as representing the beginning of a new era in the industry, in which artists were at last given space and trusted to create fresh, innovative music, rather than being stifled by out-of-touch men in suits, sitting behind desks smoking pipes, and not-so-secretly yearning for the good old days of Dickie Valentine, Winifred Atwell and Frankie Vaughan. Andrew Oldham had an eye to the future, gathering talent that would go on to produce a string of exciting and popular recordings in the 1960s. I remember passing a skinny, suited Mod I didn't recognise as he was heading down the stairs of the Immediate offices on New Oxford Street. When I asked Andrew what the bloke had wanted, he told me he'd been in to pitch himself as a singer, looking for a deal. His name was Rod Stewart. Jimmy Page was also on the books, as a session musician then, and later Fleetwood Mac released their single 'Man of the World' on Immediate.

Our game of managerial musical chairs was still in full swing when we signed with Andrew, but as each management experiment failed, we fell back on him for help. We were demanding, at times difficult to handle, ambitious in terms of how we wanted our music and ourselves presented to the public. Andrew did what he could, he liked us and wanted success for the band, and himself. By default, he became our manager, but by then, with so much of his energy spent on running the label, he couldn't really devote much time to day-to-day representation. He supported us as a band, gave us the space to be creative, but was unable to provide proper hands-on management in terms of things like tour schedules (we were still playing a lot of gigs in between studio time) and agreeing and implementing an overall strategy. In reality, and strange to say given how sticky his fingers were when it came to our money, the only proper representation the Small Faces ever had was from Don Arden.

It wasn't that we needed hand-holding. In the 18 months since the release of 'Whatcha Gonna Do About It', we had all grown far more self-assured and confident in our individual personalities. I felt it most in interviews. When we first started out, Steve used to help me a lot with the press, he helped all of us in fact. His acting and stage background gave him natural confidence, but he never looked to dominate. Instead he offered tips and advice on how to come across when being questioned by journalists or on TV or radio. At the beginning, if I'd have had my way I would have run a mile from all media, but Steve cured me of that.

Even still, when asked a question I used to think about the answer before I spoke. But by the time I'd come up with what I thought was a worthwhile response, the moment had gone. So I often didn't say anything. Yes, I was naturally reserved and shy, but not that reserved and shy. I became 'the quiet one' of the Small Faces, and from that, the 'sensible one'. That's why many people thought I was at least a couple of years older than I was. They didn't realise I was in fact the baby of the bunch by quite some margin. Steve was nearest in age, and he was 18 months ahead of me, with Ronnie more than two years and Mac more than three.

Then as the hits started to come, and my confidence grew, through experience, I started to say whatever came into my head, without first running it through a filter in my mind. I came out of my shell. I started cracking jokes, truer to the person I was when it was just the four of us.

To a lesser extent perhaps, the same applied to the other three. Publicly, they grew into their personalities. Even Steve. From the word go he'd always been bonkers in our company, and over time he began to show that side of himself more openly. You just never knew when the Artful Dodger would come out. We'd be giving a press conference, or on TV, and for no reason whatsoever he'd suddenly start blowing raspberries or pulling daft faces. 'Oh fuck, here we go again.' He loved attention.

Mac and Ronnie were the same, they grew increasingly happy to show themselves. Mac, edgy but very funny, full of wisecracks and clever one-liners; Ronnie the laid-back songsmith with a razor-sharp wit.

So we weren't looking for a big brother in Andrew. By the time we met him we could all look after ourselves. What we could have done with, though, was more attention to detail. More focus.

The musical chairs may have come to a halt with Andrew as our manager but, unknown to us, we were also participating in another parlour game – pass the parcel. More accurately, pass the debt. Much later we discovered that to secure our signatures Andrew and Tony had been required to take on Arden's 20 grand bill from Harold Davison – once again passed on to us as a de facto advance against royalties. And that wasn't the only deal agreed with Harold. He also received an additional £5,000 which had originally been earmarked to come to us.

Starting out with Immediate, however, financial issues took a back seat. We'd agreed a fair deal, we thought: seven per cent royalties for UK sales and six for overseas, plus an increase in our weekly wages. With that out of the way, we focussed on the music. Andrew's enthusiasm for what we could achieve swept us away.

Andrew himself was a sharp dresser, favouring tailored three-piece suits that he wore well. Again, that was something we could relate to, and as he was only three or four years older, he spoke our language. He wasn't one of us, however, we were never friends with Andrew. We got on well, we saw a lot of him at meetings at our homes or in the office, and he regularly appeared in the studio, but it was always a business arrangement. Andrew enjoyed playing the impresario and wanted to maintain a degree of distance.

He didn't play the big boss though, that wasn't his style. Instead he projected an image of 'Look at me, I am so cool and relaxed', while at the same time making sure everyone knew he was in charge. Sitting in his office, leaning back in his chair, he might be fiddling with a pencil and if it accidently snapped he would barely register the fact, continuing to talk as if nothing had happened, other than a brief direction to an underling: 'Bring me another one of these, please. This one doesn't work.'

Andrew's black and maroon Rolls-Royce Phantom – same as the Queen's – added to the impression he cultivated. With his chauffeur Eddie up front, Andrew would be sitting in the back, crossed legs stretched out, cigarette in hand, on the phone. Unbelievable. A phone! We'd never seen anything like that before. We were mesmerised, even if it was incredibly impractical – the whole of the boot was taken up by whatever machinery was necessary to make the bloody thing work. That didn't matter, it looked good.

Contradictions were an intrinsic part of his make-up. He managed the Rolling Stones, but was into the softer flower power world of The Mamas & The Papas; he was twitchy, but not high-strung; he offered independence in the studio, yet couldn't resist involving himself in the mixing/producing of our records. Andrew thought of himself as a supremely creative person, but in terms of his contribution to our music, although it's true he did introduce some good ideas, his influence was limited. As a big Phil Spector fan, Andrew envisaged operating at that level, but he didn't possess Spector's vision. Most of our recording ideas either came from the band or the sound engineer. In those days, there were a handful of very talented engineers, and we were fortunate to work predominantly with the best of them, Glyn Johns.

We had already begun recording new material at Olympic Studios in Barnes before finalising the Immediate deal, and now, with our new-found freedom, Olympic became our home from home. We could come and go as we pleased, almost living there for up to a week at a time if we wanted, or fitting in days between gigs, enjoying experimenting with Glyn to create new sounds.

We knew Glyn well, he'd been our engineer on the very early recordings at the IBC studios in Portland Place. We'd be playing on the ground level and I'd glance up to the control room to see Glyn sitting next to Ian Samwell at the mixing console, working the huge levers of the fader, a piece of kit that would have looked at home in the cockpit of a passenger airliner. Ian was ostensibly the producer, but it was Glyn doing most of the talking to us over the mic and creating the feel of the track. He effectively produced us.

The same was true at Olympic. We all came up with ideas for production and arrangements, but as part of the deal with Immediate Ronnie and Steve were credited as producers. That didn't reflect the true situation: Glyn contributed far too much to be assigned the role of mere engineer; co-producer would have been more accurate. I don't think Glyn was ever pissed off by this, but I suspect it would have been a very different matter had Andrew been tempted to list himself as producer. That really would have been an injustice.

I trusted Glyn. He'd be in the control room paying close attention to what was happening in the studio and if he spotted things that weren't quite working – for instance if I was on the snare drum too much – he'd come down and not only point it out, but also make a constructive suggestion. 'Kenney, when we get to the bridge, go with the side stick.' In many respects, Glyn acted like my conductor, taking an overview of the whole sound, knowing what I was capable of, pinpointing what could be improved. He understood the structure of songs and I listened to him.

Our close working relationship was a necessity given the available technology and the difficulty in recording drumming as I wanted it. Most engineers didn't like any ring on a drum, it's the same today, they demanded a clean, sharp sound. To achieve this, they would close-mic everything to pick up only the drums, taking out the room, losing the 'spillage' as they saw it. To me that doesn't have the same resonance. Glyn got that.

In my opinion, drums, the unique sound of each drum – the tom-tom or snare for instance – should come across on a record as if you were present in the room as the track was being recorded. Together Glyn and I worked out methods to capture that essence, the ambient sound.

Many studios have disappeared – Olympic included, it's now a cinema. In music terms this scarcity of recording venues is a tragedy, resulting in individuality being replaced with a generic sound. The decision to book one studio over another was not based on available equipment, as kit could be rented or mixing done off-site. The one thing that could not be sourced from elsewhere was the physical four walls, ceiling and floor. In today's digital world you can create magic in your bedroom, but you can't recreate the room. People have tried sampling mine or John Bonham's snare drums from recordings in a specific studio as an attempted shortcut to originality, but you can never replace playing in the actual space.

Abbey Road was Olympic's main competition. It offered a slightly larger room; basically a minimalist box with a high ceiling and panels on the walls for dampening the sound. It produced a fantastic noise but it never quite suited my martial-arts-snap style of playing, power without the big 'bang'. The smaller Olympic Studio One was perfect.

Olympic also offered a nice little sideline. In the basement you were only a layer of plywood away from the storeroom of the hardware shop next door. It was a simple job to push it to one side, slip through and nick anything we fancied.

After some trial and error, Glyn and I settled on placing a large mic high up in the studio to capture the acoustics of the room in stereo. The ambient sound the mic picked up was then fed back to me through my cans so that I could hear what was being recorded and any effects Glyn introduced. This was critical for me. Experiencing what would be heard on the record helped my timing and the movement on the track.

We used additional close mics where appropriate, giving us the option of picking up the drums alone, which I tuned completely differently from anyone else. Knowing how and when to combine the sound from the close mics and the one overhead was the clever bit from Glyn. Together we were a force to be reckoned with when it came to recording drums.

Glyn and I had much in common, not least the fact that neither of us saw any virtue in hanging around the studio just for the hell of it. Record and get out. Often Glyn would pack in a session around midnight, maybe one in the morning and head home. If I could see that Steve, Mac and Ronnie were set on hanging in there, just to fuck about then I'd follow. On the other hand, there were many times when I could tell they were focused and we would all stay on to develop and create songs. Those late-night hours when we were locked into that moment, absorbed by the music, were incredibly special.

Even on those highly productive occasions Glyn was quite right to bail out. There would be nothing for him to produce or engineer. These were creative sessions, crafting the songs and arrangements in advance of any recording. Just in case, though, our tape op Eddie Kramer, who went on to become a producer, would stick with us to keep the machines running and preserve what we were doing. Next day, Glyn would be there to assess the results. No doubt much of it was a load of rubbish, but that didn't matter. Songwriting and creating is usually a process to be worked through. It's rare you get it spot on at the first attempt.

Sometimes the atmosphere in the studio proved too much for me, and by atmosphere I don't mean any stifling sense of tension or frustration or anger. I mean the actual atmosphere, the air. Cigarettes and joints. You got stoned whether you wanted to or not.

Whenever I wasn't needed, if the boys were stuck on a section of a song, endlessly going back and forth, over and over and not making any real progress, as sometimes happened, I'd stagger downstairs in search of fresh air. I knew they'd call me when they were ready to start again, and in the meantime I could take the opportunity to work on customising my Mini.

Andrew Oldham had provided the inspiration. Not long after we'd signed with Immediate, we embarked on a promotional tour of interviews and TV to showcase the talent on the label, including singers PP Arnold and Chris Farlowe. Cat Stevens also joined us. One of the places we visited was Margate for a photoshoot by the seaside, pretending to play our instruments, but mainly playing frisbee with my cymbals. Andrew had brought down his Mini, a proper 'Radford' Mini, which I drove up and down the beach. I wouldn't get out of that car, I thought it was the best.

A company called Harold Radford converted standard Minis, making them posh like a Rolls-Royce, and charging thousands for it. I studied Andrew's carefully. A new paint job to match his Rolls, tinted windows, walnut-effect dashboard, leather seats, sunroof, the lot. It looked brilliant. But fuck spending the money on having someone else do it. I'd fix up my own.

That's what I did, mostly on the pavement outside Olympic Studios. The first thing to go was the instrument panel: the big unblinking eye looking at me, with its speedometer pupil. That used to give me the creeps. That was replaced by an Aston Martin dashboard I found in a breaker's yard, fitted with two fancy Smiths clocks, a rev counter and new speedo, all properly calibrated. Next came a central console with a cigarette lighter, new seat coverings, a leather-covered steering wheel and a state-of-the-art sound system. I gave it the works; it took months, but I enjoyed it – the challenge and the end result. The finishing touch was the only improvement I didn't do myself – spraying it Saluki Bronze, *the* metallic colour of the time. Or, as it's known today, brown.

I loved that car, it had been fun to build and looked flash, but ultimately it was an ordinary Mini with an ordinary Mini engine. Still, I kept it for years before finally selling it to Jimmy Horowitz, an arranger and musician who worked with us during some of the Faces' tours.

* * *

Those first months of creative freedom under Immediate produced a string of tracks that to some extent moved us away from our R&B roots, reflecting instead the world, and substances, we saw, and imagined we saw, around us. The era of kaftans, flowers in hair and LSD had arrived, and we were more than happy to embrace it musically.

It was hard going sometimes. During the spring and summer of 1967, with the sun shining, birds singing, flowers blooming – all that nice nature stuff, almost the last thing we wanted to do was be stuck in a studio with artificial light and non-existent ventilation. *Almost* the last thing we wanted to do. The actual last thing was to screw up this opportunity. So we stuck at it, determined not to waste a single hour of recording time, even though the temptations of the Summer of Love were hard to resist. We made a pact: don't fuck around; make sure we can be proud of what we achieve each day.

The resultant string of Small Faces' releases shows we stuck to our agreement. Most of the time, at least. There was a pub around the corner, after all.

Before we released anything under Immediate, however, the scorpion that was Don Arden had one more sting in his tail. Two in fact.

On 26 May, Decca put out the single 'Patterns', a Marriott–Lane composition, and one of a handful of completed recordings Don had tucked away in a dusty drawer somewhere. We were pissed off, but helpless. Arden's Contemporary Records held the rights to the song, and they licensed it to Decca. We might not have been able to stop it, but we sure as hell weren't going to support it. We ignored 'Patterns', engaged in zero publicity and enjoyed quiet satisfaction when it disappeared without inconveniencing the chart compilers for even a week. Such a shame, Don.

A week later saw the release day for our first Immediate single, 'Here Come the Nice', launched with considerable promotional fanfare, and a string of TV and radio appearances, including *Top of the Pops* and Adam Faith's short-lived ITV series *As You Like It*. Don and Decca decided to cash in on this high-profile activity by putting out what amounted to a 'Best of' album entitled *From the Beginning*, featuring the hits to date, plus various unreleased fillers. It reached number 17 in the charts, putting more money into Don's deep pockets.

'Here Come the Nice' was our first psychedelic song, stimulated by the LSD the guys were now hitting pretty hard, with the title a nod to a line in Lord Buckley's crazy monologue 'The Nazz', a favourite record at Westmoreland Terrace.

Even to the uninitiated, the lyrics clearly, and shockingly to today's ear, advocate the joys of your dealer, the Nice, turning up with a bag of speed, a powerful drug. How on earth it slipped past the BBC censors I still don't fully understand. I suspect the jolly tune and the way Steve sings it, nice and pleasant, confused the fuddy-duddies at the BBC, who didn't have a clue about amphetamines. To them it was a happy little song from a lovely bunch of lads. We'd taken a risk and it had paid off. That made us chuckle. It was the first song we'd deliberately written with a thinly disguised meaning we knew would be understood by the fans, if they were allowed to hear it.

At the end of 'Here Come the Nice', there's a crashing piano chord that proved hard to replicate on stage. It's the sound of our four arses sitting down together on the keys of an old upright. All that intense studio time had been put to good use.

In June 1967 we released our first Immediate album, *Small Faces*, with a cover featuring, well, our small faces. Given this was a month after the Beatles unleashed *Sgt Pepper's Lonely Hearts Club Band* on the world, with *that* cover, we could perhaps have been a little more imaginative.

Music-wise, I still hear a great album, commercial, with bluesy riffs in the background, underpinning the songs; an album to dispel any lingering sense that the Small Faces continued to be purveyors of disposable pop ditties. Or so we thought.

Years later, Mac said he felt the amount of acid being taken had harmed the songwriting and quality of the tracks we were recording over this period. I know what he meant, we did get a bit stuck in a rut when it came to drugs as a subject matter, but other than that I don't think their consumption did the music much harm; the songs are still powerful, even if the content is somewhat narrow. It could have been worse, we could have become fixated on the route numbers of the double-decker buses passing by. I'm counting our blessings. Not that we were analysing any of that, or even aware of it. We just wanted to go into the studio, be creative, then see what we could do with what we'd produced.

'Itchycoo Park' followed 'Here Come the Nice' as our next single. It's probably our best known and most popular song, certainly one of the most successful and the only Small Faces track to crack the American charts, but to the band at the time, it was just another song. We knew it was good, but alongside those other 1967 recordings it didn't particularly stand out.

With the penny having finally dropped too late at the BBC over 'Here Come the Nice', they were now scrutinising everything we produced for illicit drug references. Not hard to find in 'Itchycoo Park'. 'What will we do there? We'll get high; What will we touch there, we'll touch the sky.' Sure enough, word came in: it's off the airwaves. Marriott saved the day, placing a personal call to the powers-that-be at the Corporation. 'It's nothing to do with drugs,' he innocently explained. 'Itchycoo Park was the nickname of a scrappy, rundown area of the East End, a wasteland we played on as kids. It's about escaping to a happy place of childhood.' Total bollocks, but it worked. The song was reprieved.

The initial inspiration for the lyrics came from the *Alice in Wonderland* books that Steve and Ronnie were into at the time, with words sewn together because they sounded good, like, 'Over Bridge of Sighs, to rest my eyes in shades of green'. Ronnie came up with that. I think he picked up the phrase 'Bridge of Sighs' from a Lewis Carroll poem, and had no idea that in Venice you had to walk across *the* Bridge of Sighs before having your head chopped off. He thought that was hilarious when he found out. The line barely made sense initially, now it made no sense at all, but that didn't matter. There was magic in those words. That's why he'd used them in the first place.

Having come up with the basic wistful, psychedelic feel of the track, and some lyrics, it was then transformed into something more solid, a dig at privileged education, based on conversations we'd had with each other over the years, sharing tales of school-days and the very limited aspirations offered by our teachers.

A lot of Small Faces songs have their origins in the four of us sharing stories late into the night or on long tour journeys. 'Rene the Dockers' Delight' from the *Ogdens'* album is another example. Steve said it was about a woman called Rene Tungate, from the East End, but that's rubbish. It's about my aunt Rene, who was a bit of a flirt. I'd been telling the boys tales about her and about my boyhood explorations of the docks area, and Steve married the two into the song.

'Itchycoo Park' is a prime example of the innovative tech-niques we were experimenting with at Olympic, specifically the drum phasing on that track. We were making a statement about maturing as a band and musicians. Glyn Johns came up with the idea for the phasing, or the tape loop, although he discovered it by accident. As he was splicing during an editing session, looping the tape round two recording machines so he could better see what he was doing, he noticed the effect it produced on playback. For the recording of 'Itchycoo Park', Glyn looped the tape round the back of a chair, so that when the reel turned, it stretched the recorded sound.

I take some credit for making the phasing work on the record. Similar to when we were recording ambient sound, I told Glyn that I had to have the phasing in my cans so that I could play to the effect, rather than just hear it later after Glyn had cast his engineering spell. I didn't want to imagine what that sustained 'whoosh' sounded like; I needed to experience it. Most engineers would have said, 'Nah, that's not going to work'. Not Glyn, he knew what I meant and made it happen. That allowed me to delay playing for a split second, and let the effect breathe.

Everyday items such as chairs regularly featured in Small Faces recordings and performances. Look closely at some of the live TV appearances we made and you'll see something looped over the top of my cymbals. Car keys – I loved the jingling, ringing sound they added. I also didn't want to lose them.

On the Trident Studios recording of 'If I Were a Carpenter', it's my drum stool. We were sitting around learning the song and, as we needed a quiet rhythm, I started to play the stool with my brushes. That's how we ended up recording the track.

Creating an effect with whatever might be to hand was not exclusive to playing with the Small Faces. From early 1967 I'd begun to do a lot of session work. It paid decent money and I enjoyed and benefited from the exposure to other styles of music. As a session player, however, you are not in charge, you do what you are told. Fair enough.

I might have loved the sound of a drum ring but as I mentioned, not all engineers shared my enthusiasm. In sessions I found an effective way to subdue any ringing, thanks to Peter Stuyvesant cigarettes. Having the correct weight was critical, so I'd smoke a couple from a new pack, the hard packets, not the soft ones, then loosely attach it with gaffer tape to the drum. The fag packet bouncing up and down subdued the ring but kept the tone.

My introduction to session work came about as a direct result of meeting Jan Osborne on 21 December 1966, following The Who's performance at the opening night of heavyweight boxer Billy Walker's The Upper Cut Club in Forest Gate, East London. My cousin Roy and I attended the gig, after which we met up backstage with Adrienne Posta and her friend Jan.

We soon started dating, and one day in the spring of 1967 her father Tony, a famous bandleader, asked whether I read music.

'Nah, fuck off. It's too hard.'

Tony wasn't fazed. 'Ah, well, don't worry – you know what bars are, right?'

'Yeah, I drink in them.'

'Good one. Listen Kenney, it's not difficult, I promise. I'll teach you. I've got a session tomorrow that would suit you perfectly. I'm going to book you in. Come over to the flat tonight, we'll go over the song together.'

That evening, after a couple of drinks at his place in Primrose Hill, Tony explained the meaning of the lines and notes on a sheet of music.

'This one here, that's four beats to the bar. When you get to this bit, the circle with a line in it, that's a stop. And this one over here, with the cross, that's an accent. You know what an accent is, right?'

That I did know. I'm a drummer.

Sitting at his piano, Tony then ran through the song and music with me, showing how to mark up each sheet with when to come in, when to go with the high-hat, the bass, the big cymbal smashes, the gaps, the breaks, back to the accents, everything. Basically, he showed me how to learn the arrangement parrot fashion. 'Remember Kenney, you don't have to understand what everyone else is doing. Concentrate on counting the bars and knowing your sections.' It was complicated, but I got it. How the hell would I remember it though?

'Don't worry. I'll be there, conducting. I'll help you out.'

I'm sitting at my kit in Trident Studios, St Anne's Court, just off Wardour Street, Soho. I've driven there myself, in the Mini, somehow cramming in the drums. I've unpacked, set up, and now I'm waiting, watching musicians walk in with violins, cellos, trumpets. It's a fucking orchestra. What the hell am I doing here?

Oh no.

I've just seen Big Jim Sullivan saunter in with his guitar, followed by Herbie Flowers and his bass. These guys are amongst the world's best. What the fuck am I doing here? This isn't me. With the boys, we all know what to do, we've worked through it together. This is someone else's music, someone else's arrangement. Shit.

They're starting to tune up, but no one is speaking to each other. Not even acknowledging each other. It's as though the strings are in a different room to the brass, and everyone is in a different room to this rhythm section.

Tony's at his platform, baton in hand, calling us to attention.

What just happened? Suddenly everyone is focussed, together, working as one, at the tap of a baton. Impressive.

Tony's running each section through a sound check. This is where I'll get caught out, the only person here who can't read music. I'm going to stick out like a sore thumb.

Tony points to me. I start playing, eyes down. It's going okay. I risk a glance up, sure I'm going to see the room in fits of giggles. But no. Next to me Big Jim and Herbie are smiling, nodding along. These guys are alright. Maybe this will be okay.

Tony calls attention again. 'Right, everyone ready? Here we go for the first run through.'

The sound check was one thing, this is totally different. I've got to concentrate on the marks on my sheets, and Tony's baton. Sheet, Tony, sheet, Tony. Nothing else.

He counts us in and I'm following on the page. We're at the section with the first accents, when everyone is meant to come together on my beat. Here it comes. I'm screwed.

I can't believe it.

We did it. Together. In time. Everyone. Shit.

I look up, startled, shocked. And drop my sticks. All around they are still playing, making music, wonderful music. Me, I've got my mouth hanging wide open. Tony calls everyone to a halt.

'Kenney, what happened? Why'd you stop?'

I look at him, and everyone. 'I really cannot believe what just happened. I was looking at the sheet, played the accents, and at that same moment, in came the brass, everyone. Ba, ba, ba, ba, bam! Incredible. All from dots and squiggles on a little bit of paper. I knew I was going to play them, but not everyone else. Frightened the life out of me.'

The room starts laughing.

It was an amazing experience and honestly, when serious musicians like Herbie and Big Jim started raving about me, requesting I play on their sessions, it gave me so much confidence. The more sessions I did, and I did a lot, the better I became. My style of drumming changed dramatically and I had no control over it. I was just having a ball, enjoying playing, becoming less afraid to try new styles.

Andrew Oldham used me on sessions he produced of Phil Spector-type songs alongside his regular drummer Ronnie Veral. I learned a lot from Ronnie, and other drummers during sessions, but was always careful not to lose my identity. I made sure I only played as me, but even still there were little things said, tips I picked up, consciously and subconsciously, that without question improved my drumming.

For instance, Andrew once commented in a session, 'Kenney, when you are playing, play it like you mean it.' Maybe I was coasting at the time, I can't remember, but I absorbed what he said, and worked out what he meant: get into the song. Don't just tap away. Immerse yourself. Be part of the whole sound.

That's when I began to master the big orchestral drum fills, which worked well on the *Small Faces* album. By the time we came to recording our final album, *Ogden's*, a year later, I'd reached a level that I could never have dreamt of before that first session at Trident.

I benefitted from playing with a lot of exceptional musicians like Jimmy Page and John Entwistle, but the rest of the Small Faces never got into the session side of the industry. In the early days of the Faces, Mac and I did work together on an album with the legendary Chuck Berry, *London Sessions*, but that was pretty much Mac's only exposure. Probably because he'd never again have managed to be out of bed in time to make the morning call at the studio.

Session work brought more session work, and it can be a strange business. Sometimes you don't even know who else is going to end up on the track. Mike d'Abo, Manfred Mann's lead singer and the writer of 'Handbags and Gladrags', asked me to play on a demo of the song. This was around 1969. It was just him and me in the studio, Mike on piano, me on drums. I thought nothing more of it until I later hooked up with Rod Stewart when we were forming the Faces, and discovered that Mike had also called Rod in for the demo, adding his vocals after me. That was the original demo of the version Rod recorded for his album *An Old Raincoat Won't Ever Let You Down*.

Session work can also catapult you to the top of the charts – uncredited, of course. In mid-1978, as I was packing up from a recording, the songwriter and producer Mike Batt approached.

'Kenney, I need a drummer. Now. Up at the Holland Park studio. Can you make it? I'm in a bit of a panic.'

'Okay, I'll be there.'

Given the tight schedule, I was pleased to discover there wasn't a great deal of drumming involved, except a delicate turn-around, critical to the song. I worked out what was required, ran through it a couple of times, and later that day accompanied Art Garfunkel on 'Bright Eyes'.

Glyn Johns brought me in for Andy Fairweather Low's 1975 album *La Booga Rooga*, and together we experienced a flashback to Trident and the recording of 'If I Were a Carpenter'. Andy and I were in the studio, learning one of the tracks, so to keep things together I took my drumsticks and started playing on a guitar case. Glyn was listening, and decided he liked what he heard. He fixed a mic over the case. 'Carry on what you are doing. Let's see how it sounds.' That's the recording Glyn used.

Glyn and I hooked up again a couple of years later on Joan Armatrading's album *Show Some Emotion*. We almost didn't make it past the first session. It was the first time I'd met Joan.

I now know her well, she's a lovely, kind person, but on day one of that album, she must have been overcome with nerves because she just couldn't remember anyone's name. During rehearsal she continued to call the musicians by their instruments: 'Drummer, play softer', 'bass player, come in sooner'. Eventually Glyn grew so fed up with this that he had a right pop at her, 'They've all got fucking names, Joan'. An awkward moment which could have been the kiss of death to the recording, but Joan took it well and was name-perfect the following day.

I have a lot to thank Tony Osborne for, I would never have played on those records had he not shown faith in my musical ability, and my drumming might not have improved to the degree it did. My favourite claim to fame would also not have happened but for Tony. He knew a lot of people in the business, and it was through him I got to know the singer Dorothy Squires. The Small Faces had played a charity gig with Dorothy at the Royal Albert Hall on 15 December 1966, raising money for the Aberfan Disaster Fund, but we hadn't properly spoken until Tony later introduced us.

Dorothy was quite something. Gracious, generous, the centre of attention, full of life and with a foul mouth like you wouldn't believe. With Dorothy, everything was fucking this and fucking that. It was totally unexpected from someone so showbiz glamorous. I found her hilarious company.

She invited me over to one of her notoriously rowdy parties at her mansion in Bexley. I took Mum.

We had a great time, Mum especially, who throughout the evening enjoyed the charming attentions of a suave, older, English actor who we had both recently seen on television in a new series about the Home Guard during the Second World War.

Yes, my claim to fame is that Sergeant Wilson tried to pull my mum!

CHAPTER 7

NUTS GONE FLAKEY

'The Big Show' tour of Australia and New Zealand started out so well.

We landed in Sydney on 16 January 1968, following re-fuelling stopovers in Bangkok and Singapore. Stepping off the plane in Bangkok to stretch my legs, I had been immediately assaulted by the heat and humidity. I'd never experienced anything like that. It went straight to my head and my stomach.

Stumbling across the tarmac to the tiny, rickety terminal, I asked for the toilet. I thought I must have misheard. The directions led me to a door behind which I discovered two footprints, either side of a hole in the ground. The outdoor khazi in Havering Street suddenly looked like the height of modernity.

I managed a pee, and made it out in one piece, feeling even worse. Joining the others in the cafe area, I ordered a cup of tea to settle my heaving guts. Big mistake. Weather too hot, tea too milky, resulting in a weaving dash back to my footprints, just in time to throw up.

And Bangkok counts as one of the better days on 'The Big Show' tour.

On arrival at Sydney airport we were met at the foot of the plane's steps by a media scrum and a volley of aggressive questions. 'What's your opinion on the devaluation of the pound?' 'Do you take drugs?'

Don't have one. Fuck off.

We were exhausted, hungover and definitely not in the mood for serious comment or witty one-liners. The tone had been set, however, for our relationship with the Aussie press. Unbeknown to us, there'd been quite a controversy stirred in the papers ahead of our arrival, with leader articles complaining about foreign acts coming to the country to rob the weak economy of much-needed Australian dollars. And we thought we'd been invited to entertain the kids.

Despite what happened later, we're still on the highlights reel.

Having charmed the media, we checked in to our hotel, the Sheraton on Macleay Street, where I headed straight to my room to discover a genuine delight – a television. They didn't have that at the Station Hotel, Leeds. Even better, when I turned it on they were showing *Star Trek* – the first episode I ever saw. I've been hooked since.

'The Big Show' consisted of us, Paul Jones, whom we'd travelled with, and The Who, joining us a couple of days later. The first shows were scheduled for the Festival Hall, Brisbane, on 20 January. This gave us time to acclimatise, explore Sydney, and rehearse.

We hooked up with a local guide, an Aboriginal guy we nicknamed 'Boomerang', not only because he kept coming back, but because he also introduced us to those astonishing hunting weapons, trying his best to explain the proper throwing technique. That was fantastic fun, although mine never returned as it should. Cheeky so-and-so must have given me a stick.

Sydney turned out to be very manageable, small then, in comparison to London, with the different quarters – Italian, Chinese, etc. – within easy walking distance of each other. An attractive, friendly (apart from the press) place, featuring traditional streets lined with terraced houses whose little iron balconies reminded me of towns in England. It felt familiar, comfortable, while at the same time emitting a palpable sense of change. A city on the verge of transforming into a world metropolis, with the expanding skeleton of the Opera House marking the path to the future. An exciting place to be.

I was also very taken with our Sydney female fans. With our location widely known, there was a constant group of girls outside the Sheraton to welcome us back from exploring. The management may as well have fitted our rooms with revolving doors, such was the regular turnover of visitors. There was a lot of shagging generally on that tour. We were young, in a new country, and always up for a party.

When not sightseeing or entertaining, we rehearsed our set-list of 'Sha-La-La-La-Lee', 'Itchycoo Park', 'All or Nothing', 'Tin Soldier', 'Every Little Bit Hurts' and 'If I Were a Carpenter' at Sydney Stadium. 'Itchycoo Park' proved the problem. The drum phasing was impossible to reproduce live and without it the track didn't work. Steve came up with the 'solution', as we were sitting by the hotel's rooftop pool, yelling at each other over the noise of the jet airliners.

'Let's just record that bloody racket. It's near enough. The crowd won't know the difference.'

Mac produced his little tape machine, slid in a new cassette and we had our phasing at the touch of a 'play' button.

I suspect, however, that Steve was less than accurate in his assessment that the fans wouldn't spot the difference.

The lack of technology was a minor issue compared to our real problem on that tour. In plain language, our performances weren't as good as The Who. We suffered in comparison.

They arrived in Australia off the back of a major US tour, followed by a run of UK dates. Their act was polished and ready. We hadn't played a live gig since the previous October, and in the months preceding that, only sporadically.

Compared to The Who, we were flat and unprepared. Too much time spent in the studio, too much time miming hits on TV shows across Europe ... the will to tour had been fading for a while, and it showed in our performances. The truth was, our moment in front of audiences had passed.

We tried hard. We knew the fans in Australia would only want to hear the hits, the 'rinky-dink-dink tracks' as Steve liked to call them, and we weren't going to disappoint, even though we'd rather have been more authentic to our roots. As a compromise, we gave each song a heavier arrangement, which was good for us while still delivering what the paying audience expected. The crowds generally reacted positively; the press, that was another matter. These quotes are from local reviews of the Brisbane gigs:

'A boring, amateurish and altogether wasted evening. Few went home happy. Britain has more than economic problems.'

'Dullness was the only thing about the Small Faces ... both Faces guitarists showed "don't care" musicianship ... Apparently bored with having to perform anything as turned-off as a popular success, the Faces took 'Itchycoo Park' at a faster tempo than on record, ripping through it as though in pursuit of growth hormones.' At least he didn't mention Mac's tape recorder.

'The Big Show' concerts kicked off with a local band, who then doubled as Paul Jones's backing group. The Who and us would take turns in opening and closing the second half, basically alternating top of the bill, with our set lasting about half an hour, The Who's a little longer.

The press back then would have it that we were great rivals, inventing stories about how much we hated each other, but that wasn't true at all. We were good mates and got along great.

During the tour, because The Who's drummer Keith Moon was out of his tree most of the time, in the afternoons before the shows I would often end up covering his sound checks after my own. Just as I was leaving the old hook would come out, with either Pete Townshend or Roger Daltrey catching up with me. 'Eh, Kenney, guess what, Keith's not made it ...'

I didn't mind, it was fun. I enjoyed sitting behind Moonie's massive drum kit, having a thrash. His tom-toms were so far away you had to leap off the stool to reach them. That's one of the reasons why he always came across as such a flamboyant, energetic showman; it was impossible for him to remain seated if he wanted to play.

I knew Townshend pretty well. He'd taken to calling up, asking me to come and play on demos with him for Who songs he was working on. That's how Pete operated. When he was ready to take a song into the studio for The Who to record, it was near-enough finished – the arrangement, all the bits and pieces, they were basically all there. The rest of the band could hear from the demos how Pete envisaged the end product – although if I'd been involved, the drumming would have been in my style, not Keith's. That happened quite a lot during my time with the Small Faces and then later with the Faces.

Pete's highly prepared approach was very, very different to what I was used to. Especially with the Faces. Studio time there was far more haphazard, more like, 'What shall we do today?' Then someone would play something. 'Oh, that's a nice riff, but we might try ...' 'Fuck any "but"! We'd better get on with it. It's the only one we've got!'

The fact we were mates with The Who didn't mean there wasn't a degree of rivalry, especially during that Australian tour when they regularly got one over on us by attacking our main weakness. They were also playing their hits, same as us, but unlike our commercial catalogue, even after we'd tweaked the arrangements, The Who's most popular songs – 'Substitute', 'Pictures of Lily', 'I'm a Boy', 'My Generation', etc. – better represented the music they wanted to make. That provided an added dimension to their performances that perhaps we lacked. As Daltrey once said, 'If you put a Who record on at a party, it will kill it stone dead'. He's right, you listen to The Who, you don't dance to them. Their tracks and delivery suited the big stadium sound; ours did not. That was our Achilles heel on the tour.

Adding to the fun and games, we regularly faced technical difficulties. The sound equipment was ropey at best. The amps weren't powerful enough for the venues, microphones didn't work and spare parts were almost impossible to source, which given that Pete had taken to smashing up his equipment once again, proved a considerable headache for their crew.

Then, on our return to Sydney after Brisbane, for two nights at the old Sydney Stadium, originally constructed as a boxing arena with wooden seating circling the ring, the revolving stage refused to revolve. Half the audience could only see our amps, or at best our backsides. They were not happy and showed their displeasure in a hail of penny coins. Good luck at weddings apparently, but on this occasion not for me. One struck me hard. Right on my nuts. I hit the roof. Fuck that was painful. I can still feel it now. Steve noticed me double over in agony and was understandably angry and called out to the crowd to give it a rest.

An unfortunate incident not of our making? You would think so, but here's how our friends the Australian press reported the gig, under the headline 'Who! What? Why?':

'Five thousand teenagers booed the English pop group, the Small Faces, from Sydney Stadium last night after their lead singer swore at the audience. The singer, Steve Marriott, became upset when coins were thrown on to the stage during one number. The audience was stunned to silence when Marriott stopped singing and threatened to get down from the stage and "clip some bleedin' ears if it don't stop".'

Hold on Steve! That's appalling bleedin' language. And you can't go around intimidating people like bleedin' that. Threatening to clip someone's ear is one small step away from actually wagging your finger at them. Steady on.

Apparently, however, this was such a serious incident that Australian politicians stepped in:

'Crackdown on pop show louts. The [New South Wales] Premier, Mr Askin, has ordered police to watch closely the conduct of both performers and audiences at teenage pop shows. His edict followed a police enquiry into alleged indecent language by the English pop groups the Small Faces and The Who at Sydney Stadium on January 23.'

Accepting that Steve may well have used far stronger language than bleedin' this or bleedin' that, this reaction was still far in excess of what was appropriate. They were out to get us. And they could have, if they had merely opened their eyes.

Two days after Sydney we were in Melbourne on the third leg of our tour. I was in my hotel room when the phone rang. Moonie.

'What you doin', Ken? Let's go get drunk in the bar.'

'Sure Keith, you're on.'

'First though, come on up here. I want to show you something.'

Opening the door to Keith's room, the first thing I saw was a row of 10 Premier snare drums.

'What are you going to do with them?'

'I'll show you.'

Laughing, he picked one up and threw it towards the closed window. Stop! Keith! Smash!!! Straight through. Did he think it would bounce back? Maybe. Too late now. We rushed to the window in time to watch the snare drum crash on to Melbourne's High Street and bounce off down the road, disintegrating as it went.

'Fuck that!' said Keith. 'Let's get that drink!'

Moonie and his snare drum was the least of the items that exited hotel windows during that tour. In New Zealand, on Marriott's twenty-first birthday, a record player, chairs, doors, televisions, a sofa and mirrors all took flight over the balcony. I'd escaped by then, back to my room, only hearing about it next morning. I thought we'd be in big trouble, but no charges were ever brought and once damages had been paid, it was all forgotten.

The same could not be said for a far less dramatic incident on a flight from Adelaide to Sydney two days previously.

We'd been up late the night before, partying after two shows at Centennial Hall, which marked the end of the Australian concerts. We were tired, hungover and ready for sleep. We certainly were not looking for trouble. We didn't have the energy.

I was sitting next to Paul Jones, who was asleep before takeoff. Moonie was in front of us, also out for the count. On reaching cruising altitude the air stewardess started down the aisle with her drinks trolley. Internal flights in Australia then were dry, we knew that, and anyway, the last thing any of us wanted was alcohol. We'd had plenty.

The noise of the trolley woke Paul, who tried to attract the stewardess's attention. She ignored him, walking right past. Paul pressed the call button, she stopped, and came back.

'Yes?'

'A coffee, please.'

'You don't need a coffee. You can't have a coffee. You've got your booze – drink that.'

'Now just hold on a second,' Paul came back at her, in that well-spoken manner of his. I always thought he was quite posh. 'Listen, I don't have any booze. I just want a coffee.'

'Well you can't have one.'

'Excuse me. I've paid my ticket. I want a coffee.'

We discovered later that she'd seen one of Paul's backing band, an Australian bloke sitting towards the rear of the plane, who had smuggled on a can of beer from the all-night party.

By now the altercation had woken the others, including Moonie. Fatal. Everyone started shouting and chanting, 'We want coffee! We want coffee!'

Up to this point, hardly the stuff of rock 'n' roll legend.

Bob Pridden, The Who's sound engineer, and our monitor mixer on the tour, then helpfully intervened. Bob was always a bit dishevelled, long fingernails, generally unkempt, and a ball of fun. He sang to himself as he was working, 'Root-dee-doo-dee-doo, A root-dee-doot-dee-die-day'. It made us laugh, and as a happy memory we worked it into the 'Lazy Sunday' track later that year.

I can't remember Bob's words exactly, but he stood up and shouted across to the girl something along the lines of, 'If that man wants a coffee, bring him one! Do you know who I am? I'm next in line to the throne of England!'

Not exactly, Bob. Yes, he married an earl's daughter, but that's not quite the same.

Perhaps the stewardess was an Australian republican, I don't know, but she didn't take kindly to Bob's royal command.

'If you don't sit down, and you lot don't shut up, I am getting the captain.'

'Get the captain! Get the captain!'

Sure enough, out he came to explain that if we didn't quieten down, he was going to divert the plane to Melbourne.

'Fine. Can we have a coffee there?'

The stewardess told him we'd been drinking. We said we hadn't. He didn't believe us. We wouldn't shut up.

Welcome to Melbourne.

As we disembarked, we walked down the steps with our hands in the air, as if we were coming off a hijacked plane. Well, we thought it was funny.

In the terminal calmer heads took over. Townshend, John 'Wiggy' Wolff, The Who's tour manager, and Paul Jones sat down with the guy who ran the airport to explain what had happened. He seemed to understand, accepted there'd been a huge over-reaction (we later received an apology from the airline) and arranged for a separate plane to take us all to Sydney in time for our connecting flight to New Zealand. I guess they were happy to see the back of us.

Nothing much had really happened, except for the flight being diverted, and yet we were slaughtered in the press. Australia's *The Showman* called for a ban on 'these scruffy, guitar-twanging urchins once and for all'. Me? Guitar-twanging? That's an insult. Meanwhile, the *New Zealand Truth* offered this verdict. 'We really don't want them back again. They are just unwashed, foul-smelling, booze-swilling no-hopers.' I take exception to the 'foul-smelling'. Finally, leading Australian concert promoter Kenn Brodziak, who in 1964 had brought over the Beatles, couldn't resist a comment, declaring he was now reluctant to book British pop groups.

We were not sorry to be heading home after the final shows in Wellington, although the tour still managed to deliver a last moment of drama. The scheduled route to London involved brief stopovers in some US states, but as we wouldn't be passing through immigration at any of these locations the fact that Mac was barred from entry on account of his drugs bust wasn't a problem. Until bad weather forced us to divert to San Francisco, requiring an overnight stay. Now there was a serious possibility of Mac being arrested as an illegal alien. We were all worried, but the bus that arrived to transport us off the plane drove straight to the Holiday Inn outside the airport complex with no checks whatsoever on our passports. Straight through. Same in reverse the following morning. Mac remained a free man.

One final shock.

Walking into my room in the Holiday Inn, I saw a TV attached to the wall. How the hell does that work? It's great! I switched it on. Colour! Even better! A news report about the Vietnam War. I stood transfixed as the newscaster introduced some footage. Soldiers on a street. A Vietnamese policeman with a gun. A prisoner with hands tied behind his back. The gun pointed at his head. Bang! My God! He shot him! The blood seemed to pour from a high-pressure tap straight towards me, out from the television.

Finally, the Small Faces make it to America, and this is my first impression.

* * *

Steve, Ronnie and Mac brought back some unwelcome presents from our trip Down Under. Down under. I remember the moment vividly.

We'd gone up in the world. The Black Maria was long gone and we were now travelling to gigs and media appearances in our Mark 10 Jaguar. It wasn't long after our return from Australia, and for once I was in the back between Steve and Mac. Normally I sat in the front of the Jag, but on this occasion Ronnie, for some reason, had insisted on sitting there. I soon found out why.

Steve turned to Mac, 'Did it work for you?' I didn't know what they were talking about.

'No, not yet,' replied Mac, 'I'm going to try a different cream tomorrow.'

What the hell was that all about? Then they mentioned the word 'crabs' and immediately I pushed up off my seat, desperate to distance myself from them, horrified at the thought of picking up something very unwanted.

Next day, on our way to another engagement, we pulled up outside Mac's house to pick him up. He appeared at his front door with head down, a hand shading his eyes. Odd. It was cloudy, not sunny. Slipping into the back of the car, Mac then looked up, a sheepish grin on his face. What the hell?

'The bloody things have got into my eyebrows. I tried that new cream and this is what happened.' It was impossible not to laugh. Mac's eyebrows had turned purple.

I only realised I'd been infected while on a flight from London to Rome, a few weeks later. Within days of arriving home, we'd hidden ourselves away for an extended period of studio work at Olympic. It was hot in there, airless, and we thought nothing of sharing towels to wipe off the sweat. I'm certain that's where they came from. The timing made sense. I'd had no symptoms before then.

We were flying to Italy for a series of gigs in the prestigious Piper clubs, a chain of discos with high-concept design and modern architecture, incorporating small stages for bands. On the plane over with Jan, I began to feel increasingly itchy and soon desperate to get to our hotel room. The cab ride there was a nightmare. I just wanted to scratch and scratch and scratch. I checked in as quickly as possible, sprinted across the lobby to the lifts, and once in the room, dived straight into the bathroom to see what the hell was going on. I pulled down my trousers and had a good old root around to see what I could see. I feared the worse.

I spotted a little black dot. Plucking it out, I put it on to the white tiles surrounding the basin for closer inspection. As I peered down, it scuttled away. I nearly had a heart attack. *Shit! I have to get rid of these. Now!* I called out to Jan, explaining the situation and pleading with her to find a chemist. 'Get me anything! I don't care. But make sure it's strong!' She headed out immediately, no fuss, locating a chemist next to the hotel. She later told me that as soon as she said the word 'crabs' the pharmacist knew exactly what she meant and gave her some DDT powder. While she was away I'd been so disgusted by myself that I'd shaved off my pubic hair. The worst thing I could have done.

At the time I was relieved, I thought I'd sorted the problem, or at least was over the worst. No more itching, and the DDT would do the rest. Then at the gig in the evening, I started to sweat. Oh my God. I was in agony. The sweat was stinging like hell and added to that, my style of drumming meant the insides of my legs were being rubbed raw against the shaven area below my knob – sensitive skin on what was in effect sandpaper. Nasty.

It's not a remedy I'd recommend. Far safer to put the razor away, and instead mix whisky and sand, pour that over your Old Chap, and leave the crabs to get pissed and start throwing rocks at each other!

* * *

We were touring in Europe when we heard a familiar sound, although we didn't fully recognise it at the time. Bang, bang, bang. A nail being driven into another coffin. This time it's not our relationship with a manager that's being buried, it's the band's future.

The hammering echoed out of an article that caught our eyes as we absentmindedly flicked through one of the music papers. Apparently, the Small Faces were set to release a new single, 'Lazy Sunday'. News to us. We were supposed to be involved in all such decisions. Not this time.

We'd recorded the track at Olympic, a throwaway song that Steve had come up with after one too many noise complaints from his Chiswick neighbours. It was his second, and lesser, act of revenge against what he saw as the constant and unreasonable thumping on his wall. He and his mate Mick O'Sullivan had already spiked the water tank that supplied the terrace at Eyot Green in which Steve lived. With LSD. For a short time, the now-tripping genteel folk next door were no doubt wandering aimlessly around their house 'sussing out the moon, man'.

We liked the song, for what it was – a fun nod to the old East End music halls, with Marriott giving it the full Cockney in response to an argument he'd had with one of The Hollies about why Steve never sang in his natural voice. We'd laughed our way through the lyrics, Bob Pridden's root-dee-doo-dee-doo, the daft jingle-jangle tune and me taking the piss with silly rim shots. The whole thing was a muck-around in the studio, with the end product an album track, if anything. That's all we ever thought of it.

Andrew Oldham, however, smelled money.

What we hadn't known was that while we were on the road, Andrew had been going into the studio, asking Glyn to play him whatever we'd recorded. He heard 'Lazy Sunday', and, recognising its potential, worked on the mix, edited it down to radio-play length, then had it pressed and ready to go. Without telling us.

We went fucking mad.

Yes, it was a hit, fine, but it worked against us. We were forever trying to lose that boy-band, teeny-bopper image; 'Lazy Sunday' sealed our fate.

It reached number two in the charts. Great, another smash. From the outside it must have looked like we'd just taken another big step up the ladder of fame and fortune, when in fact our sure-footed upwards climb was an illusion. The rungs on the ladder were rotting, soon to snap and send us tumbling into the dirt.

For a while we had all been growing increasingly frustrated, Steve perhaps most acutely, whenever we bumped into people like Eric Clapton or Jeff Beck, guys who were playing heavier, rawer music. We'd be chatting with them, cracking jokes, laughing, being the Small Faces that everyone expected, but inwardly we were groaning, desperately wanting the equivalent of the musical recognition and respect they received. 'Lazy Sunday' all but ensured it was never going to happen.

At the time, I sensed there would be repercussions following Andrew's decision to release the single, although when they came their severity shocked me.

Taking a step back, trying to assess the situation dispassionately, I can understand why Andrew, and previously Arden, acted as they did. Both wanted to keep the Small Faces' name in lights, using chart hits as the energy source. Fine, but they could have done that without resorting to underhand methods, by giving more thought to us as individuals, trusting us musically and, crucially, not panicking. Instead, they rushed into decisions unilaterally and favoured short-term gains over more-fulfilling long-term success.

It was based on the mindset that promoter Ron King explained to me once, well before then, when he gave me a lift back home to Stepney in his brand-new Mercedes after a meeting in Arden's office. For the entire journey, he'd been bending my ear about his achievements and wealth. As his bragging droned on, to pass the time I found myself wondering about the Merc's ivory steering wheel, and how realistic it looked. *It didn't really come from an elephant, surely?*

The contemplation of such important issues summed up my level of interest in Ron's monologue, until he suddenly caught my attention with a comment. 'You know Kenney, you will only have three months in this business so make the most of it. Cash in while you can.' Interesting attitude.

Then as he pulled up to drop me off, Ron said, 'What you want Kenney, is to end up like me, with a car like this'. I thanked him for the lift, shut the door, waved goodbye and thought, 'What a load of bollocks. That's not us. We're different. We're going to be around for a long time. Your car's alright, though. I could live with that. But the last thing I want to do is end up like you.'

With 'Lazy Sunday' already in the warehouse, set for distribution, there wasn't much we could do other than adopt an attitude of, if we can't beat Andrew, we may as well join him. There was demand from television shows for a film clip to accompany the track, so why not do it on our terms and have a laugh while we're at it. We filmed at my parents' house in Havering Street, it's their front door in the video and their outside loo that Steve steps into with a roll of toilet paper. A neighbour, Peggy Dawson, plays 'Mum'. ('Hello Mrs Jones, how's your Bert's lumbago,' Bert being a reference to my Uncle Bert who married one of Mum's cousins and lived next door.)

Mum and Dad were very happy to be involved in that video, albeit not in person. They were very proud of my success and enjoyed sharing in it, but only to a limited extent. They had no wish for their lives to be turned upside down. The *East End Advertiser* would occasionally knock on Mum's door, looking for a comment, and she was always happy to oblige. That was about the extent of it.

Mum used to love telling me whenever she and Dad heard one of our songs on the radio. 'And I said to your father, "That's our son, Sam." And your dad would nod, a big smile on his face.' They liked our music, and came to a number of concerts, Mum especially. The only thing Dad ever had a problem with was my clothes and accent. And then only to have fun, taking the piss. He used to tell me that the thing he was most proud of was that success hadn't changed me, apart from how I dressed and spoke. 'You're more polished now, son. You don't sound like the rest of us anymore. I can hardly understand you.' Then there was how I looked.

The fact that I lived at home for such a long time meant that on days off I would often meet up with Dad in the local pub for a couple of pints. Wearing pink jeans. Or green shoes. Or a flowery shirt. 'Can't you afford a proper outfit?' he'd say. 'Affectionately embarrassed' I think sums up how he felt. His mates thought it was a right laugh, taking the mickey mercilessly. But I knew they all understood. Life had been conducted in black and white for so long that it was well overdue for the kids to start doing their own thing, brightening up the world a bit.

On the day of the video recording, for an extra little dig, Steve also insisted on filming a dance sequence in the garden outside his place on Eyot Green, with the 'offending' neighbours' house in the background. It was giggle, and to top off a good day out, we all ended up in the pub after filming.

Despite those happy memories, and the single's success, I have conflicting feelings when I think of the song. I understand that for some fans 'Lazy Sunday' represents a sort of youth anthem for rebellious teenagers, and that's great. I like that, I really do, but on the other hand I can't shift the sense that the track stands as something of an epitaph for the band. That drives me nuts and makes me feel sad. It's too jokey, too Cockney, a bit too much fun when we wanted to be taken more seriously.

* * *

The lid of the coffin was almost secure, but not quite. We still had one last big breath to take.

The album we'd been working on for the previous 12 months or so was released in May 1968. A lot has been made of the time we spent in the studio, mainly at Olympic, sweating over the concept for the album, recording and re-recording tracks. In fact, *Ogdens' Nut Gone Flake* didn't take anything like a year to record, not in terms of hours in the studio. We had the one extended run in February, but other than that, it was a case of finding days here and there when gigs, tours, and TV and radio commitments allowed. If we'd had one straight hit I reckon we'd have been done inside three weeks.

As for the idea of creating a 'concept' album, that had never entered our heads. Not until the story found us, through Ronnie.

On our return from Australia we already had some tracks recorded, which ended up filling side one, but not yet enough for a complete album. Andrew Oldham suggested we take time out to clear our heads, in the hope of kindling inspiration, and hired each of us a motor boat for a cruise down the Thames. Great.

Off we went, wives and girlfriends accompanying, for a long weekend gently pottering along the river, chilling out, enjoying a few smokes. Crashing into things. I was first, and it was an extremely unfair contest. My little motor cruiser versus a bloody big destroyer or frigate or some such naval vessel, presumably purchased after the war, with people now living on it.

We were up by Windsor Bridge, and I was attempting to turn my boat around, with absolutely zero knowledge of steering or currents. It was not a happy experience. Very quickly I was out of control, and helpless to avoid drifting at some speed into the side of that huge, great steel monster. The force of the impact smashed part of the steering wheel cabin, where I was standing doing very little other than panicking and knocked out the window completely, which crashed over my head. As we came to a crunching halt, I found myself staring through a porthole at what looked like a very nice family enjoying, until that moment, a delicious looking Sunday lunch.

I made my apologies, at least there was no damage to their vessel, and we continued on our way. A little further up the river Mac was in the lead, travelling too fast, as another boat was heading towards him in the opposite direction, with a very cross-looking gentleman standing on the bow, ramrod straight, dressed head to foot in a white, shoes, trousers, blazer and cap, like the Admiral of the Fleet, gesticulating wildly. Politely, Mac gave him a friendly wave back.

'Move aside! Move aside!'

Too late Mac realised that his speed was not going to allow him to take the evasive action required to avoid contact. He did his best, and almost got away with it. Almost, but not quite. You could barely hear the screech of Mac's cruiser scraping down the side of the Admiral's pride and joy above the howls of laughter from Steve, Ronnie and me.

As the two boats separated, the Admiral turned back towards Mac, shaking his fists wildly as he screamed, 'Scourge of the seas! Scourge of the seas!'

Such mishaps aside, the trip was a great success, mooring overnight on the bank, lighting fires, talking, Steve and Ronnie playing their guitars. One evening Ronnie was lying on the grass, looking up at the dark sky, when he came out with, 'Where's the other half of the moon?'

From there, the story of Happiness Stan's quest to find the rest of the moon took off. We played around with ideas on that trip, but the actual songs were written back in the studio, with Mac and me pitching in, feeding off Ronnie and Steve's imaginations which had been wonderfully reignited.

Initially, Steve was keen on hiring Spike Milligan to narrate Stan's story, but Spike's schedule made that impossible. It was a shame, as Spike would have been excellent, but his replacement, Stanley Unwin, the Professor of Gobbledegook, proved an inspired choice.

Having accepted our invitation, Stanley sat down with us individually while we were recording at Olympic so he could understand us better. He told me the story of how he first decided to use his Unwinism language as an act. He was a television producer in Birmingham when the Bullring Centre had just opened, and was heading to work one day in a convertible with a friend when, unfamiliar with the new road layout, they ended up driving the wrong direction down a one-way street. A policeman pulled them over and Stanley's mate said to him, 'Why don't you do that funny talk you do when he speaks to us, just for a laugh.'

Why not? 'Ah, deep folly, for this Mr Spokenman. To and fro and we will drive out the back road.'

Gibberish, but the young constable started smiling and said, 'Alright, alright, just fuck off the two of you!'

Stanley thought, 'Ah, that was an interesting reaction'. According to him, that's when he started to really work on it.

We didn't give Stanley a script. How could we? We explained the basic storyline and he listened to us talking to each other, scribbling down notes on the things we were saying, which he then wove into his narrative. That was a touch of genius, especially as these were not phrases Stanley would use naturally, things like 'Oh blow your cool, man,' 'What's been your hang-up, man.' What I found most astonishing about Stanley's narrative, however, was that for all it mainly consisted of made-up words, you can still follow the story. Amazing.

He was a lovely bloke. Many years later I did a TV talkshow with him in Leeds. He appeared not to have aged a day. 'Stanley, you look great, just the same,' I told him, to which he replied, 'You see Kenney, the thing is, you are right. I haven't changed. I looked old back then.'

We'd both walked into the reception area together, carrying our changes of clothes and he said to me, 'Right Kenney, let's go drop off the gear in the dressing rooms and pop across the road for a couple of pints of tilty-elbow.' Who could resist such a wonderful invitation.

Only seven songs on *Ogdens'* tell Stan's story, side two, plus the title track, the instrumental. The genesis of that track came from our flop single, 'I've Got Mine'. I had always felt it was a great song and so I took it as my inspiration in developing that opening number. I brought in my big band experience not only to that instrumental, but to all the other Happiness Stan tracks. As we were working on that side of the album I found myself being drawn more and more into the music, immersed in the whole idea of *Ogdens'*. I was determined not just to be a drummer, keeping everything together in the background, I wanted the songs to come alive, to use all that I'd been learning during my session work to make Steve, Ronnie and Mac's compositions even more meaningful, the lyrics even more powerful. What made that possible, of course, was that the songs were so good. If you have an average song, one that's not inspirational, you play averagely. For me, to play my best, I must love the song; I don't necessarily need to understand it.

Take the final track on the album for instance, Mac's 'Happy-Days ToyTown'. It's about the secret of life, apparently, how every day you come to the same conclusion that, 'Life is just a bowl of All-Bran, you wake up every morning and it's there. So live as only you can. It's all about enjoy it, cos ever since you saw it, there ain't no one can take it away.'

Eh? That never made sense to me, but that's immaterial, I never worried about that. What was important was that it sounded great and it fitted into *Ogdens'*. Yes, it has that Cockney sing-a-long feel to it, but unlike 'Lazy Sunday' it has its place on the album, bidding the listener goodbye with an upbeat chorus.

The side one tracks were all recorded around the same time and you can hear the similarities, which does mean they flow together on the album, except perhaps 'Lazy Sunday'. That's on the album because of Andrew. Having accepted its release as a single, we would have rather have left it at that. Andrew, however, insisted. With his commercial hat on, no doubt he was thinking that we've got the album coming out, it's got a weird cover, we don't know if it is going to sell even though we all love it, so as insurance let's stick on 'Lazy Sunday' as it's a hit already.

Side one should have closed with Ronnie's 'Son of a Baker', which had been inspired by his interest and involvement in the spiritual teacher Meher Baba's form of Sufism. Another great song, but its original arrangement was a bit flat. I felt it had to move, otherwise it would have been too basic – up and down, up and down, with nothing to lift it. I worked closely with Ronnie on the track and came up with something I thought would work: a quick left-hand triplet coming down on the snare, giving a flick to the standard beat, so that at those moments the listener is taken to a different place. It's not that difficult to do, but tricky to invent. And it sounds great.

The way that song developed is another good example of the strong telepathy we shared as a band. I could hear what Ronnie's song needed, and Ronnie recognised that. Perhaps more than most drummers, I've always paid close attention to lyrics and how they are being sung, looking to augment the words to provide opportunities for the singer to deliver the best vocals possible. I focussed on that with Marriott, and the same applied when I was in the Faces. Rod Stewart and I used to connect like mad, he'd be looking at me as I was playing and sometimes when he turned away to sing to the audience, for a split second I'd stop, which made him pause for an instant. Like he'd been given a jolt, 'Shit! What just happened?!' He loved that.

An innovative album deserved innovative packaging. We'd recorded all the tracks but didn't yet have a title, let alone a design, until we were sitting around having a couple of joints and one of us pointed at the items on the coffee table in front of us – a round tin of Ogden's Flake tobacco and a blue packet of Rizla rolling papers. That's the album right there. Immediately ideas started flowing, not doubt with the help of the spliffs. A round tin, a round album, how about a round sleeve? Ogden's, a great name, old-fashioned, we like that, but let's change the brand to 'Nut Gone Flake'. 'Like my nut,' suggested Steve; and the name on the rolling papers, that became 'Sus', for 'suspect activity'. A mad rush of ideas. Perfect.

We needed permission to use the name of the tobacco firm, and when Andrew contacted the company in Liverpool to find out how they felt about it they were delighted, supplying us with vintage art books featuring their various designs from which we could choose our favourite for the front and back covers. Sticking with the initial inspiration of the round tin, we produced the first-ever circular album sleeve, which folded out into four additional panels, one of which was illustrated by two of Mac's mates who produced an image of Happiness Stan smoking a pipe in a psychedelic setting, very much in tune with the times. The front cover showed the lid of the tobacco tin, and on the back it read '1lb Box', again using original artwork from Ogden's tobacco.

The result was a brilliant package for what proved to be our most successful LP, spending six weeks at the top of the UK charts.

We never played *Ogdens'* live. That was a mistake. Yes, it would have been complicated, but I wish we'd tried to find a way to make it work. A great regret. We were supposed to record a new 'live' version of the second side for a performance on the BBC's *Late-Night Line-Up: Colour Me Pop*, to comply with the Corporation's rules on miming. Even that we didn't manage. We couldn't face it. Instead, as we had done many times in the past, we went into the studio and pretended to record, supplying the BBC with a slightly remixed version of the album. A wrong decision. We should at least have tried to produce a new version. Better still, we should have insisted on playing live on the show, even if the performance hadn't matched the quality of the record, given the over-dubbing and additional effects. Instead, we took up our instruments – Steve with his Gibson SJ-200 acoustic and

Ronnie on his beloved Harmony H-22 with the black pickguard –
and mimed to tracks it was almost impossible to mime.

It was an odd evening in other respects. Stanley Unwin joined
us to record the narrative, which turned out slightly different
from the original. Hardly surprising, as replicating it would have
been virtually impossible. He captured the gist brilliantly, and
sounded great. He didn't look so good, however.

We wanted him decked out in a wizard's costume, but ended
up with King Stanley sitting on a throne. We'd searched the
props department for an appropriate outfit but all we found was
a crown and an ermine robe, which Stanley was game enough to
pull on. You can clearly see he's wearing a shirt and tie underneath. Not exactly Gandalf.

Then when presenter Michael Dean introduced us, he said
that we were there to play our 'idiosyncratic' new album. *What?
Is that good or bad?* I'd never heard the word before.

The tape of the show was rescued from being wiped by an
engineer, thank God, and looking at it again now it makes me
feel weird. I see the boys happy, laughing, yet I know what is just
around the corner.

* * *

We were incredibly proud of *Ogdens'*. During the recording
sessions, we knew it was special, but we had no idea what anyone
else would think. Then when it became a huge success, we must
surely have felt the world was at our feet. Invincible. Strong.
Independent. Masters of our own future. Didn't we?

Nothing could be further from the truth.

After the release of the album we played a series of gigs, but
nothing had changed. The girls were still screaming. Ripping at
our clothes. Not listening to the music. What's the point? We

were still a teeny-bop pop band. Even after *Ogdens'* we hadn't shaken off the image. The realisation began to sink in that we would never do so. The band the public saw, and wanted, was not the band we aspired to.

In addition, for the first time internal pressure began to build when thoughts turned to a new album. We started to record, but made very little progress. The only meaningful refrain we came up with was: 'How do we top *Ogdens'*?'

We didn't know what to do. Try another concept album? Or something in a totally different style? We should have just gone into the studio to see what happened, allowed ourselves to be creative without a preconceived idea of what to produce. But we didn't, we were lost and couldn't find the way back to our music.

As all this was happening, Immediate Records was beginning to implode. Financial concerns were overwhelming Andrew and he was unable to offer even the limited guidance and advice of the past. By the end of the decade they were in receivership, owing us a great deal in unpaid royalties. It was many years before any payments were made.

Despite the problems we had with them, I was still amazed to see Immediate fold. Perhaps the big contemporary labels of the time didn't like the idea of this successful upstart and called in some loans, I don't know. Immediate should have been the Virgin of its day, going from strength to strength for years, but instead they went bust for only £250,000. A lot of money, sure, which Immediate had spent on creating music, and on themselves and the image, but it shouldn't have been insurmountable. And yet, for whatever reason, they found it impossible to garner enough financial support to keep them afloat.

Mac and I never made much money at all out of Immediate – Steve and Ronnie did, and it caused the first major argument we'd had in the band. They bought a house in Epping Forest courtesy of Immediate – Beehive Cottage, in Ongar. Steve lived in the main house, while Ronnie took the flat above the garage. Ronnie always drew the short straw in life. When Ronnie moved out, Steve converted the flat into a recording studio.

We only found out about the payment they received after the deal was signed, as we were looking into setting up our publishing company, Avakak (or 'have a cack', as we made sure to pronounce it; Steve's idea for the name, needless to say). It was something like 12 grand, quite a lot of money in those days. They tried to excuse themselves by saying it had been offered as an advance solely against their songwriting royalties. Well, even if that was correct, they were wrong to snaffle it. The cash should have been split four ways and viewed as a band payment for the recordings we were going to make. We were really pissed off, and fell out with the two of them over it, for a bit.

Getting stiffed on that money was one thing, but what really hurt us all was when we later started to look into the Immediate accounts, trying to identify down which hole our royalties had disappeared. It turned out that Andrew's liberating, 'Take as long as you want in the studio, lads,' should have been followed up with, 'because we aren't paying for it, you are'.

Immediate was deducting studio time from our royalties, and much else besides – giving with one hand and taking with the other. We weren't aware of any of this. To us, Immediate had portrayed themselves as nurturing and giving, allowing us all this studio time to be creative because we were so great. When I eventually discovered the truth, I couldn't sit down for a week. The knife in my back kept getting in the way.

Of the four of us, Steve was the most affected by our post-*Ogdens'* situation. He was a complex guy who internalised problems, letting them stew over time without properly discussing how he was feeling with either me, Ronnie or Mac. It was only after the excitement of the album's release had died down that we began to realise just how badly the build-up of his frustrations was hurting him. We still didn't understand the wounds were terminal.

His intense dissatisfaction turned into independent action. And the final nails sealed the coffin.

First, he insisted on releasing a song he had recorded on his own at home, basically in his back garden, while his dogs ran around barking. You can hear them on the track, 'The Universal'. It was a poor choice, it didn't even reflect the band as we saw ourselves, but Steve had a bee in his bonnet about it. He wanted to show that he could put out anything after *Ogdens'* and it would be a success, to prove a point. Either that, or he had a death wish for the Small Faces, fighting for the single's release because he knew it would crash, providing an excuse to split the band.

Entering the UK charts in July 1968, 'The Universal' stuttered to number 16, then faded away. As Steve said in the song, 'So I continue to play, and if I'm so bad why don't they take me away.' He did that himself.

If 'The Universal' was Steve's genuine last throw of the dice to create a new beginning for the Small Faces, it failed to come up with the number he wanted. I think that's when he finally convinced himself that his only option for escaping the pop image was to form a new, heavier band – his version of Zeppelin. We could have gone down that road with him, maybe not as the Small Faces, but the four of us together, had he talked to us and given us the chance.

He didn't. Instead, behind our backs, he started working with guitarist Peter Frampton of The Herd. We knew nothing about this.

We knew Peter, however. As a mate of Steve's, he'd played a couple of gigs with us towards the end of 1968, staying in the background, and I'd played on sessions with him. We liked Peter and admired his guitar playing. The three of us never held a grudge against Peter for what was about to happen.

* * *

The gloom and frustration that was beginning to suffocate our once happy band was briefly lifted in November, during a six-date UK tour that also featured The Who, The Crazy World of Arthur Brown and Joe Cocker. Keith Moon provided the much-needed antidote.

Moonie was on imperious form during that brief run of concerts, picking up exactly where he'd left off in Australia, relishing in unleashing one madcap antic after another. We opened in London, at the Roundhouse, Chalk Farm, and from there stopped off at Birmingham, Newcastle, Glasgow and Liverpool. Arriving in Newcastle during the afternoon before the gig, I'd decided to take advantage of a few hours of free time to rest up in my hotel room, and perhaps grab an hour's shut eye so I'd be fresh for the evening performance. I was lying on my bed, beginning to drift off when I heard a strange scratching sound coming from beneath the desk that was pushed up against the wall next to my bed. Got to be mice, I thought. What a pain in the arse. I hope they don't keep me awake. The noise grew louder, I reassessed my thinking. Rats. The wall started to shake, plaster crumbling. Fucking elephants!

As I got up to investigate properly, there was a loud crunch, followed by an explosion of dust and clattering of bricks. I bent down to take a look under the desk, and found myself staring into the bulging eyes of Keith, his head poking through the hole in the wall between our adjacent rooms. 'Fancy a drink, Ken?'

Keith had decided to travel on the tour in his purple Rolls-Royce, with chauffeur Dougal Butler. We all arrived in Glasgow at the same time, outside the Albany hotel, Bothwell Street, in the city centre. Dougal pulled up the Rolls by the entrance, and began to unpack Keith's gear as we checked in.

'I am sorry, Sir,' Keith was informed, 'but you can't park your car there. You will have to move it, I'm afraid.' Keith stood quietly for a moment, then nodded. 'Fine. No problem. Whatever you say.' He then took the keys off Dougal, slipped behind the wheel and drove the Rolls straight through the front doors, right up to desk, at which point he casually got out, threw the keys to the startled receptionist and said, 'Can you park this please.' I can only assume Keith offered to pay for the damage to the doors because we weren't thrown out. I suspect the hotel staff wished they had.

After the concert at the Paisley Ice Rink we were all back in the hotel bar, hitting it pretty hard, until at around one in the morning I decided to bail out first, as usual, leaving the others to it. Back in my room, I was half asleep when I heard whispering and giggling outside the door. What the hell? I got up and was tiptoeing slowly to the door, not wanting to make a sound, when all of a sudden a massive torrent of water erupted into the room from underneath the door. It hit me square on the chest, knocking me backwards, off my feet, and planting me on my arse in an open suitcase. Soaking wet. It turned out Keith had stuck the hose from the fire extinguisher under the door to wake me. 'I just wanted to double check you really didn't want another brandy and Coke, Ken.' Thanks Keith.

That poor hotel. Or more precisely the poor chambermaid who came to clean my room the next morning after we'd checked out. Not only was there still a puddle of water on the carpet, but when she entered the bathroom she would have been confronted by what appeared to be a woman drowned in the bath, with just her bare legs visible, sticking out of the tub. The previous afternoon, Keith had found a local joke shop and bought two pairs of inflatable legs. Not a blow-up dolls, just legs. I can't imagine they sold very many of them in a week, and certainly not two sets in one afternoon.

Foolishly, Mac and I had agreed to Moonie's offer of a lift to the next gig, down in Liverpool. We should have known better, but what a laugh. Keith had customised his Rolls with a hidden speaker behind the front grill, attached to a microphone inside. With Mac and me in the back, and Dougal driving, Keith was crouched down in the passenger seat with the mic, shouting rude comments at passers-by and old dears standing at bus stops. 'Up yours, Mrs!' that sort of thing, giving them a hell of a fright.

The second pair of inflatable legs almost had us arrested. Stuck in traffic on one of the main streets in Glasgow, Keith poked the legs out of his window and started to shout in a woman's voice. 'Help! Help! I'm being attacked!' We were next to a bus at the time, and the driver saw what he thought was a terrible crime being committed and jumped out of his seat to come to the rescue. Fortunately, the jam cleared just in time and we sped away, the legs still clearly visible.

Through the other side of the city, and into the countryside heading south, with the legs now safely tucked away, we pulled into a petrol station to fill up. Out of nowhere, four squad cars appeared, screeching to a halt, surrounding us, truncheons at the ready. They'd been following at a discreet distance, waiting for their opportunity to swoop. 'Out the car, all of you! Now! What have you done with the girl!' They did not see the funny side when the 'girl' was produced, nor when Keith started rolling around on the ground in stitches. 'Bugger off! And don't ever come back!'

I never accepted a lift from Moonie again.

* * *

The final death throes of the Small Faces began in Paris a short time after that tour.

Glyn Johns invited us over to work on an album with French rock star Johnny Hallyday. We were in limbo. Paris. Decent money. Let's go. Then Steve invited Frampton to join the ride.

Peter was great in the studio, a joy to watch up close. The only way I can describe how I felt when Peter was playing is that it was like listening to a flower opening – wonderful little riffs that slowly blossomed into something special, bringing those tracks to life.

Peter was a highlight of that trip. We also had good times with Johnny. He was fun. He loved driving around the streets of his city in a black Lamborghini, making sure he was seen, very much the French king of rock 'n' roll until it broke down one afternoon and we had to push it back to the studio, laughing our heads off.

My memories of Paris are marred, however, by the second, but not last, argument we had within the group, when Steve announced he was going to ask Peter to join the band. Ronnie and Mac went mad, refusing to even consider the idea. To them, we were a four-piece or nothing. I think they were probably right, even though Frampton's style of playing would have given us a new, welcome dimension, and taken some of the pressure off Steve, allowing him to take a further step forward as lead singer. The problem, however, was that we would have ended up with two frontmen, and that's a recipe for disaster.

Many years later, and I don't know how true this is, I heard that after our bust-up it was Glyn Johns who suggested to Marriott that he and Frampton go off together and form a band.

Not long after Paris we were playing a New Year's Eve gig at Alexandra Palace. Steve had invited the highly respected bluesman Alexis Korner to join us on stage. Alexis was someone we looked up to, a British version of Muddy Waters, and we were honoured that he was willing to play with our band. Whether this was a deliberate ploy or not I can't be sure, but Steve asked Alexis to accompany us on absolutely the worst song imaginable, 'Lazy Sunday' of all things. Something like Smokey Robinson's 'You Really Got a Hold On Me' which formed part of the set would have been great. But fucking 'Lazy Sunday'? What's a blues guitarist meant to do on that? Embarrassing.

The song fades away towards the end, with a drum solo to see it out. As Steve sung the final words, 'Close my eyes and drift away', he threw down his guitar and stormed off stage. Planned? I don't know.

We didn't have a clue what was going on. We looked at each other, continuing to play and hoping that Steve would reappear. Then Alexis, no doubt wondering what the hell he'd got himself into, slipped away, soon followed by Mac, then Ronnie, who whispered to me as he passed, 'Keep playing, we'll go and try bring him back'. After a minute or two, when no one returned, I put down my sticks and quietly walked off. There was no cheering, no clapping, no calls for 'More!' from the audience. Just a stunned silence.

I stepped into the middle of a huge row in the dressing room, Mac going crazy, laying into Steve, shouting and swearing, while Steve kept repeating, 'I can't do it any more'.

We sat there for a while after Steve left, in that little box room, not speaking, empty inside, staring at the dark mauve walls. A horrible colour that matched the mood. Then we packed up and went home.

For me, the worst thing was Steve not waiting until we'd finished the gig. I would still have been upset, but it would have been okay if he had just said he'd had enough after we'd finished. But to mess with us, and the audience, in the way he did – I found that unforgiveable.

We had a handful of shows in January 1969 to which we were committed. We agreed with Steve that he would complete those gigs, then that was it. We said goodbye to each other and went our separate ways.

Marriott at least had somewhere to go – into the arms of Peter Frampton and their new band, Humble Pie.

On the surface, Steve appeared to have had his wishes granted. He was stepping away from the frustrations of how the Small Faces were perceived and into the new world of authentic rock music, guaranteed to deliver respect and recognition. I do wonder, though, how happy it made him. To me, Humble Pie felt like a band trying too hard to escape their past. Music-wise, they had all the talent you could ask for, but they were over-arranged – too clever, too many twiddles. They'd just be getting into the groove when they would veer off somewhere else, accents coming out of nowhere. I wanted to say to them, 'Alright, you've done it once, don't keep doing it. What are you trying to prove?'

As for Steve, his voice was increasingly becoming a carica-ture of the hardened rock star, an over-exaggerated image that he then allowed to influence him physically, taking to extremes the perceived necessity to be wasted all the time.

The concern which surfaced in Paris, the problem of the dual frontmen, was evident in Humble Pie. I liked Peter's voice in the songs, but it was clear what was happening. Steve was trying to overpower Frampton; Frampton was fighting back. Ultimately, that was going to take them nowhere.

I didn't see Steve again until the summer of 1972, when the Faces played a huge festival in America, Concert 10 at Pocono International Raceway, Pennsylvania. Humble Pie were on the bill – alongside Emerson, Lake & Palmer and Three Dog Night – and Steve and I bumped into each other backstage. Steve was cocky, a bit of an ass, but I remember thinking, 'Sod it, it's okay. It's done'. We were now two different bands. We were successful, they were successful. Water under the bridge. It did make me think, though, how ironic it was that the Small Faces never played in the States but here we were, the four of us, not together. It felt weird, not right. It should never have come to that.

I do still feel short changed with regard to the Small Faces, and I lay the blame for that on Marriott. It's the only thing I've ever not liked about Steve – that his actions deprived the Small Faces of a future. It was so stupid. We could have, and would have, evolved into the band he was searching for. We did with the Faces.

We should have taken a deep breath, maybe some time off. Later, when bands that came after us told me that following a couple of hit records their lead singer was leaving or the band was splitting, I'd say to them, 'You don't need to break up. Fine, go off, do solo material, but come back together. No one will ever be bigger than this band you've created.' Groups that stick together through their problems, like The Who or the Stones, evolve into a kind of business, an entity that can continue, allowing individual members to be perfectly fulfilled doing other projects, while still making the band work. I've always been jealous of those bands.

In that period between the Alexandra Palace gig and saying our goodbyes, I tried to get the Small Faces to see that, but I couldn't. I didn't have the experience then, or the balls to stick up for myself and speak to a lawyer or accountant to try to find a way to make it work. I should have done.

Steve walking out came as a complete shock to Mac, Ronnie and me. We hadn't seen it coming, even after Paris. We felt that had been dealt with. The fact that Steve might continue hanging around with Frampton wasn't an issue. We trusted each other, we'd never had a problem with one of us taking time out to play with other musicians.

We were devastated, and to make matters worse, unlike Steve, we had nothing lined up. *Thanks Steve, for dropping us in the shit.* I left the Small Faces with £800 in my bank account, failing in an aspiration I'd been harbouring to make it to a thousand. If I'd reached that amount, I'd persuaded myself it would be a sign I was doing okay. Assuming, of course, that the band was still together. But now, having fallen short of my target and facing this musical divorce, £800 was little money to fall back on, with no gigs and, it felt, at the age of 20, no future. All my hopes for the next stage of the band had disintegrated in an instant.

It felt as though there'd been a death in the family. Up to that point we'd done everything together. Millions of photos, hundreds of gigs, TV shows, hotels. They had looked after me; we'd looked after each other. When I was homesick on our early tours abroad, carrying my little brown suitcase, they had stood by me, supported me. When I came out of a loo in France on our first visit, shocked by the fact I'd seen a woman in there, they'd laughed at me, and then with me. The memories came tumbling. My band of brothers.

Now, after Alexandra Palace, one of us was gone and none of us would ever be the same.

CHAPTER 8

FANCY A DRINK?

We were lost. The only people Ronnie, Mac and I could face speaking to were each other. We couldn't bear contact with anyone else. No one could understand how we were feeling. Did Steve really mean it? Was this the end of the Small Faces?

As the weeks drifted by, it became clear that he did; and it was.

Humpty Dumpties. We had to put ourselves back together again. We achieved it through music. The Rolling Stones kindly offered an outlet: their equipment warehouse at 47 Bermondsey Street, a couple of minutes' drive from Havering Street. A damp sound-proofed room provided our refuge. We could play there, talk there, hide there and, in time, emerge stronger from there.

At the start, we were only filling hours in the day. We didn't want to say goodbye to each other, but we didn't know what to do next. Coming together to jam, laugh and piss around, reminded us that music can heal, as well as tear apart.

Then Ronnie brought down a new pal, his neighbour Ronnie Wood, bass player with the Jeff Beck Group. Woody was also looking for a new beginning, a break from the bass in favour of playing lead. As soon as he walked in, I recognised him as the guy from Selmer's. Now and again, the Selmer's owners would invite bands to come in, to try out some amps which they were going to be given for free, as a marketing ploy. Woody had arrived with his band The Birds and there was a big fuss made over them. Ronnie Lane and I were so excited. Real-life musicians. Of course I'd heard of Ronnie Wood over the years since, but our paths hadn't crossed again, until that day.

Woody was great. Exactly the fillip we required.

After a month or so of playing once or twice a week, Woody said he'd like to bring over a friend from the Jeff Beck Group. Like Woody, he was at a loose end. The band had a short US tour on the horizon, but other than that they had time on their hands and his mate was looking for a bit of fun.

Of course. No problem Woody. Bring him along. What's his name?

Rod Stewart.

I didn't know Rod, but I knew of him – initially as that skinny Mod on the stairs of Immediate Records, but mainly from his pre-Jeff Beck life in the blues band Steampacket, with Long John Baldry, Brian Auger and Julie Driscoll.

Rod was shy. He wasn't pushing to be involved in what may or may not be the embryonic days of a new band. Rather, he was there to pre-empt the Double Diamond advertising slogan of a year later. 'I'm only here for the beer.' Or more accurately, the rum and Cokes. Rod would sit on the amps watching us play, until every now and again we'd take a break and all disappear up the road to the King's Arms pub for a few drinks and a giggle. Then we'd head back to the warehouse to make more music, Rod continuing to act as our one-man audience.

In time, it reached the point that we couldn't continue messing around, we had to do something more. We started writing songs. Now we required a vocalist. I had the best seat in the house to watch all this. Ronnie had a great voice, but it wasn't strong, not after we'd been used to Marriott. Mac had a go, then Woody, but throughout I kept thinking something was missing. All the time I was looking over at Rod. Wondering.

'Rod, come on, give it a shot.'

We played Muddy Waters, Rod on lead vocals.

Shit!

In a really good way.

In the 1974 film *Stardust*, when Adam Faith, as the road manager, asks one of the guys in the group, 'Fancy a drink?', that bloke is for the chop. In the King's Arms, early summer 1969, the opposite happened.

'Fancy a quiet drink, Rod? Round the other side of the bar?'

'Sure Kenney.'

'Rod, do you fancy joining the band?'

'Shit, yeah. But what about the others? Do they want me? Would they let me in?'

'Don't see why not. You heard us together. I heard us. They heard us. It'd be great. I'll suss them out.'

That night, Alvin Lee, singer with Ten Years After, was throwing a party at his mews flat in Marylebone. Early on, I called Mac and Ronnie into the kitchen for a talk. I knew I didn't need to worry about Woody. He was up for the idea of a new band and would be cool with this, no question.

'Boys, I've asked Rod to join.'

They didn't look happy. Mac especially. I could guess why. After Marriott, he didn't want another prima donna. Rod wasn't a threat though, I was sure of that. And his potential was huge. I knew this was a big opportunity. Since he started singing with Jeff Beck, even though he wasn't yet a name, everyone in the industry recognised his talent.

'Kenney, I am not sure I like this.'

'I get it. I really do. But think about it a moment. You both saw, felt more like, what happened when he sang the other day. I'm convinced he's the difference between success and failure. With Rod, we can forget Marriott. Make him eat humble pie.'

That brought a smile.

It was just a line. It wasn't really about Steve. Not much anyway. It was about the three of us. The last thing I wanted was to stop working with Ronnie and Mac. In a music sense, they were all I had. When Steve fucked off we could have gone our separate ways, but we didn't. There's a reason for that. We needed each other. We were stronger together and we would come through this, better than ever, but we needed Rod and Woody.

'Think about it. Please, think about it.'

They did, and after a few days of badgering I had my way. Rod was in, but into what? We weren't anything at that stage. Five guys with an idea, but no plan.

Woody's brother Art stepped in, offering to organise gigs. We were shuffling around at best, Rod and Woody were still officially with Jeff Beck, but yeah, go ahead Art.

Art insisted on being involved. He was a decent singer, he'd been in a band called the Artwoods which hadn't quite made it, and as he was doing all the legwork, it seemed more than fair. Art arranged for us to play some Oxford and Cambridge University May Balls, bringing in a mate, Kim Gardner, as cover on bass for the Cambridge dates while Ronnie was off in India visiting the mystic Meher Baba's shrine, who'd died in January.

We appeared under the name Quiet Melon. Where did that come from? Well, when we were talking about what to call ourselves there was a particularly uncommunicative large green-skinned fruit sitting on the table. As good a reason as any.

The gigs were a riot. Booze and blues. Muddy Waters' 'Hoochie Coochie Man' and 'I Got My Mojo Working', plus Ray Charles' 'What'd I Say'. And if the students wanted more, we'd do them again.

By August, Rod and Woody had returned from their US tour commitments with the Jeff Beck Group. Woody was by then an ex-member, having been chucked out. Not long after that, Rod himself left and Jeff broke up the band for a while. With Ronnie Lane now back from India, Art booked us into the Philips Recording Studio near Marble Arch. We laid down a handful of tracks, including 'Diamond Joe' and 'Engine 4444'. Apparently, the Fontana label had shown some interest in signing us, until they heard the tape. Fontana weren't alone in their comprehensive lack of enthusiasm. No one gave a monkey's about Quiet Melon, and our brief collaboration with Art Wood ended.

Four significant events occurred around this time.

First, Rod kept going on and on about the car of his dreams, a yellow Marcos. Then out of the blue, he bought one. It cost £1,300. A lot of money. Especially for a car with a wooden chassis. I thought every time it went over a bump that it would snap. More importantly, it also happened to be the exact amount Rod had agreed with Mercury Records to sign on as a solo artist. It must have slipped his mind to mention that to the rest of us.

Second, it's announced in the music press that Rod is joining our still unnamed band.

Third, late one night down in the Speakeasy Club on Margaret Street, off Oxford Circus, my girlfriend's brother, Gary Osborne, an A&R man at RCA Records, introduced me to Billy Gaff. Billy was a short Irishman with thinning hair and pinched nostrils who worked for Bee Gees' manager Robert Stigwood. Billy and I began chatting and after one, or probably five, too many drinks,

I offered more detail than intended about our financial mess, thanks to the Small Faces legacy. The pass-the-parcel music had finally stopped, and Mac, Ronnie and I were left holding the unwanted gift of a big debt. Billy offered to help, to extricate us from Immediate and find a new recording deal. I said I'd run it past the others. Billy became our manager.

Finally, I had a meeting with the Small Faces accountant, a nice guy called Milton Marks. He sat behind his huge desk while I perched on a seat in front of him, feeling and looking small and insignificant.

'Kenney, what you've got to do, now that the band has finished, is earn some money. Quickly.'

'I know Milton, I know. But we are going to be okay. We're getting a new group together. We'll get a record advance. We'll tour.'

'But how do you know it's going to work? You need cash now. How do you know you're going to get an advance? And even if you do, realistically, how much will you get?'

Out of nowhere, the figure £30,000 popped into my head and out of my mouth.

'Kenney, that's telephone numbers. You'll never get that much. You're smart Kenney. You should think about sessions again. That's where you can be successful. A new band, is that wise ...?'

'But ...'

'Sessions, Kenney.'

'But ...'

'Sessions.'

Billy was as good as his word. He got us out of the Immediate contract. Not particularly tricky, as it turned out. Given their financial situation, on a fast train to receivership, the Immediate contract was null and void anyway. We didn't know that at the time.

Billy Gaff set up a meeting with Warner Brothers, something I could probably have managed myself as I knew the label's boss, Ian Ralfini, through Tony Osborne, but I was still a little too shy of business at the time. I left it to Billy. However, I did at least ask if he'd pitched for an advance yet. No.

'Well, ask for 30,000 quid. I don't want a penny more or a penny less.'

'Are you serious?'

'I'm fucking serious. Thirty thousand. Don't forget.' I kept nagging and sure enough when he came out of his negotiations, we had our £30,000.

A new beginning.

We were ready to sign, happy to sign, until we saw the contractual parties. Warner Brothers and the Small Faces. That's not us. We haven't got a name yet. Negotiations ricocheted back and forth. They kept insisting we had to be commercial and the name 'Small Faces' would sell. We kept reiterating we're a new, different band. In a nutshell, it came down to the fact that if we didn't go out as the Small Faces, we wouldn't receive the £30,000.

Who won? A draw probably. We compromised on our debut album *First Step* being released in North America under the name Small Faces, and everywhere else as the Faces.

After that, we insisted. Forget the 'Small' entirely. We are the Faces.

Once again, we were ready and happy to sign. If not entirely kicking off as a *new* beginning, it was a beginning. Hand over the pen.

Wait.

When we received the contract there was only space for four signatures. Billy? Rod? Mr Ralfini? What the fuck?

LET THE GOOD TIMES ROLL

Rod's solo contract precluded him from signing. That pissed us off. Not the fact that he'd already made his deal, but the fact we hadn't been informed. With the band's future on the line (but not the dotted line, thanks Rod), Mo Ostin, boss at Warner Brothers in Los Angeles, became involved. He and the head of Mercury Records were great mates and they agreed a satisfactory compromise. Rod could work with us as a full member of the Faces and still do his solo stuff if we promised to give a live album to Mercury. That's why *Coast to Coast* is on that label.

Yes, we were annoyed with Rod at the time, Mac more than anyone else and their relationship continued to have an edge throughout the lifetime of the band, but for the rest of us the feeling was fleeting. As for me, I was delighted to have him involved. He was magnificent, a knight in shining armour, a paragon of virtue, a guiding light ... eh, no. He was one of the boys, and all the better for that. Not only had we lucked out with a fabulous singer who had a powerful voice that matched our music, he was also a great mate, slotting in instantly. Nothing flash. I took him round to my parents' often when we were rehearsing, and one time he said to Mum, 'Excuse me Mrs Jones, you don't happen to have a piece of cardboard, do you?'

'What do you want that for Rod?'

'I've got a hole in my shoe.'

* * *

In early 1970, Billy Gaff arranged a series of gigs in England and across Scandinavia, to work ourselves in. The English audiences didn't really want to know us then, but we weren't bothered. Our sights were set on the US, and in the meantime we were happy to tighten the act and enjoy ourselves.

There was a lot of drinking in the early days, but I wouldn't say it was wild, more a bunch of mates up for a laugh, getting along with each other. After what Mac, Ronnie and I had been through, we felt liberated, and it was a fantastic feeling, to be part of a five-piece setting out to conquer the world. Or at least give it a good go. It's true that we rarely performed a gig sober, but because we were young it affected us less. We could still play, up to a point.

Our first North American tour began in March, at the Varsity Arena, Toronto, supporting Canned Heat. From there we moved on to the States, and a series of small clubs and theatres; hot and sweaty places, like the Northern Virginia Community College, the Wharton Youth Centre and the Eastown Theatre, Detroit. We were loud, bluesy, ballsy and word-of-mouth spread like wildfire. When we hit New York in April, it was everything I hoped it would be. Just like in the movies. Arm-whirling cops directing traffic, shimmering skyscrapers, yellow taxis and steam billowing out of manhole covers. And the people, they were so welcoming, all across the States. Have a nice day. We sure did, many of them. Mac, I remember, was particularly taken with one aspect of New York life. Across from our hotel there was a little deli that sold freshly squeezed orange juice. He said he'd never tasted anything as good. Apart from brandy.

Playing live with the Faces proved a revelation. A different image: less Mod, more rock; longer hair, colourful clothes and more fun on stage. And an unheard-of reaction from the crowd, or unheard of for me, Ronnie Lane and Mac at least. No high-pitched screaming; instead it was cheering and shouting, appreciating the music.

On our return from the US, we made a series of festival appearances in England and Scandinavia, plus some back in the States, interspersed with smaller concerts at venues such as the

Cooks Ferry Inn, Edmonton, and the Civic Hall, Dunstable. Half the time, though, I didn't have a clue where we were going or where we'd been, although one particular gig does stick in my memory from this period – the Open-Air Love + Peace Festival in September on the island of Fehmarn, off the coast of West Germany. The idea was to recreate Woodstock in Europe; they got the weather right, but not much else.

We played on the Saturday night, 5 September, in a wild storm. Drenched by the horizontal rain and electrical equipment shorting as we tried to perform, I spent most of the set either grabbing at my cymbals, which were continually being whipped up and down by the vicious gale, or chasing them across the stage before they disappeared into the crowd. Despite the genuine danger, we thought the whole thing was a blast.

The situation became potentially less amusing after we'd finished, when Billy Gaff went to collect our payment from the festival manager's office – a suitcase full of US dollars – and had to negotiate his way back to our caravan through the hordes of bikers who'd congregated at the site and started a riot during the night. If they'd realised what he was carrying he'd have been set upon, I'm certain.

Jimi Hendrix was scheduled to come on after us, but the deteriorating weather made that impossible. He played the following afternoon. By that time we were home and thankfully dry. We hadn't hung around the night before, especially after word filtered through that Jimi had been postponed. We were happy to have made it out of there in one piece, and that's no exaggeration. Reports afterwards talked of machine gunfire and the promoter's trailer being set alight.

Despite the undoubted need for a speedy escape, I wish we'd stayed on for that extra day to watch Hendrix. There would never be another opportunity. Two weeks later I picked up a newspaper and read of his death.

* * *

That first State-side tour had lasted 10 weeks. When we returned there in October we graduated in part to what we called 'sheds', the larger auditoriums like the Civic in Santa Monica. By the third tour, in February 1971, we were selling out stadiums. We'd grown bigger than the Stones, and real money started to roll in.

As the arenas increased in size, I developed a different, more powerful way of playing. The sound systems weren't very sophisticated, and for the PA to pick up and project my drums, I had to keep it simple.

If I tried to play anything a little complicated, like a roll or a paradiddle, it would disappear in the wall of sound. I'd be able to hear it, but no one else. Initially I found it hard to play in that style, to keep the discipline. It was totally different from the Small Faces. Back then, my drums were loud enough in the smaller venues that the audience could hear everything I was doing. I grew to like the Faces style, though. Very much.

By 1971, our stadium concerts were not the only things increasing in popularity and size. With the release of his album *Every Picture Tells a Story* in May and the single 'Reason to Believe'/ 'Maggie May' in July, Rod's solo career had gone crazy, resulting in a not-so-subtle change to our billing. Rod says he was pissed off that we became known as 'Rod Stewart and the Faces' and I believe him. It wasn't his doing. Some marketing genius quietly began to alter the promotional material without telling us.

It was fine. I wasn't bothered. We were having too much fun, and success, for it to matter. On stage, the Faces were a band whose primary motive was to please the crowd. If the audience wanted to hear 'Maggie May', we were happy to oblige. That's certainly how I felt, and Rod wasn't about to complain. We made that song for him in the States.

I did once get caught out, however, when performing one of Rod's songs, '(I Know) I'm Losing You' from *Every Picture.*

On one of the evenings that Rod was recording the album in a studio in Willesden, he tracked me down at Jan's mother's house in Hampstead. I was watching a movie at the time. By then we'd already been playing 'I'm Losing You' live, so when he called the house to ask me to come over and play on the recording, I happily agreed. Knowing the song backwards, I drove there, sat at the kit he had set up, nailed the recording, and was back on the sofa in time to catch the end of the film.

'I'm Losing You' contains a big drum break, which is one of the reasons Rod was so keen for me to play on the recording. It had become something of a speciality. On stage with the Faces we had built it into a near epic. It started with Rod chanting over two or three bars, but it soon became longer and longer and longer until it turned into a massive solo. Great. Until the day they left me onstage to dive across the road for a drink in a pub opposite the venue while I gave it everything I had. I was a physical wreck by the time they merrily sauntered back to pick up the song again. That pissed me off. Funny though.

The four of them leaving me to it was not unusual, but normally they just wandered over to the bar we had on stage, so I could see them and give the nod when the time was ready for them to get back into it.

Yes, the Faces set up a bar on stage. Not only that, it came with a barman – our roadie Royden Walter Magee (known as 'Chuch', much easier to handle) in full penguin outfit, towel draped over his arm, the works. During the concert, you could catch his eye and, as he knew each of our preferences, your beverage of choice would be duly delivered on a tray. Very sophisticated. Or for a change, if one or more of us wasn't performing at a particular point in the show, for instance the boys during my drum solo, they could walk over to the bar, pull up a stool, enjoy a drink and watch the action.

The audience loved it. It contributed to breaking down the barrier between them and us, which is what we always wanted. At those moments, the band and the fans merged; we became part of the crowd, Jack the Lads, just the same as them. That's why Faces' gigs were so amazing. There was no sense of detachment, of us playing, the audience applauding, then us playing, the audience again applauding ... Instead we were in it together, part of the same show, and that created a wild, joyous atmosphere.

In the Small Faces days I wasn't really a big drinker – just the odd lager now and again, but in the Faces, fucking hell. Brandy and Coke normally. Not exactly a health drink, but I never put on weight. Whenever I came offstage, I was sopping wet and pounds lighter. I never needed to worry about developing a Coke belly. You rarely see a heavy drummer.

My drinking did once lead to a potentially dangerous incident. Not for me, but for our publicist, the wonderfully named Tony Toon. He was a great laugh Tony, flamboyant, camp and full of fun, we all liked him, but boy did we take the piss.

We had a late-afternoon band meeting around Christmas in an underground club near Shepherd Market in central London. Tony had arranged to meet there because he knew how hard it was to first gather everyone in one place, and secondly to keep us focussed on business. Previously we had tried holding meetings at Billy Gaff's, er, gaff, but there we would just muck around the whole time, drinking and generally wrecking his flat, filling his bedroom drawers with jam, stuffing things down the toilet. Like schoolboys. Tony must have felt the club was a safer bet. More chance of us all showing up and concentrating, with the prospect of some harmless nightclub fun acting as an incentive to deal as quickly as possible with the matters at hand.

To a large extent, Tony's ploy worked. We ran through our agenda, then relaxed into the evening. The music was loud and we were getting merrier and merrier. Tony was by now on the dance floor, trying to persuade us to join him, 'Come on boys, let's have a boogie'. As we watched him cavort around, I had a thought. The club had placed festive streamers on all the tables. Wouldn't it be a brilliant idea to thrown them all over Tony. I was on top form, obviously. The boys agreed, and started dancing around Tony, covering him in so many streamers that he looked like a Christmas tree. He was loving it. Tony liked nothing more than being the centre of attention.

Then I had my second brilliant idea of day. I took out my lighter and set fire to the paper streamers. Whoosh! Tony went up like a roman candle, prancing around shrieking, 'I'm on fire! I'm on fire!' Disco Inferno. Especially when I tried to douse the flames with a brandy! Tony wasn't hurt, thanks goodness. His pride may have been a little singed, but nothing else.

It wasn't all fun and games and raucous live performances with the Faces. We did make some records, of variable quality. 'Stay With Me' and 'Cindy Incidentally' were single successes, but even if they hadn't been, it wouldn't have mattered. We weren't after hits, we only cared about playing together.

We made albums that were alright, with some great tracks on them. Rod, Woody and Ronnie brought ideas and riffs to the studio and then we all contributed to making them work.

The albums could have been a lot better though if Rod hadn't pocketed a lot of good songs that we could have had. When I heard his solo material I often thought, hang on Rod, that should have been ours.

A similar situation occurred when I joined The Who, at a time when Pete Townshend was recording his *Empty Glass* album, which I played on. I heard the track 'Rough Boys' and immediately thought that it should have been a Who song. I said that to Pete and, although I am sure he knew I was right, he refused to acknowledge the fact. It wasn't the only time it happened and I think it damaged The Who, as unlike with the Faces, their recordings held a greater importance to their fans. Rod squirreling away his best material for personal use didn't really matter; Pete doing the same was more detrimental.

Two of the Faces albums, *A Nod Is As Good As a Wink … To a Blind Horse* and *Ooh La La*, which charted at number two and number one respectively in the UK, and were successful in the US as well, were recorded back at Olympic Studios in Barnes. One of those sessions, for *Ooh La La* I think, cost me a small fortune.

We were on good money by then and had all bought ourselves flash cars, which we parked outside the studio. Well, me, Rod, Mac and Woody had smart motors: mine was a brand-new Dino Ferrari Spyder, Rod's a Lamborghini, Mac and Woody something like a Triumph sports and a Jag. The gypsy that was Ronnie Lane, however, had settled on a scruffy Land Rover.

We were in the upstairs studio at around six or seven o'clock in the evening, and had just finished a track when Glyn Johns said, 'I think we need an acoustic on this. Ronnie, have you got your J-200?' He didn't, but as he lived in nearby Richmond he was happy to nip back and get it. While he was away the rest of us shot over to the Red Lion pub for a few jars. We used to do that quite often when Glyn and Ronnie were overdubbing tracks or splicing in additional sections.

We returned before Ronnie and were sitting listening to the song when he walked in with his guitar and a huge smile on his face. Laughing, he said 'Kenney, I've just smashed into your car'. No one believed him, but he kept on laughing and insisting it was true. Eventually I went down to have a look, and sure enough, there was my gorgeous Spyder with its bonnet crumpled. His Land Rover had this great big tow-bar sticking out of it, and as he'd reversed into his spot, from where he was sitting, up high, he hadn't noticed my brand new low-slung coupé.

Ronnie offered to pay for it but I told him not to worry. I was just pissed off that I had to get it fixed and couldn't play with it. I'd only had it a few days.

My poor Spyder. That wasn't the only time it was in the wars. I used to love rehearsing at Shepperton Studios. There was a great little pub down the road where we would go for beers, and in the massive complex itself there was a full stage, which meant that after we'd finished rehearsals, we could have a complete run-through of a concert with lights and the whole set-up. Fantastic.

During one rehearsal, Rod and I started bragging about whose car was the fastest, his Lamborghini or my Spyder. Very mature. We put it to the test inside the studio grounds. All the road crew were there to watch as we lined up against each other, revving our engines to the max ... and beyond. I won the race, but burned out my clutch. Expensive. Again.

Rehearsals at Shepperton signalled an up-coming tour, which usually delivered a lot of fun and games. Not always, though. There were poignant moments as well.

The first time I came across American GIs was in Sydney with the Small Faces, when we met a group of them in their hotel bar.

They were a similar age to us, in their early twenties, some even still teenagers, like me, and over drinks they described the horrific events of the Vietnam War. I couldn't understand why they were in Australia until they explained it was a weekend furlough. After a few days leave to touch life again, before returning to the jungles and swamps and the same battles they had just left. That really affected me.

Then, touring the States with the Faces, travelling on internal flights to and from small domestic airports, we met a lot of GIs, and later veterans, some with missing limbs. Had it not been for the war, these boys would have been the same as us, trying to make their way in the world and having a good old time doing it. But they weren't the same. They couldn't be, not after what they had been through. There I was, famous, fooling around, earning money, girls everywhere, drinking – and they'd fought for their country, killed people, lost friends. It's an obvious thing to say, but it struck me hard just how lucky I was. On the spectrum of life experiences, for no reason other than good fortune, I was at the extreme end from them, doing something that I loved, incredibly privileged. To many people we were heroes, living the rock-star dream. True heroes were those young men.

Through chatting with those guys, we learned that there were lots of Faces fans who listened to us on their radios in Vietnam. When they attended gigs, whenever possible we let it be known they were welcome back at our hotel for a few drinks after the concert. A small gesture, but it was something we could do. These soldiers, no older than us, were desperate to break away from what was happening in their lives, or their nightmare memories, and music could play a part in that. We opened our doors to them in the hope we might help or offer some relief, however fleeting and inconsequential.

Touring brought many surprises.

On our first US visit we were staying at Loews Regency Hotel, Midtown Manhattan, where we bumped into Led Zeppelin at the end of their North American tour. As drummers do, John Bonham and I hooked up, heading around the corner to a 'proper' English pub to talk fills and drink gallons of Watney's Red Barrel. John did, anyway, I couldn't keep up. I sat there watching him down pint after pint. I have no idea where he put it all, but I know where it went. To his head. We were smashed at the end of the evening, struggling to find our way back to the hotel, no more than two minutes away. What a fantastic night though. Bonham was loud, brash and always interesting. And a brilliant drummer.

Next day, the who's who of the lobby became even more starry.

Muhammad Ali. 'Hey boys, where you going? Where you touring?' He knew who we were! We were so excited as we craned our necks to look up at him. Huge bloke.

In traditional rock 'n' roll fashion, Faces' tours could also involve an element of destruction, although not in the classic smashing up hotel rooms vein. We were more original than that, or so we liked to think. On our third major trip to the US, we had played a gig at the Sam Houston Coliseum, in Houston, and were scheduled to appear the following night in Fort Worth, around 300 miles away. One of the record execs who was accompanying us kindly offered to give the band a lift, in his brand-new Chevy Camero. Big mistake.

We all piled in, four squeezed tight in the back and one up front, and immediately started fucking about. 'Oh I don't like the back of your seat.' 'That headrest looks funny.' 'This carpet is a weird colour.' 'My ashtray lid squeaks.' One by one, we decided to chuck the things we didn't like out of the window. By the time we reached Fort Worth, we were sitting on sheet metal, tears running down our cheeks from laughing so much. Well, not the driver.

That same tour also brought me marriage, in spring 1971. I had been dating Jan Osborne since we met at The Upper Cut Club in December 1966, and she, along with the other girlfriends and wives, flew out to Los Angeles to meet up with us during the band's mid-tour break at the beginning of March. That often happened when we were settled in one location for a few days – but it was only ever meant to be for a few days. Jan, however, had other ideas and refused to leave for home unless we got married. So that's what we did, on 9 March at the Little Brown Church, Coldwater Canyon. That night, Mo Ostin threw us a party on the set of the film *Grand Hotel* at MGM Studios. There was a cake, speeches and no one talked me out of it. (Nine years later, Jan and I divorced in unhappy circumstances, but had we not married that day we wouldn't have our two wonderful sons, Dylan and Jesse. That's too dreadful to contemplate.)

Wives and girlfriends insisting on joining the band on tour was understandable, of course, but not always welcome. For one thing, their presence cramped our style; we couldn't get up to mischief. Not something to be proud of, but a reality of life on the road. Secondly, they packed tension in their holiday luggage. While the boys were mates, getting along great, looking out for each other; the girls created all sorts of jealousy, constantly attempting to outdo each other. 'I know something you don't know' – that sort of thing. At times, it felt as though they were trying to force us to take sides, to drive wedges between us. Yes, we should have been more understanding, more supportive, faithful, but in truth, having them around for too long wore us down.

We did have some laughs, mind you. At the Finsbury Park Astoria, someone backstage upset Woody's wife Krissy. We knew nothing about this, until just as Woody was in the middle of an electrifying solo, Krissy walked across the stage and tapped him on the shoulder. Woody jumped a mile. She was fuming, totally lost it, and shouted at him, 'If you do to me what she has done to me, I'm leaving you'. Then she spun round and walked off. The rest of us were in hysterics, and next day got T-shirts made up with that phrase. Woody wore his proudly. Out of sight of Krissy.

In fact, Krissy was a lovely person. I liked her and never thought she and Woody would split. They seemed good together. I was so sad when she died in 2005. I also got on well with Rod's girlfriend, Britt Ekland. She was fun, and we're still friends. Of all the girls, she was the one who seamlessly slipped into the piss-talking spirit of the band.

Despite what some of the wives and girlfriends might have hoped, the five of us were always happy to mess around together like naughty boys whenever we had the chance. In July 1973, after a Faces gig in Rome, we went out to a posh restaurant up in the hills with the promoter. Naturally, we started throwing bread rolls at each other. Then my steak arrived. Rare? It was practically raw. No way was I eating that. Fuck it. I skewered it on the end of my fork and catapulted it across the restaurant. We watched it fly towards the next table, smack on to the plate of guy also having a steak. With his head turned at the time, talking to the person next to him, he didn't notice it land. Then he turned back to his meal and carried on eating, my steak. We pissed ourselves.

One of the things you learned from the very early days of touring with the Faces was never to fall asleep on a plane. Ronnie made that mistake. Once. When we were coming back from Scotland on a private jet. He received the butter treatment – knobs of it delicately placed in his hair while he snoozed, oblivious. As the butter slowly melted, dripping down his face and inside his collar, we were rolling around, hugely impressed with ourselves. Ronnie did not see the funny side. When he woke, he went berserk, he was really narked. I'd never seen him like that before. I think he was angry because he felt that you should never pick on your own. Don't fall asleep then, Ron. You know the rules.

He was so pissed off that he stood up and threatened to open the rear exit door. At that point, although each of us denied responsibility, we all started to apologise. 'Eh, okay Ronnie, you've got our attention now. We're really, really sorry. Now please, sit down. Please!'

Did we learn a lesson? Did we hell. It's too good a game. Jimmy Horowitz, a mate of Billy Gaff's and the strings arranger on our last tour, was subjected to something similar when he dozed off. Fatal. He had a sort of wild, afro-style hairdo, which stuck out a mile, giving us plenty of places to insert things – ash, cigarette butts and, naturally, butter. He also went ape-shit, although like Tony Toon before him he loved being the centre of attention.

For the record, I never, ever fell asleep on a plane with the Faces.

CHAPTER 9

MEN OF THE WORLD

'Party back at our hotel!'

Rod's announcement at the end of gigs wasn't the least bit subtle. It was an invitation to girls looking for some fun. To begin with the parties would take place in one of our rooms, and on one memorable occasion, in Billy Gaff's.

After the concert we'd gone ahead of Billy and decided to try an experiment. How many Faces, roadies and girls could we pack into one motel room? Answer, well over a hundred.

We were all there, squeezed very close together in the dark, and ready to leap out screaming and shouting the moment Billy entered. The poor man got such a fright. And very little sleep that night.

It was a huge pain if the party formed in your room, because it tended to remain there for the duration of that stay, however long. It wasn't uncommon for people you'd never seen before to be crashing on your floor, and bed, for three or four days on the trot. Privacy was impossible. That never bothered our roadies, mind you, they were far worse than us band members. At least when we'd hooked up with one of the girls we looked for an unoccupied bed to jump into, even if it wasn't our own. With most of the road crew, sex in the open didn't seem to worry them in the slightest.

Eventually, we organised ourselves better. We held a band meeting and agreed that we would pay for an extra suite, and designate it the 'Party Room'. That meant after each gig we could take our time, have a shower, get changed and one by one make our way to the Party Room. The fans would be there already, and it really was a case of walking in, having a few drinks, taking your pick of the girls and disappearing to your own room. An hour later, the others were most likely back at party HQ for a second sitting, but not me. Once I was out of there, I was out of there.

Looking back through today's eyes, our antics might appear debauched, but for everyone – us, the girls, anyone else present – it was regarded purely as a bit of fun. Wild fun, perhaps. But fun, without question. There was no pretence. Coming back to a Faces party, you knew the score: sex, spliffs, drinks. Any order would do. Everyone was there to enjoy themselves and enjoy themselves they did. Hedonistic days on the road. Living the rock 'n' roll dream. A separate person from the man you were at home – the land where the wives and children lived. Stepping off the plane at Heathrow, you reverted. No fooling around in your own backyard. Warped morals maybe, but that's how it was.

You can't create Party Rooms without gaining a reputation, and before long ours travelled ahead of us. Certainly to the southern US states. When playing gigs there, we'd be met at the airport by the County Sheriff, plus a police escort. Impressive welcome. Thank you. But stationing guards outside our hotel rooms, is that entirely necessary, officer? I don't think we're in any danger. Oh, I see. You're not looking after *us*, you are looking after your town and the welfare of your impressionable citizens. Quiet night for us, and you'll make sure we're on our way nice and sharp in the morning. Got it.

At least we were welcome to visit those states, provided we behaved. The same couldn't be said for the Holiday Inn chain of hotels, from which we were banned entirely. I can't imagine why.

The ban wasn't a big deal in the major cities, there were always other hotel options, but occasionally a Holiday would be the only inn in town. In those circumstances, we resorted to subtlety and subterfuge. We kept Rod to the back on those occasions.

The April 1972 'Mar Y Sol' Pop Festival in Puerto Rico was the first time we were forced into such tactics. The ban must have only recently come into effect, because we'd been able to book rooms in advance for our 3 April performance. We were left in no doubt about its existence, however, when Pete Buckland, our tour manager, tried to check in.

'They told me at reception that you are banned. We're all banned. They won't give us the rooms. They're adamant. We're screwed.'

There's got to be a way.

'Who else is staying here this evening?'

'Fleetwood Mac. They're due to arrive later.'

'That's it then. The hotel staff won't have a clue what we look like. Okay, Mick Fleetwood's six foot six, a slight problem, but they'll still never know. Let's check in as Fleetwood Mac.'

It worked. We were given the keys to 'our' rooms and up we went, even though we knew it wouldn't last. We'd be sussed the moment the real Fleetwood Mac turned up. Sure enough, that's what happened, by which time Pete had found accommodation in a golf course hotel not too far away. But if the ploy worked once, it was bound to again. We became Fleetwood Mac on numerous occasions over the coming years.

It was a strange event that one. Music-wise it was great. The *New York Times* described our set as the highlight of the evening.

'With Emerson, Lake & Palmer, [the Faces] were the only certifiable supergroup at the festival.'

Off stage, however, there were major problems. There had been considerable disquiet in advance, with the local populace unhappy that a bunch of rock bands and hippies were set to invade the island over the holy week of Easter. An injunction was issued to stop the event but it failed in court. At the festival itself, traffic congestion forced Black Sabbath to cancel their performance; Fleetwood Mac also never took to the stage. Blistering sun resulted in several cases of severe sunstroke that stretched the limited medical support to breaking point and the promoter had to escape the island in fear of arrest by the tax authorities. Add to that extremely basic toilet and washing facilities, hard-to-come-by water and provisions, and promised transport home that never materialised, leaving thousands of stranded, unhappy, unwashed and underfed music fans at San Juan airport. Worst of all, knife-wielding gangs apparently roamed the campsite, two people drowned, and a teenager from the Virgin Islands was murdered.

Although nowhere near of the same magnitude, we also faced a disquieting experience. While out for a walk we came across a guy schooling a beautiful black stallion to trot between massive, hard-edged railway sleepers, using a steel noseband with jagged edges and a very severe bit. There was blood dripping down the horse's head and flies buzzing around him. A horrible sight that affected everyone, Ronnie Lane's wife Sue most of all. She was extremely distressed. We had a go at the bloke, but he told us to fuck off and mind our own business, then ignored us. We complained at the hotel, but that didn't achieve anything either. We were told it had nothing to do with us and not to get involved.

On a lighter note, Puerto Rico was beautiful, and we were fortunate with the accommodation we ended up with, a lovely hotel, with gorgeous views and excellent facilities. I decided on a facial. Well, I wanted to look my best for the gig. I was lying on the table, cucumber slices covering my eyes as the masseuse worked her relaxing magic. Wonderful. I began to drift away as she moved on to my scalp ... harder than before, and less effective. Less relaxing. Much less relaxing. Hang on. I whipped off the cucumber to find myself staring into Rod's beaming face.

'Hi Kenney. Thought I'd take over for a bit. Enjoying yourself?'

* * *

Around the time of the Puerto Rico festival, I began to sense that Ronnie Lane wasn't happy. He'd become withdrawn. He'd been agitating for a more prominent role in the band, singing and songwriting, but it wasn't happening. Not in the way he hoped. In vocal terms, his gentle voice was great for a handful of our songs, with Rod supporting, but for the vast majority of Faces' tracks, Rod was always going to be number one. Realistically, Ronnie had no chance in a competition for frontman.

In writing terms, we recorded a number of Ronnie's songs, they offered an ideal counterbalance to the heavier material, and some of them were excellent. 'Debris' was always a favourite of mine. It fitted nicely with the Faces. Others, although they sounded great, were not really representative of where the rest of us saw the band. 'Stone' is a good example. It's a gentle, quirky, almost mystical song, perhaps a touch self-indulgent, about being a stone thrown into a pool, then a sword, a daisy, and God knows what else. It's on our first album, with Ronnie singing, and its lovely, but perhaps better for a Lane solo recording. Even right at the beginning, he was kind of going in a different direction from the rest of us. And as his other songs began to get knocked back, he began to realise that himself.

In May 1973, Ronnie quit the Faces. His departure left a big hole, so large, in fact, that it ended up swallowing the band, although I didn't fully realise the implications at the time.

I think he felt he'd taken his involvement as far as he could. Deep down he wanted to be a solo artist and he reasoned the time had come to flex his muscles. Even though I knew the writing had been on the wall, I was upset. Not at Ronnie, I wished him well. It was the brotherhood breaking up that got to me and I found Ronnie's absence difficult to deal with.

We brought in the Japanese bass player Tetsu Yamauchi to replace Ronnie. He was talented and in one major aspect fitted perfectly with the Faces' ethos. Perhaps, too well. In those days, Tetsu was basically a bottle of Teacher's whisky on the stage. You just lifted his head and filled him with scotch.

Even with Ronnie gone, we remained a close-knit band personally and, for three of us, geographically.

The first house I bought was a little cottage in Temple Fortune, north of Golders Green, for £9,400. It was lovely, like something out of a cartoon, a tiny little place surrounded by huge houses looking down on it. Prior to that I'd been living with Mum and Dad in Havering Street, or crashing at Jan's family home. I stayed in the cottage for about a year, but because I was now earning decent money from Faces tours I had my eye out for the next step. I saw it advertised in *Country Life*, a house called Kingsmeadows on Coombe Wood Road. Love at first sight. That was the place in Kingston Hill, near to which I tried to buy Mum and Dad a house. Kingsmeadows meant a big jump in price, £48,000, but I sold Temple Fortune for £16,800 which helped, although I wish I'd realised at the time the real value of that plot, nestling there between those big houses. I could have made a fortune if I'd held on to it for a while.

I liked Kingsmeadows, it was a lovely looking property in an ideal location, with the added bonus of comedians Jimmy Tarbuck and Bernie Winters living nearby.

Jimmy and I became good friends. We complemented each other. We've enjoyed a great deal of fun over the years; lots of house parties and pranks, such as turning on garden sprinklers to soak one another when we came visiting. We both drove white Rolls-Royce Corniche convertibles at the time, his with a personalised number plate, COMIC, and I was forever getting pulled over by the police because they confused me for him. For some reason, they seemed to be out to get Tarby for drink driving, although as far as I'm aware that's not something he ever did. Jimmy used to love it when I would report that once again I'd been mistaken for him. He's eight-and-a-half years older, with a Scouse accent. Give me a break, guvnor.

When I first moved into Kingsmeadows, Ronnie Lane was living in Richmond in a flat next door to the singer Billy Nicholls, who recorded an album on Immediate called *Would You Believe* that was never properly released at the time thanks to the label's financial meltdown, while Woody was near me in Ravenswood Court. Then in 1971, Woody learned that the actor Sir John Mills was placing his wonderful eighteenth-century Richmond Hill house, The Wick, on the market. Woody was smitten, but at an asking price of £100,000, plus 40 grand for the cottage at the foot of the garden belonging to Sir John's wife Mary Hayley Bell, it was beyond him. Until he asked Ronnie Lane to come in on the deal. Somehow Woody pulled together enough cash to buy The Wick, with Ronnie purchasing Wick Cottage at the same time. For Ronnie, this at least was a step up from the flat above the garage that he'd bought with Steve, and he lived there happily until he left the Faces, selling the cottage to Woody.

Meanwhile, Mac lived on Fife Road, near Richmond Park's Sheen Gate, close enough for me to jog over for a visit, so for a while we had three of the park's gates covered. I enjoyed the fact we lived so close to each other, it strengthened the bonds. Although, at times, it could be a pain.

Almost the first thing Woody did on moving into The Wick was to install a recording studio, after which I could never be guaranteed a good night's sleep. He always seemed to call around midnight, as I had one foot in my bed.

'Kenney, we haven't got a drummer. We need you. Please!'

I always said yes and would drive over, not knowing who else would be there. One night it might be Bob Dylan, the next Eric Clapton, or Townshend or Bowie. We all used to mingle. On one particularly memorable occasion in late 1973, it was Mick Jagger.

Woody had recently fitted all sorts of gizmos in the control room and was like a pig in shit, playing with his new knobs and buttons. Mick had a riff he was working on, and I started to play along, doing my own thing, enjoying the sound we were making. Mick then got it into his head that he wanted something different. He started insisting, but I told him to let it go. 'Don't worry Mick. It's only rock and roll.'

'But I like it,' he fired straight back.

Ding! We started to work around Mick's original riff, getting to know it better, and the track began to take shape. Woody noticed and hit the record button before joining us.

Mick had been developing lyrics, with help from Woody, which were not yet complete, but good enough for us to pull together a song, with Woody and Jagger on guitar. We had a laugh, it sounded okay at the time, for a demo, and then I went off home, thinking no more about it.

Next thing I knew it was a Rolling Stones single. With me drumming. That's nuts. I couldn't understand why it was my drums on the track, but apparently they'd tried it in the studio with Charlie Watts, and they couldn't replicate the same sound and feel. I felt bad. Charlie was a friend, still is, and I never intended stepping on his toes. I gave him a ring.

'Charlie mate. I'm really sorry. I didn't meant for that to happen.'

'Oh, don't worry Kenney. It sounds like me anyway.' Typical Charlie. Lovely man.

'It's Only Rock and Roll (But I Like It)' wasn't my only non-Faces release in 1974. In the spring of that year I'd heard about Keith Moon's version of the Beach Boys' 'Don't Worry Baby', and that he was also working on a solo album.

If Moonie can do it ...

I recorded Jackson Browne's 'Ready or Not' at drummer Barry Morgan's studio in Willesden, with my brother-in-law Gary Osborne. I didn't realistically set out to be a solo singer. Recording that track was more an exercise in challenging myself, trying to find out if I could do something other than drumming. Turns out I could, up to a point. The single was released. Not many people noticed and I confirmed what I already knew. I was never going to be a great singer, decent maybe, but that route offered nothing in comparison to what I could achieve on the drums. Stick to the night job, Kenney. I chalked it off my To Do list as an interesting experiment and moved on.

Only I didn't. Not quite.

The following year, Billy Gaff launched his own label, Riva Records. He was looking for product, and as he was one of the very few people who registered that I'd released 'Ready or Not', he suggested I try recording some more tracks, possibly for an album.

Maybe. I'll think about it.

Word somehow got out. Thanks Billy. In LA, after a Faces gig, Mentor Williams approached me with a couple of new songs he'd written, 'So High' and 'Baby Blue Eyes'. Interesting. This was the man behind Dobie Gray's smash 'Drift Away'.

I'd met Mentor previously in London through friends and found him to be a great guy, a wonderfully, typically 1970s California Man – laid-back, big moustache, at home on Sunset Strip. Lovely.

I also knew, and liked, his actor and songwriter brother Paul, who was responsible for such classics as 'Evergreen' and 'We've Only Just Begun'. This was a talented family. Mentor's offer wasn't something to be idly dismissed.

But had he heard 'Ready or Not'?

Apparently yes. He knew the level of my talent and offered to help. 'Everyone can sing Kenney.'

'Yes, but not necessarily very well, Mentor.'

He persuaded me to give it another go. What the hell. He booked a studio in LA. Now all we needed was a band.

Mentor enlisted the wonderful guitarist Danny 'Kootch' Kortchmar, and brilliant all-rounder Al Kooper. This was becoming serious. I thought I'd better contribute something, other than my voice. Paul and Linda McCartney, plus Denny Laine, were staying in my hotel, having a break after recording the Wings album *Venus and Mars*, and, as I knew them all well, I asked if they fancied playing on the record.

'Love to.'

In the studio, Paul enquired, while pointedly sitting at the piano, 'Kenney, what do you want me to play?'

'Bass.' His faced dropped.

We recorded 'So High' first. It's a slow song with a good, but strange, feel. Mentor talked us through it and off we went, Paul on bass, Linda on keyboards, Denny and Kootch on guitar, and Al on everything else. I then added the words, with Mentor assisting with the phrasing, while the others enthusiastically got stuck into the two-word backing vocals. 'So high!!!'

In no time, we had the track nailed, quickly followed by Mentor's 'Baby Blue Eyes', featuring a line that no East End Herbert should never be caught singing. 'In the canyons of my mind ... ' Yuck.

Fortunately, I never was caught. Paul still asks to this day when those songs are going to be released.

Never.

And that, ladies and gentlemen, was the end of my solo career. Thank you very much.

* * *

The Faces were seriously cracking by the spring of 1975. We were drifting apart, Rod was spending more time on his solo career, and when we did get together, drink and drugs were adversely impacting our performances more than ever before. Where previously we'd all been half-cut on stage, but at a 'we're having a right laugh, but we can still produce the goods' level, now we were screwing up. Woody and Mac were the worst culprits.

Booze played its part, although it wasn't the primary problem. When we were together, the alcohol intake was pretty much even across the band – bucket loads. The difference was in the down-time moments. Neither Rod nor I would drink on our days off, and we didn't miss it. We enjoyed getting up early, being out and about, enjoying a relatively normal life. Mac and

Woody, on the other hand, they were still hitting it hard away from the studio, rehearsals and gigs. That was up to them, of course, but it did begin to show. They became more sluggish, even less on top of things.

. Drugs, coke specifically, was the real issue. Rod wasn't interested, and neither was I. But Mac and Woody, they were all over the white powder, which would keep them up for days, with barely any sleep at all. Fine, again totally up to them, until it messed with the music. We'd be on stage and Woody would count in a song, or be playing the intro, and the tempo would be all over the shop, way too slow, because he was knackered, although he thought it was bang on. Rod would be standing with his back to the audience, looking at me, his hand hidden from view, giving it a rolling gesture, and mouthing, 'Speed it up, speed it up'. But I couldn't just leap into it, I had to do it slowly so it wasn't obvious, but even then Woody would shout across at me, 'It's too fast. Too fast!' That's what drugs do for you. Frustration was building.

The first signs are there in this quote Rod gave to *New Musical Express* the previous August: 'We've tried in the studio four times, and it's never really worked the way it should. My albums have always been better than Faces albums, always. We won't make another Faces album; I think we'll just put out singles from now on. But maybe I shouldn't be saying this ... maybe the lads want to make another album ...'

Then in April 1975, Rod moved to LA, with Britt Ekland joining him four months later. We now had a transatlantic gap adding to our problems. Telephone calls took an hour to set up. Our drifting had become continental. Communications were breaking down, tension growing.

At the same time as Rod's move, Woody announced that the Stones had asked him to fill in for Mick Taylor, who'd quit. They were embarking on a major North American tour at the beginning of June and needed a guitarist. Woody asked if that was okay. We said fine, but when you get back our tour starts immediately. Keep yourself together.

The timings worked out, just about. With the Stones tour ending on 8 August and ours beginning on 19 August in North Carolina, there was a sufficient window of opportunity for Woody to join us in Miami where we were rehearsing.

For those couple of weeks, we rented the house at 461 Ocean Boulevard, made famous by Eric Clapton's album. What a place, right on the beach, with a view from your bedroom of the vast Atlantic ocean dipping out of sight over the horizon. Stunning. Although if I went back tomorrow, you wouldn't catch me with even my little toe in that water.

On one of our days free from rehearsing, I got up early while everyone else was still in bed. Although I could barely swim I wanted to experience the ocean. I found a blow-up dingy and spent two idyllic hours stretched out on it, feet dangling over the side. Lovely. Apart from being burnt to a crisp, of course. Later in the evening I came down for dinner and watched the news, which was reporting on a shark attack earlier in the day, about a mile up the coast. The guy had been bitten while lying on an inflatable. Fucking hell.

Just then our new rhythm guitarist, Jesse Ed Davis wandered into the room, and I over-excitedly told him all about the report. 'It could have been me!'

'Man, that's tough,' he agreed, sighing and slowly shaking his head. Then he promptly suggested we all go and see the new film at the local cinema, *Jaws*. Thanks Jesse, that's bound to make me feel better. I went along and, like everyone else, was scared shitless. On the way home, Jesse admitted he'd seen the film three times already and only wanted to go again so he could watch us jumping out of our seats.

On arriving back at the house, I immediately called Jan, who was back in the UK with our three-year-old son Dylan. 'Whatever you do,' I told her, 'don't put him anywhere near water. Not even the sink!'

Rod had wanted to introduce changes for our up-coming tour, changes that resulted in ratcheting up the existing tension. The first was the addition of a 12-piece string section conducted by Jimmy Horowitz, to accompany the songs from Rod's very recent *Atlantic Crossing* album that would feature in our set list. Mac, and to an extent Woody, hated the idea. This was us taking the first step on the path to becoming Vegas Faces according to Mac, but Rod had his way.

The second issue was the addition of Jesse to the tour line-up. He was an excellent guitarist and Rod felt his presence would support Woody. The thing is, the way Woody played then, picking his strings, meant that when he was on rhythm, he was brilliant, but when he had to switch to lead, there could be some empty air. It wasn't a big problem, but that's why Rod wanted Jesse, to fill that hole. It was certainly an observation that could accurately have been made of the Small Faces pre-Mac, when Steve was struggling to keep both lead and rhythm alive. Mac's arrival had been necessary to plug that gap, but Marriott was not in Woody's league, certainly not back in 1965. Perhaps that's why Mac took such exception to Rod's suggestion. Was Rod having a dig at him? Was he suggesting that even with the brilliance of Woody, there remained a space in our performances that Mac should have been occupying?

I don't believe it was that at all, but it doesn't really matter. Justified or not, Mac was pissed off, big time. It wasn't anything against Jesse, we all liked him, Mac included – he was charming and funny and gentle, with great talent. Mac articulated his anger by claiming that Rod bringing in Jesse amounted to an unwarranted slap in the face for Woody. Mac couldn't keep his mouth shut on the subject and it caused problems. He'd been like that from the start of the Faces, as if he carried around a great big chip permanently balanced on his shoulder, which he would grab from time to time and hurl at Rod. In that respect, he was a different Mac to the one in the Small Faces. I think perhaps he never fully recovered from Steve walking out. Lead singers. Don't trust them.

As for Woody, I suspect he didn't really give a toss about Jesse, or the strings, not after he returned from being Stoned. When Woody strolled into 461 Ocean Boulevard, he wasn't the same person. Rod and I both saw it and looked at each other as if to say, 'This is the last tour, isn't it?' Woody had left a Face and come back a Rolling Stone. The writing was on the wall. The show must go on, though. And go on it did.

Early September found the Faces, their wives, families and girlfriends on the Hawaiian island of Oahu, after two performances at the Honolulu International Center. Hawaii is truly beautiful. I've made a few mistakes in life and one of them is not moving there to live. One afternoon we took a trip up the hills and as we looked out over Honolulu harbour a magical, warm, tranquil wind gently stirred, blowing across my face. I was mesmerised, completely at peace with everything. It is perhaps the most amazing place I've ever visited.

We were all captivated by Hawaii, so much so that at the end of our short break Rod, Britt, Jan and I didn't want to leave. So what did we do? On check-out day we ran away of course, hiding further down the beach. Brilliant. No one could find us. Until we had to come back. Not so brilliant, especially when we walked into the middle of a scene in the lobby.

Australian singer Helen Reddy and her husband and manager Jeff Wald were booked into Rod and Britt's suite, which of course was not ready. Jeff, who frankly came across as a right prick, was throwing a wobbly at the concierge. Best we make ourselves scarce.

We weren't quick enough. Wald noticed us and began yelling abuse, rather nasty abuse. The girls were both quite shaken. Rod and I were livid.

Fuck it.

Having been hassled by the hotel manager to pack our gear, we quickly sent word out to rally the troops. Messing with hotel rooms was a Faces speciality.

Rod and Britt's suite was the target. The telephone was dismantled, dimes put in the lamp socket, so they would blow the moment they were turned on, towels down the loo, the bed rigged to collapse as soon as someone sat on it. Whatever we could think of, we did, leaving the room, on the surface, immaculate. Then good as gold, and as fast as possible, we checked out.

We were still down in the lobby waiting for our cars when Wald came flying down from the room, which he'd obviously gone to look over. Cue more swearing and shouting. Lots more. Mac was there, to wave us off as he was staying on for an extra day, and foolishly Wald picked him as his target, snarling in his face, pointing his finger, calling him a 'punk'. Mac hated that.

Oh dear. What's going to happen now.

Sure enough, Wald lunged and Mac threw a punch, knocking Wald backwards against the wall, dislodging a big painting, which fell on top of him, leaving his head poking through the canvas. You had to laugh. And we did. Then we pulled Mac away.

Inevitably the police were called, and as entirely reliable witnesses Rod and I blamed it all on Jeff. Then we legged it. Our taxis had arrived.

Mac later told us that the police knew Wald as a hothead who'd been involved in similar trouble on the island previously. The incident was quietly forgotten. A fair outcome. While Wald had been the aggressor, we'd not exactly been innocent little angels.

On that occasion, Mac had certainly been provoked into throwing the punch, but the fact that he'd lost it was not a surprise. Mac could have a dreadful temper. Great fun most of the time, but when he lost his rag – never with us – he could be awful. Billy Gaff was afraid of him. If Mac wasn't happy about something, he wouldn't hold back, often chasing after a fast retreating Billy to make his point.

Promoters were also shit scared of Mac. Ahead of Faces gigs he would demand a certain make and size of piano be made available at the venue, say a nine-foot Steinway. If, on arrival, it did not match Mac's specifications precisely, the promoter was potentially facing the cost of a replacement. More than once, on stage at the end of a gig, offended by what he saw as an inadequate instrument, Mac turned it into firewood. With an axe.

* * *

On 18 December 1975, Rod announced to the press that he was leaving the Faces. I was show jumping in a Christmas do at Olympia. Jan showed me the headline a day later. She'd kept it from me so as not to ruin my enjoyment of the show.

I was annoyed. Not because he was leaving, I knew that was coming, but because he hadn't given me the courtesy of a call to explain that he was about to make a statement concerning the band. Rod has admitted that the situation wasn't very well handled, and that's true. Mac in particular was very angry about the circumstances, complaining that it showed a lack of respect on Rod's part, although that may have had a lot to do with their testy relationship. In all honestly, how it unfolded didn't really matter, not then and it certainly doesn't matter now. The end was inevitable; how it was made public is largely irrelevant.

I never felt jealous of Rod going off on his solo career, my emotion at the time was more one of disappointment. I felt he could have made his solo albums and still allocated proper time to the Faces. Perhaps he would have, had Ronnie Lane still been with the band. Rod said at the time of Ronnie's leaving that the spirit of the Faces went with him. Rod was absolutely correct. Ronnie was unmistakably at the heart of the group. We were never quite the same without him, and that eventually took its toll.

When it finally came, the split was unavoidable. Rod was getting fed the 'Rod Stewart, Rod Stewart, Rod Stewart' line the whole time by Billy Gaff, and it wore him down. I think Rod genuinely cared about the Faces, but by the end it had grown into an irritant, something with its teeth clamped firmly around his ankle. His life as a solo artist would only grow more and more complicated unless he succeeded in shaking the band free. Rod loved being a Face, but having to deal with Mac and Woody being out of their trees the whole time eventually became too much.

For a short period we contemplated carrying on without Rod, but it was never a realistic possibility. We might have managed it if at the time of Rod's move to the US I'd been able to persuade the others, and I did try, to play as a band without Rod when he was off doing his solo thing. His departure to LA precipitated the band's disintegration. The separation was always going to be a huge strain, we all recognised that, but if we could have begun to build a name for us as the Faces without Rod, we would have been more independent. The distances wouldn't have mattered as much. We could have played with Rod when he was available, and perhaps brought in other singers when he wasn't. But it never happened.

* * *

With the Faces no more, Rod and I began talking about forming something new. We knew we worked well together, with a lot in common in terms of our professional attitude. Simple things like turning up on time ready to play, and capable of doing so.

Rod mentioned this in an interview he gave to *NME* in September 1974.

'What's wrong is the Faces recording schedule is completely alien to what I'm used to. I go in the studio at twelve and finish at seven no matter what happens. On a Faces session everybody falls into the public house. I can't cope with that, and Kenney can't either.'

Our new band began to take shape, with guitarists Billy Peek and a guy called Gary Grainger, who we'd noticed playing in one of our support groups, plus Phil Chen on bass. Our early rehearsals were in London, in a studio behind King's Cross, where on our first day together Rod turned to me with a genuine look of surprise on his face.

'Kenney, I've never heard you play like that.'

'Well, there are a hell of a lot of ways I play that you haven't heard. I do loads of sessions and can adapt my drumming to as many styles as you can think of. All you've ever known is me with the Faces, where I was compelled to play one way only, to fit the feel of the band. That was fine, but with other musicians on stage, who are not stumbling around drunk, I play differently.'

Billy Gaff was going to manage us and the plan was for Rod and me to split everything 50:50. That was critical. I refused to be part of Rod's backing band. Rod was happy with that, and it was all systems go for three months of rehearsal and writing in Los Angeles.

Another beginning. *Okay, this is good. Isn't it?*

The vans arrived to transport my drums to Heathrow, where they were booked on a flight to LA. That's when I began to think about what this actually meant. It was a great deal for me financially. No question about that. But standing there, watching my new career making its way to the airport, my feet turned cold. Was I trying to hold on to a part of the Faces that no longer existed? Had I agreed to this only out of fear that I would have nothing else to do? If so, I realised I had to stop thinking like that. I had to listen to my heart, not my head. The band was wonderful, all exciting musicians to play with. That registered on the plus side. But deep down, I knew if I went ahead I'd always be regarded as a traitor who had sold out, somehow poisoning the Faces from the inside to manufacture this opportunity. That did not sit well with me, at all. A major negative. In the end it was simple really. I couldn't live with myself if I let this continue.

I called Billy Gaff. I told him that I really didn't want to let anyone down, but it just didn't feel right and although I would probably regret the decision, I wasn't going to go. I said to him to ask Rod to give me a call so I could explain.

On putting down the phone to Billy, the relief was immediate. I knew I'd made the right decision. Now I had to retrieve my drums. The Corniche and Spyder were of no use, but fortunately I also had an ancient Volvo, fitted with a roof rack. Perfect. I drove as fast I could to the cargo handling area of Heathrow. I knew it well from all the years of touring. I had the paperwork they'd left with me, but I was told I'd arrived too late. The drums had been booked onto a flight. There was no way to recall them now.

Watch me. Those are my drums and they are coming home with me.

Three trips later and I was settled back in Kingston. With my drums. Unemployed.

Rod phoned to find out what the hell was going on. He was upset and disappointed, but cool about it. He understood. I felt guilty that I'd messed him around. I was relieved when in time it was announced they had enlisted Carmine Appice from Vanilla Fudge as my replacement. Good drummer.

Do I regret the decision? Well, I don't live in regret. It's pointless. You can't undo the past. Do I think I did the right thing for me? Yes. I liked being a Face, and I am glad I didn't tarnish that. It would have come across as though the Faces hadn't mattered to me. Instead, I kept my pride and didn't let down the fans. Also, I suspect the new band would have been a five-minute wonder. As Rod's popularity soared his individual fame would have sucked the life out of the rest of us. Not his fault, but a reality, as witnessed by the fact that it wasn't too long before it was all change with that band. Despite our friendship and respect for each other, I'd have ended up as a line in a sleeve note, an 'also featuring ... ' I doubt we'd still be such good mates today if that had happened.

* * *

On 5 July 1986, myself, Mac, Woody and a frail Ronnie Lane in a wheelchair – shrunk in stature but not spirit by the multiple sclerosis that would eventually kill him – joined Rod on stage for a surprise encore at his Wembley Stadium concert. Ronnie by then was unable to play his bass so Bill Wyman kindly stepped in, with Ronnie sticking to vocals. We hardly rehearsed, but it didn't matter. Bill winged it and the crowd love it. A hugely emotional night, with over 60,000 people singing, 'We love you Ronnie, we do ... ', then cheering and clapping as we pummelled our way through 'I'm Losing You', 'Twisting the Night Away' and 'Stay With Me'. Never mind the quality, feel the love.

It was another seven years before we played our second reunion gig. Ronnie was too ill to attend, and, adding to the poignancy, we played Alexandra Palace. It was a coming together, on the same stage where, 24 years earlier, Mac and I experienced a ripping apart. The occasion was the Brit Awards, with Rod set to receive an Outstanding Contribution gong. We were there to make him sound good. I hoped.

We rehearsed at John Henry's studio, off the Caledonian Road, Holloway, and Bill Wyman's joined us again.

I'd been so looking forward to this moment. We were back as a band, but at a different level from the past. Rod's solo career had gone from strength to strength, seeing him play countless arena concerts to vast audiences; when once he commanded a stage he now owned it outright. Woody had spent years with the Stones, playing at an incredible level. Since we were last together, Mac had played with Bob Dylan, the Everly Brothers and many other musical geniuses. I'd toured the world with The Who. And while Bill could never be Ronnie, and wouldn't try, he's no slouch on bass. We were older and calmer and booze was no longer a dominant force in our lives. We were going to rock.

'Here we go. One, two, one, two, three, four ... '

Oh shit. Just as dishevelled as ever.

'Pub?'

'Let's go.'

Nothing changes.

Reunion number three should have happened at the 2009 PRS For Music Members Benevolent Fund Concert, taking place at the Royal Albert Hall on 25 October. It was a big deal. We hadn't played together in more than 15 years and this would mark the first gig for the remaining Faces since Ronnie's death. We were also to receive an Icon Award, an honour which I believe had only been bestowed twice previously in the Fund's 75-year history – to Paul McCartney and Andrew Lloyd Webber. Great. Only problem was, Rod didn't show up, even though he said he would. His manager informed us only days before that Rod couldn't make it. Fuck.

I called the organisers to explain that we wouldn't be able to accept the award because the whole group couldn't be there. 'Not a problem,' they informed me. 'Icon awards are for individual contributions, not the band as a whole. Please come along. We'd love you to play, even without Rod.'

I was thinking fast now. 'Who else is on the bill?'

'Mel C, Paul Carrack, Kiki Dee, Georgie Fame, Andy Fairweather Low, Robin Gibb, Rick Wakeman, Bill Wyman's Rhythm Kings, Mick Hucknall ...' The list went on.

'Okay, here's an idea. How would it be if we contacted some of the acts and asked if they would agree to join us for a Faces song. Would that work?'

It worked.

Paul Carrrack sang 'Cindy Incidentally', Andy Fairweather Low plus star-studded backing singers performed 'Ooh La La', and finally Mick Hucknall belted out 'Stay With Me'. It turned out that Mick was a massive Faces fan with a great voice, ideal for the band. He said himself that when he got to play with us he truly felt like a kid in a candy store. Well, ours was a candy store more than happy to welcome him in, and over the next couple of years we had great fun, with Mick and Glen Matlock, first bass player with the Sex Pistols, playing a series of festival gigs as the Faces.

Mick stepped in to replace Rod again on 14 April 2012, when the Small Faces and Faces were inducted into the American Rock & Roll Hall of Fame. I was thrilled when I received the news. Honestly, I thought we'd been forgotten. It was a big deal for all of us, a great honour. As Mac said on the day, it's the music equivalent of a knighthood. Definitely the only one of those I'm going to receive.

Rod had intended to be there but two days before the event he was struck down with a nasty dose of strep throat. Jayne, my wife, received the email from Rod's management team informing her of Rod's illness as she stood at the tip of Manhattan, looking out at the Statue of Liberty.

We were in New York in advance of the induction in order for Woody and me to do a series of PR engagements, and also to enjoy a few days of sightseeing with two of our kids, Cody and Erin.

On receiving the news about Rod, Jayne rushed back to the hotel and together with Woody's manager, Sherry Daly, they stayed up all night trying to work out the logistics of flying Mick over to Cleveland, Ohio, where the Hall of Fame is located.

Mick was brilliant. When Jayne finally got hold of him, on the Friday morning in the UK, he didn't hesitate. With barely minutes to spare, he made it to Heathrow in time to catch his flight. Thanks Mick. I can't tell you how much we all appreciated your efforts.

While in New York, Woody was also attending an exhibition of his paintings, on the Thursday night, 12 April, which ended too late to catch a commercial flight to Cleveland. That wasn't a problem, fortunately, as a friend of Woody's had kindly offered to fly us there in his private plane. I think Erin was a little apprehensive about boarding such a small aircraft, but her worries were soon dispelled as we cranked up some classic albums over the PA system and all started to sing along. It was so much fun and just the thing to get us in the mood for the event ahead. It was only a short flight, but it was rocking the whole way.

We had such a laugh in Cleveland. Our hotel was like a who's who of rock music. The kids had a ball, from having breakfast with Guns N' Roses' bassist Duff, to getting in a lift with Alice Cooper. I don't think he was wearing his make-up or had a snake draped around his shoulders – I'm sure they would have mentioned that.

I also enjoyed a rare moment of being one up on my children during the trip. In the foyer of the hotel I bumped into Chad Smith, drummer with the Red Hot Chili Peppers. I've met Chad before and when I mentioned to Cody and Erin a little later that I'd been chatting to him, they burst out laughing. 'Dad, you're such a nutter! We saw you. That wasn't Chad Smith, it was Will Ferrell!' Eh, sorry kids. I know they look alike, but for once your dad is right. I hardly mentioned it again all trip. Well, maybe only a couple of hundred times ...

I found the ceremony itself very emotional. Standing in the wings, ready to walk out, I listened to Steve Van Zandt begin his introduction with the words, 'Not too many bands get a second life. In this case I'm sure it helped having not just one, but miraculously two of the greatest white soul singers in the history of rock 'n' roll, Steve Marriott and Rod Stewart.' I glanced to my right. Steve's daughter Mollie was right next to me, smiling as she gently squeezed my arm. A cherished moment, for both of us.

We walked on stage together, Woody, Mac, Mollie and me. I introduced Mollie and she received a huge round of applause. I could imagine Steve with his cheeky grin, looking down on us, knowing his other kids were in the audience, and loving every moment.

Then the music started to rock. Mick had made it over in time, and with Rod's bass player, Conrad Korsch, taking the place of Ronnie Lane, we blasted out 'All or Nothing' and 'Stay With Me'. What a thing. From the Ruskin Arms and a Bermondsey Street warehouse, to Cleveland, Ohio, and the Hall of Fame. It didn't seem possible. And yet, there I was.

My brief reverie did not last long. Following our two numbers, Woody and I joined Slash, George Clinton, Green Day's Billie Joe Armstrong and the Red Hot Chili Peppers (featuring Will Ferrell, apparently) on stage for a wild, jamming rendition of Stevie Wonder's 'Higher Ground'. A brilliant end to the show.

As exciting as the whole experience was, the most important part of that trip came at the end, when Jayne, Cody, Erin and myself drove the three hours from Cleveland to Windsor, Ontario, to see Jayne's dad, for what turned out to be our final visit. He hadn't been well recently, so we didn't stay long. But long enough. He knew we all loved him very much.

* * *

Mac died in Texas in 2014 and the original Faces were down to three. At Rod's seventieth birthday party in LA, I mentioned a concert I was organising for that summer in aid of prostate cancer research at my Hurtwood Park Polo Club. Would he be interested in joining me and Woody?

Yes he would.

I didn't hold my breath. Rod says yes to everything, then checks his diary. I knew he was sincere, however, and although it turned out there was a clash for the June date, he could be with us in September. Any good?

Great.

We've run various concerts at the club over the years and have gathered together a fantastic house band, members of which would readily stand in for Ronnie and Mac. They were brilliant and the concert was a huge success. For perhaps the first time in the history of the Faces, the band played sober. It showed.

Woody being off the booze and drugs was a big part of how tight we were that night. He'd been through a terrible spell over the previous years, but had been strong enough to pull himself around after his manager Sherry and I sat him down and read him the riot act. He was killing himself. We couldn't stand by and do nothing.

Not only was Woody clean and sharp, but we properly rehearsed, in a studio near the Rotherhithe Tunnel. We sounded great. Had age finally straightened out the Faces?

Rod turned to me after the session.

'You haven't given up drinking, have you Kenney?'

'No.'

'Thank God for that.'

CHAPTER 10

NOT HIGH,
NOT HAPPY

Mac and I glanced across at each other. We knew what we were both thinking.

How the hell did we get here? How did it come to this?

It was early 1976 and we were standing in what could loosely be described as a farmhouse, though it was more like a large stone cowshed. Outside in the yard an open fire was burning, ramshackle, crumbling outbuildings and barns were dotted around, and various caravans had been parked to one side and people we don't know were wandering about. The feel was of some post-apocalyptic refuge – mankind trying to start all over again – apart from the large gleaming, silver Airstream trailer we could see through the window, now kitted out as a mobile recording studio. This was Ronnie Lane's home, Fishpool Farm in Wales, and he was standing next to us, complete with beard, neckerchief, waistcoat, cords and sturdy boots. Ronnie the Traveller. Ronnie the Troubadour. Ronnie the Penniless.

Since quitting the Faces, Ronnie had enjoyed some decent hits and endured some shattering misses. The single 'How Come?' with his band Slim Chance reached number 11 in the charts, and he'd released two albums. Great. He'd also all but ruined himself financially chasing a dream. Ronnie Lane's 'Passing Show', was a carnival of music, misfits and circus acts, travelling from town to town, performing under a Big Tent to handfuls of people. I don't know if magicians formed part of the Passing Show, but if they did they performed a brilliant disappearing act. With Ronnie's money.

I hadn't been surprised that this was how Ronnie chose to live. Ronnie was always searching for something, some connection – to the land, to his soul – always asking deep questions. What's the secret of life? How can I be a better person? That's why he turned to Meher Baba, seeking the path to a more fulfilled, gentle life. Pete Townshend did as well. They were both consumed with a spiritual curiosity, to find a guiding principle that would bring inner peace. The farm was Ronnie's attempt to create his own reality, based on what he had learned from Baba. I admired his ambition. Whether it was working for him was hard to tell. On the surface he seemed happy enough, but there was an edge to Ronnie that hadn't been there before.

We'd arrived in good spirits. While driving there I'd turned to Mac and asked if he wanted to take over. He'd declined. 'Alright, but I'm done,' I said, letting go of the steering wheel and climbing into the back. I loved winding Mac up like that. It totally freaked him out. He was panicking as he tried to clamber across into the driver's seat, but once he had the car under control he couldn't stop laughing. We had to pull over until we got hold of ourselves. We had still been smiling about it as we pulled into the farmyard.

After a few beers with Ronnie, listening to him procrastinate – 'Oh, I don't know if I want to. But I love you guys. I just don't.' – we found ourselves in the kitchen, with Ronnie's wife Katie cooking something in a big cauldron. Someone's head, by the look of it. I hoped I was wrong; I'm allergic to heads. We watched her

© Richard Young

```
928723 PO HA 3
299992 PO TS G
H37 AP6 1015 LONDON T 18

GREETINGS

KENNY JONES DRUMMER OF THE WHO WEMBLEY STADIUM
WEMBLEY

GOOD LUCK FOR TONIGHT
        MRS MOON AND FAMILY

COL NIL

299992 PO TS G
928723 PO HA 3
```

HARROW
MIDDX

© New York Daily News Archive/Contributor/Getty

1: You'd never guess this was the 1970s, would you? With Keith Moon and Woody.

2: Peppermint Park Club, London, the night of 6 September 1978. The last time I saw Keith.

3: My treasured telegram from Mrs Moon.

4: With my good friend and drum tech, the late Bill Harrison. Bill, you are very sadly missed.

5: With Roger at the Mudd Club, New York, on 30 October 1979, celebrating the release of the *Quadrophenia* film. I didn't spill a drop!

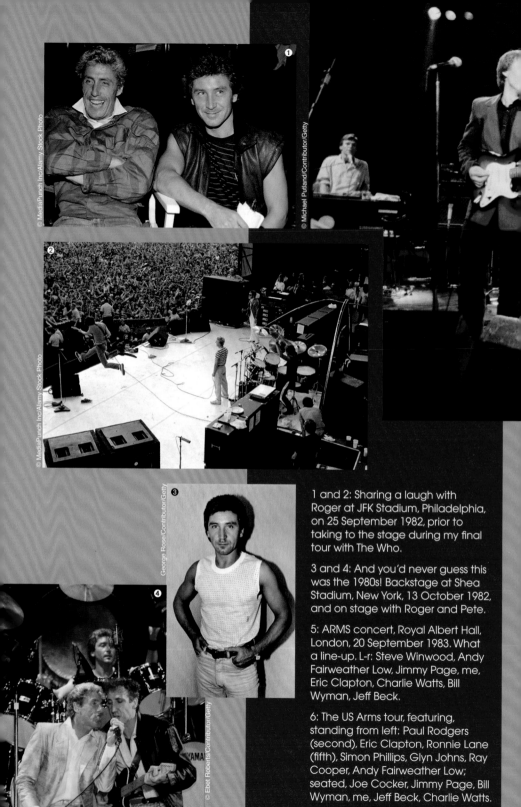

1 and 2: Sharing a laugh with Roger at JFK Stadium, Philadelphia, on 25 September 1982, prior to taking to the stage during my final tour with The Who.

3 and 4: And you'd never guess this was the 1980s! Backstage at Shea Stadium, New York, 13 October 1982, and on stage with Roger and Pete.

5: ARMS concert, Royal Albert Hall, London, 20 September 1983. What a line-up. L-r: Steve Winwood, Andy Fairweather Low, Jimmy Page, me, Eric Clapton, Charlie Watts, Bill Wyman, Jeff Beck.

6: The US Arms tour, featuring, standing from left: Paul Rodgers (second), Eric Clapton, Ronnie Lane (fifth), Simon Phillips, Glyn Johns, Ray Cooper, Andy Fairweather Low; seated, Joe Cocker, Jimmy Page, Bill Wyman, me, Jeff Beck, Charlie Watts.

7: The Who, after our Live Aid appearance.

⑤

⑥

⑦

1: Paul Rodgers and I had a plan. One successful album, *The Law*, enjoy recording it, then done. We stuck to that.

2: The Jones Gang album, *Any Day Now*, takes off in the US. On a fleet of over 30 planes. The artwork of me, Robert Hart and Rick Wills is by Woody.

3: The ever-changing Jones Gang, in August 2006 featuring Dave (Bucket) Colwell and Nick Cook, with Oliver Tobias right, at a charity concert in Wales.

4: The Jones Gang is very much active. Here we are in 2017. L-r: Mark Read, Pat Davey, me, Robert Hart, Nick Cook (hidden), Johnson Jay.

5: Celebrating my sixtieth birthday with Ringo, Woody, Rod and Jim Cregan.

6: Small Faces and Faces inducted into the Rock 'n' Roll Hall of Fame, 14 April 2012. Mick Hucknall brilliantly stood in for Rod, unable to attend through illness.

7 and 8: Back on stage with Roger and Pete at the 2014 Rock 'n' Horsepower concert at Hurtwood Park Polo Club, in aid of Prostate Cancer UK.

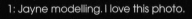

1: Jayne modelling. I love this photo.

2: Come fly with me. One of the great joys of my life, flying helicopters.

3: Very happily and very proudly hitched to my beautiful Jayne.

4: Sharing the moment with our parents. My mum Violet, and Jayne's mum and dad, Stuart and Joan. My dad sadly passed away five years earlier.

5 and 6: With two great friends who have helped me enormously. Top, Mark Singer and below, Rod Cousens.

7: The Jones family and partners, at Jay and Harriet's wedding in 2017. L-r: Dylan, Amber, Cody, me, Jay, Harriet, Zac (Harriet holding), Jayne, Jason, Casey, Fin (Casey holding) Jesse, Poppy and Erin.

© John Periam

1: Horse riding, another great passion in my life.

2: The first rock 'n' roll polo team. Mike Rutherford on the left, me, and Stewart Copeland far right, with the late Bryan Morrison.

3: The Guv'nor. Sometimes at Hurtwood Park Polo Club. Never at home.

4: Walking across the Hurtwood polo pitch with Prince Charles, shadowed by security. His, not mine.

5: Getting the better of Prince Harry. I like to think so, anyway.

pick up some massive tongs and grasp hold of whatever it was, pulling it clear of the bubbling water. A ham. Thank God. She tried to turn it over, but it was heavy. Too heavy. It dropped to the floor. No big deal, clearly. Unperturbed, Katie bent down and successfully secured the ham once again in the tongs, holding it up triumphantly. I could clearly see the dog hair, droppings, dirt and God knows what else stuck to the ham. She popped it back into the cauldron. Mac and I looked at each other.

'I hope you're staying for dinner?' Katie said.

'Er, thanks, but I think we've got to get back early tonight unfortunately.' We legged it.

In the car, I turned to Mac. 'Burger?'

He nodded. 'And chips.'

* * *

How did we get there?

This is how, and it will be a brief telling. This episode of my life still pains me.

Having turned down the chance to join Rod and the band in Los Angeles, with the prospect of tours and hit singles and albums, I did the next best thing. I moved house, to Gainsborough Gardens in Hampstead. Next door to the mother-in-law.

I had a few quid in the bank, but it wasn't going to last forever. Or even very long. I began to look around for what to do next. I picked up session work, which I enjoyed, but it was only ever pin money. I half thought of touring with my mate David Essex after the two of us, plus Mac and a great guitarist called Chris Spedding, enjoyed a casual gig together at the Speakeasy Club. But it was never a serious proposition.

I really didn't know what to do, and to rub salt into my somewhat self-inflicted wounds 'Itchycoo Park' had just been re-released and seemed to be climbing the charts. Great, for someone. Not us. We weren't going to see a penny from this unexpected hit.

Not until, that is, I received a call from our old Immediate pal Tony Calder, now with management company NEMS, founded by Brian Epstein back in the 1960s. NEMS had bought up the Small Faces back catalogue, released 'Itchycoo Park', and now, according to Tony, there was demand for a video. The four of us. ASAP. A grand each. Interested?

We recorded the video, plus a second for the soon-to-be-released 'Lazy Sunday', in one afternoon. We had a laugh. Yes, awkward tension to begin with, but that quickly faded. If not exactly like old times, there was still a spark. And we were wanted again ...

That's how Mac and I ended up at Fishpool, to try and persuade Ronnie to join us and Steve in re-forming the Small Faces. I wish we'd never gone.

We were all at a bit of a loose end. Perhaps with the exception of Ronnie, who at least had a plan, even if it was proving unworkable. Whereas Mac, Steve and I, we were casting around for the next thing. The Faces were gone, Humble Pie had split and Steve's solo career was faltering. We all needed something new in our lives. Instead we hooked on to something old. And as we should have known, you can never recreate the past.

Steve, and separately Mac, had recently joined Ronnie on stage for a couple of one-off appearances with Slim Chance, and they seemed to have gone well – positive vibes as Steve had kept reminding him – but Ronnie remained reluctant. He had a band. Did he need a second?

Eventually Ronnie's financial situation carried the day. He agreed to our proposition.

Early summer 1976 found us in Chigwell, at Joe Brown's recording studio, located in his garden. Steve was friends with Joe, both living up Epping way, and Joe had offered the use of his studio, on the agreement that we'd pay for the time should we land a recording deal.

That afternoon marks the final time Steve, Ronnie, Mac and myself played music together.

Ronnie was drunk, but not as drunk as he looked. He was occasionally stumbling, sometimes slurring his words, and I now realise this had more to do with his multiple sclerosis than alcohol. Whether Ronnie knew he had the disease at that stage, I don't know. I think he probably did, or at least suspected, but was in denial. Ronnie had changed, no question, more angry, belligerent, frustrated and upset. I'm now certain it grew from his physical decline. That fragile frame of mind, combined with his drinking, produced a toxic mix that could be difficult to deal with. And on that summer's afternoon in Chigwell, Steve reacted badly.

Marriott himself was acting like an ass, constantly taking the piss, overly confident and arrogant. Strutting. The two of them clashed. Verbally and physically. Ronnie stormed off, and did not return. As Steve said in an interview a few months afterwards, 'We sent him out for a packet of Rothmans cigarettes and he never came back'.

It's a good line, funny, but it also reveals a truth about what happened. Of course, no one 'sent' Ronnie out for cigarettes, but Steve was bossing him around and Ronnie did not respond well to that. Their personalities locked horns and there was nothing Mac or I could do to prevent it. Our band was crumbling in front of us before it had even been properly re-formed.

As it turned out, Ronnie was the wise one that day. When he walked out, I kept thinking how sad it was, that the four of us had come to that point. What I should have been thinking was, 'Hold on a second Ronnie, I'll join you'. We all should have thought that.

Instead, Steve phoned a mate. The following morning Rick Wills arrived at the studio. Until recently he'd been touring with Roxy Music, but when that came to an end Rick had been forced to find work on a construction site to earn a living. His circumstances, however, were no reflection on his ability. Rick was a good bass player who would later find fame and success with Foreigner.

At the time, I saw Rick's arrival as a positive development. We all got on well and began to record an album. Those weeks of recording felt better than they should have. The material wasn't particularly strong and Steve was over-exaggerating his rock 'n' roll persona, but even still I was enjoying making music with Mac again. Better to be playing than not, I reasoned. I was wrong.

There's an irony in the title of the first track on the album, 'High and Happy'. I was neither.

Recording at Joe Brown's place was a genuinely positive experience, at least. Joe had been generous in letting us use the studio and he was great fun to be around, very complimentary about my drumming. His wife Vicki was also a delight. A lovely person with a great singing voice who had enjoyed a successful career in the 1950s and '60s as a member of The Vernons Girls and then The Breakaways, before becoming a much in-demand backing singer. She's there on our album. Vicki sadly died in 1991, when she was just 50 years old. Awful. She was such a warm, giving person.

With the album recorded, promoter Mel Bush, who ended up managing us, negotiated a deal with Atlantic Records for two LPs and a decent advance. However, much of this evaporated when we discovered that Steve was not in fact a free agent. Yes, sounds familiar. He had an ongoing management and record deal, which had to be bought out before we could release any material. This took months. It wasn't until March 1977 that we officially re-formed. In April we began touring, and our album *Playmates* eventually came out in August. By then punk had smashed its way into the charts, leaving the Small Faces very much a once-was band, out of sync with the music scene and out of favour with the record-buying public. *Playmates*, and the follow-up *78 In the Shade*, released posthumously, sank without trace.

Steve's contractual mess was not the only reason for the delays. In December 1976, following too many drinks in the local pub after a long day of rehearsal, I was driving home with Rick in my convertible VW Beetle, through Epping Forest. We were on a winding country lane, leaves covering the surface, ice beginning to form and approaching a tight bend, when, literally, the wheels came off.

Maybe the axle snapped, I'm not sure, but whatever the reason, we were suddenly helplessly tramlining off the road. Smash! Head-on into a great big sturdy tree. I wasn't wearing a seat belt and sailed through the windscreen. Thank God we were in a convertible. The windscreen disintegrated, rather than breaking into lethal shards. That saved me from serious injury, I am certain.

Strange the things that stick with you. I was wearing a pair of red cowboy boots at the time, and as I flew through the air, I remember thinking fleetingly, I bet I look just like Superman ... then smack, I was tumbling through a jagged holly bush. I don't think Superman ever did that.

When I opened my eyes, I couldn't see a thing. Pitch black, no lights anywhere. I thought for a moment I was blind, until my sight began to adjust. I patted myself down, to check if anything was broken and then clambered back to where I thought I'd find the car. I couldn't see it. Disorientated, I stumbled around in circles until I eventually came across the road and, following that, tracked down the VW, the entire front of which was crumpled into the dashboard. The force of the initial impact had obviously sent the car into a spin, ending up with it lodged sideways against a second tree, the passenger door buckled inwards.

Rick! Rick!!

I could feel panic rising.

He was still in the car, groaning. I dragged him out and we collapsed by the side of the road. The smell of petrol was so strong you could taste it. I fumbled in my pocket and pulled out a packet of cigarettes, lighting one to calm myself. Smart thinking, Kenney.

The beam of a torch found us, attached to a bloke who lived nearby. He'd heard the crash and came to investigate. Taking one look at the wreck he asked. 'The driver. Is he dead?'

I squinted at him. 'Me. I'm the driver.'

'No way. No one could get out of that.'

I eventually persuaded him not to go searching for anyone else. He'd called the emergency services before venturing out and we sat together, waiting for them to arrive. As my head slowly began to clear, realisation struck. Shit, that could mean trouble. I'm still half pissed. Fortunately, the ambulance appeared first and having dealt with Rick, and what turned out to be a broken collar bone, the paramedic turned to me.

'Are you okay, Sir?'

By then I'd caught a glimpse of my reflection in the ambulance window. I looked like death, blood oozing from dozens of pinpricks caused by the shattered glass. No cuts, but dramatic on the surface. A possible escape.

'No, no I'm not. Not really. I can't see. Glass in my eye.'

He wrapped my face in a bloody great bandage. Perfect. The Old Bill won't smell my breath now.

At the hospital, following an initial assessment, we were settled behind a curtain, me on one stretcher bed, Rick on the other. We looked at each other and burst out laughing – and the more Rick laughed the more it hurt. He was relieved when they took him off to get sorted.

Left alone for ages, I began to wonder what was going on. The curtains didn't go all the way to the floor and I noticed these big old policeman's boots on the other side. They are coming to arrest me, that's what's happening, I thought. I started groaning and moaning, eyes shut, as the curtains were pulled back and the officer walked in.

'I know you've had a traumatic time, but we really should discuss what happened tonight. And you will have to produce your driving licence and insurance.' I didn't respond, but continued my distressed and in-pain act, ramping it up. He stood there for a minute or two, clearly unsure how to proceed. At last, he gave up. 'I'll leave you then, Sir. I'll just slip this ticket into your jeans' pocket. Here you are. That tells you what's needed. If you can produce the required documentation tomorrow, that will be fine.'

Having got away with it so far, I wasn't about to hang around, just in case. The doctor who had examined me earlier had obviously decided I wasn't an urgent case. He was right. There was nothing much wrong with me. Even so, someone was bound to pop their head in soon. Not worth the risk. Checking my watch, I saw it was two in the morning. Time to go. I got up and peeked out the curtains. Dead quiet, so I tiptoed over to the loos and caught a look at myself in the mirror. Claret all over. I gently washed my face, and looked again. Right as rain, some scratches, but handsome as ever. Head down, I strolled out of that hospital unchallenged.

The cab home cost a fortune, and the next day I had to go to the breaker's yard to pick up what I'd left in the car. When I saw the wreck, I couldn't believe we got out of there alive. Then I went to see Rick in hospital, now in a private room, and as I put my head round the door the laughter hit us again. It took me a good few attempts before I could make it in there without dissolving into hysterics. Must have been awfully painful for poor Rick.

When this second incarnation of the Small Faces did eventually set off on tour, the early gigs were particularly bad. Marriott was all over the place, drunk. I was dreading playing, and I hated feeling like that. We told Steve we weren't going to put up with it and he did eventually listen. He pulled himself together and the gigs improved. I would have walked if they hadn't, but I could see threads of hope.

These threads were well and truly snapped on the second tour, in September. In an ill-fated attempt to connect with the youth culture of the times, Steve turned punk. Swearing and spitting at the audiences. Horribly unpleasant. I wanted to be professional, but instead found myself playing on a stage that I wished would open up and swallow me.

What made Steve's behaviour even more disappointing is that the tour should, could, have been good. PP Arnold had joined us as a backing singer. We knew her from the Immediate days and she still had a hell of a voice. In addition, Jimmy McCulloch from Wings was added to the line-up, giving us a much bigger sound. But Marriott blew it. It was such a shame. I don't like to think of him in those days. He was so much better than that.

Mac was the main reason I hung on. For all the downsides, it was still fun being with him, playing together. Rick also helped.

He was a good guy and I enjoyed his company, but it wasn't enough. Not after the gobbing. I told Mac I was cringing every time we stepped out on stage. He agreed. We fulfilled our contractual obligations, then we were done. No final flourish. No fanfare. No announcement. With barely a whimper, the Small Faces were once again no more.

The accountants distributed what money was left. We were each owed £15,000 from our deal, but we didn't receive that. Of course we didn't. We were the Small Faces. Once again, nothing changes. Steve's share was eaten up with more contractual problems and Mac and I had agreed to pay production on the albums. With that settled, we were left with pennies. Only Rick walked away with any cash. The full 15,000 quid. Good luck to him. Right place, right time.

I was pleased when it over. Especially stepping back from touring, as I'd had enough for a while. By the middle of 1978 I liked the position in which I found myself. I had space to clear my head, keep my hand in with session work, and in time turn my thoughts towards starting a new band, maybe something with a different feel. And on a smaller scale. I needed a break from the madness.

CHAPTER 11

TRADING PLACES

Drama free. Limited touring. Different feel.

When Glyn Johns approached me with the idea of forming a transatlantic band, it ticked all the boxes. Glyn spoke about a guy he knew in the US, Bill Lamb, a great singer and songwriter, with a folk-rock feel. 'You'll enjoy working with him, Kenney,' Glyn assured me. He had also earmarked two other Americans, an excellent keyboard player called Tim Gorman, who became a good mate of mine when he toured with The Who in 1982, plus singer Kelly Harland.

Was I interested?

Yes.

We enlisted another couple of very talented guys, this time from the UK – Tim Renwick on guitar and Dave Markee, a bass player and Robert Mitchum look-a-like, whom I'd worked with before on many sessions. Suddenly we had a band with a laid-back vibe, as though half the Eagles had married their UK cousins, and were now looking to chill in the studio and on the road.

At rehearsals, I felt very comfortable with this group of musicians. The more we played, the more excited I became. The sound was melodic, it was great to have Glyn involved and the other band members were decent, straightforward people. Exactly what I was looking for. There would be no outbursts or tantrums with this group, no spitting.

A face from the past then entered the scene. Another positive. Eric Kronfeld was a music lawyer from New York – well-connected, a hard negotiator, tough but fair – who'd helped the Small Faces in the transition from Don Arden to Immediate, via Tito Burns. Eric would go on to become president of Polygram Records, but at this point in his career he was still in private practice, with Glyn as one of his clients. Eric took it upon himself to find this unheard of, fledgling band a record deal. He succeeded. Very well. He negotiated a $1.5 million contract with A&M for us.

My life was turning a corner. After the frantic, hedonistic whirlwind of the past few years, the offer of a period of creative calm appealed enormously. I wasn't looking to slow down permanently, just take a breather. I was tired. The suggested name of the band kind of summed up my feelings: Lazy Racer.

On 6 September 1978, I stepped off a plane at Heathrow and straight into a waiting car, which transported me directly to the Peppermint Park Club in Covent Garden. I was buzzing, excited. The past few days had been very productive. I'd been in the States with Bill Lamb, talking over ideas for the album we would shortly begin recording, and now I was on my way to a party hosted by Paul and Linda McCartney, prior to Paul screening a preview of the film *The Buddy Holly Story*.

I arrived around 7 pm, and soon found myself at a table with Paul, Linda, Paul's brother Peter, David Frost, plus Moonie and his lovely girlfriend Annette Walter-Lax. Keith and I were sitting next to each other, and when he asked what I'd been up to, I explained how I'd come directly off a flight from America, where I was working with a new band.

'Sounds good, Kenney. Best of luck.'

'And how are you doing, Keith? Haven't seen you in a while.'

'I know Kenney. I was away. Out of it. Malibu. Fucking great, but too much. Back now, for good. Off the booze and drugs, the lot. Had to, you know? I can't do it anymore.'

'So you're in good shape?'

'Yeah, I am. Great. I'm together. At last. The Doc's giving me pills, you see. If I have alcohol, or anything, man I'm screwed. Crazy reaction. And not even fun. What's the point?'

'Oh. Right ... eh, you don't mind if I have a drink, do you?'

He laughed. 'You go ahead.'

It was good to see Keith looking so well. Yes, he was a little overweight, and still with that mad look in his eyes, but he appeared much better than I had seen him for a long time. I was pleased. Very pleased. We were mates from way back, long before the ill-fated Australian tour. I cared a lot about Keith, even though he was nuts and could drive you mental at times.

* * *

We used to drink in a pub on the corner of Wardour Street in Soho. Keith would often be hyper when we arrived. 'Yeah, yeah, let's go, let's go. Let's sit there. No there. Here, this one.' It could be hard to settle him.

We knew a lot of people in that pub, it was a kind of a magnet for musicians in the mid-1960s, and our quiet drink would sometimes mushroom into a session with a big crowd, everyone chatting over each other. That wasn't always Keith's scene. When too pumped up, he couldn't deal with conversation, couldn't cope with the rapid back and forth, and would become withdrawn and isolated. On those nights he didn't want to chat, but just as much he didn't want to not be involved. A complicated man.

In that state, Keith's eyeballs would begin to bulge as he grew more and more agitated and, because of the leapers he was popping, all you could see were his big black pupils. That was the giveaway. Something was brewing. On more than one occasion I watched him go to the bar, order a big drink, maybe a treble brandy and Coke, come back to the table, take a sip, and tip the rest over his head. Then he would just sit there, dripping and grinning. Look at me everyone. I'm over here. I'm Keith Moon. Pay attention. I need it.

Towards the end of 1973, Keith was spiralling out of control, out of shape and out of his box. At a gig in Cow Palace in California he'd collapsed on stage, and the situation wasn't improving going into 1974. That's when, on my return from a Faces tour of New Zealand, Australia and Japan, I received a call from Pete Townshend asking if I would play some sessions for the *Tommy* soundtrack. The Who had a studio in a converted church in Battersea, Ramport Studios, and as I was living on Kingston Hill at the time it was easy to nip along. Sure Pete. Happy to. I arranged for my drums to be delivered and turned up at the time requested.

'What's up with Keith?' I asked as soon as I arrived.

There was a bit of, 'Well, er ...', before Pete finally said, 'it's partly that he's away filming *Stardust* with Adam Faith. He could make it back, I guess, but the truth is, Keith's out of it. So we're looking to use a couple of different drummers.'

'Oh, right.'

Given the circumstances, Pete approaching me wasn't a big surprise. He knew my drumming from working on his various demos over the years, plus sometimes jamming together when our paths crossed. He recognised what I could bring to the recording, and which songs would suit my style of drumming.

I played on several tracks, and because I was used to drumming with Pete, I knew how to adapt to his style. I could follow his guitar, which he quickly picked up on. After a couple of run-throughs, Pete turned to me and asked, 'Why are you emphasising everything I do?'

I shrugged. 'Because it is good.'

'Oh. Fuck. Fine.'

Tony Newman, the drummer with Sounds Incorporated, also played on the album and our recording schedules sometimes overlapped.

Now, if Moon was a loon, Tony was even worse. A total nutjob who, when he put two drumsticks up behind his head as antennae, was a dead ringer for the alien character 'Uncle Martin' in the TV show *My Favourite Martian*. He did that a lot. If Keith picked up his crazy behaviour from anyone, it was Tony Newman.

Tony loved practical jokes and daft pranks, forever winding up his poor wife, Margot Quantrell, who sang with Vicki Brown in The Vernons Girls and The Breakaways. Just for a laugh, Tony might announce that he was planning on committing suicide. Hilarious. Eventually Margot had enough, and decided to get her own back. They say revenge is a dish best served cold; in Margot's case, it was served red hot.

Tony drank all the time, often in the big shed at the bottom of his garden, which he'd kitted out with a loo so he could spend hours in there, smoking, getting hammered. Tony's vanishing acts began to annoy Margot as much as his daft jokes, so to teach him a lesson she poured a load of paraffin into the toilet. She knew his habits well. Sure enough, Tony was soon back in his shed, sitting on the loo, pissed as a newt no doubt, puffing away and, yes, he flicked the smouldering cigarette end down into the bowl. Whoosh! A burst of flame. Blew his arse off!

I'm sure Margot hadn't intended the butt to inflict so much butt damage, and when she heard his shriek she came rushing out to help, managing somehow to manoeuvre her husband upstairs to the bedroom, so he could lie there, face down of course, and wait for the ambulance. When it arrived, the guys put Tony on a stretcher to transport him to the burns unit, and as they were carrying him down the stairs, one of them asked what happened. Tony told them exactly, ending with ' ... and when I threw my cigarette down there, it just went bang!' The two paramedics were laughing so much they dropped the stretcher, sending Tony tumbling. That's a bad day. That's a Tony Newman day. Just as he described it to me.

During one of the sessions at which Tony and I were both present, Moonie popped in to check out what was happening. If excluding Keith from the recording had been Pete's way of reading his erratic drummer the riot act, it hadn't worked. Keith wasn't the least bothered about the soundtrack. He'd played on the original album; that's the one that mattered as far as Keith was concerned. Moonie was upbeat when he appeared, even more so when he spotted Tony and myself. With Moon and Newman in the same room, anything could happen.

There was a bar set up at Ramport Studios, in the main room where we played. Keith, Tony and I were chatting in there – or to be accurate, I was listening to two motormouths bouncing off each other; you could never get a word in whenever Moonie and Newman were around – when Keith spotted the well-stocked larder. 'Ahh, great. Just the things guys. Just the thing. But before we get stuck in, a moment. Things to do.' And with that he walked over to the only door into the room and locked it. Three drummers. Two nutters. Three drinkers. 'Now, what can I pour you?' Everyone else was up in the control room, helpless. They were desperate to get back to work, but Keith wasn't having it. 'Fuck 'em. Another round, Kenney? This one's on me.' There was nothing the rest of them could do except watch us party.

My work on the soundtrack took about a week all in. Unpaid labour, as it should have been. This was helping out mates. I was delighted to be involved and happy with the outcome. I felt part of that album, as did all the other non-Who musicians, Pete made sure of that. By chance the Faces happened to be in LA in March 1975, on the day of the film's premiere there, and Pete was keen for me to attend. I was pleased about that – the public recognition that I'd been involved. Needless to say, the rest of the Faces came along as well. You couldn't have stopped them – not when they realised there was a party afterwards. I enjoyed myself so much that a few days later, back in London I pitched up at the UK premiere too, proud of my association with the album.

* * *

Back at Peppermint Park, Moonie seemed to have moved a million miles away from those *Tommy* days. He appeared relaxed and content. I didn't see him drink.

From the club, we walked in convoy to the cinema. There, at the brief drinks reception ahead of Paul's screening, I spoke to Keith again, wishing him all the best and saying my goodbyes, as I was keen to make a quick exit after the movie. It was the last exchange we ever had. I never saw him again.

In the morning, Keith's death dominated the television news. I thought it had to be a prank, something crazy Keith had cooked up for a bit of fun. It couldn't be real. I'd just seen him.

The reality then began to sink in. Keith was gone, his body found in the apartment he was renting from the singer Harry Nilsson, the same flat in which Cass Elliot of The Mamas & The

Papas had died in July 1974. Cursed? I knew that flat well, I'd visited Mickey Dolenz of The Monkees there when he was renting it. It seemed impossible that we could have had so many laughs in the very place where now a close friend lay dead. Those happy memories made the crushing news even more surreal.

The exact details of what happened are still unclear to me. From what I've been told, it seems Keith may have been confused when he woke in the night and, thinking it morning, swallowed down a second batch of pills, too close to his previous dosage. This was the medication he'd mentioned at Peppermint Park, to combat the effects of alcohol withdrawal. An accidental overdose.

It was so sad. People ask me to this day what I think of Keith Moon and the answer is easy. I loved him like a brother. I wish he was still here. There is only one drummer for The Who and that's Keith Moon.

I didn't attend Keith's funeral. I was invited, if that's the correct word – it seems too upbeat. It was held at Golders Green Crematorium, north London, not far from where his mum still lived. I decided not to go because I felt that it should be for Keith's family and The Who. Not me. I didn't want to be involved in a rock 'n' roll song and dance, and somehow be seen to be playing a part in the inevitable media circus. I felt having too many names present might take away from what the occasion meant to those closest to Moonie. I didn't feel comfortable with that. Instead, I chose to pay my respects privately. I slipped in an hour before it began, with a wreath and a little poem that I read to Keith. I then placed them both at the plot, and said farewell.

It never crossed my mind that Keith's death would have any impact on me other than sadness. Then, shortly after the funeral, my drum roadie Bill Harrison, who had also worked with Keith, telephoned.

'I think you'll be getting the call.'

'What call?'

'From The Who.'

I didn't believe him.

At the time, Lazy Racer was rehearsing in England. We were gelling as a band, something positive in an otherwise bleak period. The record deal was all but signed. Anticipating the future, I felt energised. Time to look ahead, not back.

Then during late autumn 1978 one, two, three things happened.

One.

I've just had my hair cut by a guy called Dallas at his salon, Smile, opposite The Scotch House in Knightsbridge. I'm walking down the street, when a gypsy woman appears out of nowhere, standing in my way, bringing me to an abrupt halt.

I step one way, to pass; she mirrors my move. Now she's thrusting a bunch of white heather in my face.

'Have it. You need it. Please Sir.' Startled, I take two steps back, trying to escape. She presses forward. She's about my height. I can't see her face. It's covered by a scarf and she's keeping her head down.

'Listen, I'm sorry, but I don't need it.'

'You do. You must.' She continues to insist, taking a half-step nearer, now pinning me against a shop front. She then reaches up and lowers her scarf.

I'm mesmerized by her eyes, intense, penetrating. They aren't those of an elderly woman. I swear to God it's Keith, his look, his face, his mad stare.

Taken aback, I splutter, 'Yeah ... yeah ... okay,' and thrust a fiver into her hand in exchange for the heather. She disappears into the crowd of shoppers, milling around and oblivious to what has just happened. I'm shaken and confused. What the hell was Keith trying to say?

Two.

It's shortly afterwards, and I'm in my car driving home, taking a shortcut around the back of London Zoo. I'm still thinking about the gypsy woman as I turn a corner and suddenly, speeding towards me on my side of the road is a Rolls-Royce, clearly out of control. There's no time to avoid it. We're colliding. Fuck, this is it. I screw my eyes closed and prepare for impact.

Nothing.

I jolt myself back to attention. I'm still driving. Glancing in the rear mirror I can't see the Rolls. Did it swerve at the last second and speed around the corner? Or did it pass right through me? Moonie? I don't know.

Three.

Having made it home in one piece, I'm sitting having a much-needed drink when the phone rings. It's Bill Curbishley, The Who's manager.

'Hi Bill, how're you doing?'

'Fine Kenney, fine. Listen, I'll come straight to the point. The Who have had a meeting and they want the band to continue, with you as drummer. They want you to join. They're not considering anyone else.'

'Well, that's a statement, Bill. But I'm sorry, I can't join. I'll have to say no.'

'What do you mean?'

'I'm forming a band. We've got a deal. We'll be signing any day.'

'Listen Kenney, Pete's going to be in the office this evening. Why don't you come round? Let's all have a chat.'

'Okay Bill. I'll be there.'

My chat with Pete started out a good laugh, remembering all the things we used to do. Then the tone changed. Pete leant across the table, face to face, suddenly serious. 'Look, you've got to join. We've come through the ranks together. You're one of us.'

That struck home. Was I suited to a transatlantic version of the Eagles? Did I really want a peaceful, easy feeling? Or was I one hundred per cent London Mod? Just like The Who. Was that the message being sent with the gypsy and the lucky heather? The Rolls? Good luck Kenney. Keith's not blocking the way. He's supporting you. Take the chance.

It wasn't that simple. I liked working with Glyn, he had huge credibility as a producer and I enjoyed playing alongside what had proved to be a great bunch of musicians. I felt positive and fired up about recording our first album with a great label. I didn't want to let anyone down. I didn't know what to do.

Pete could see the dilemma in my eyes. 'Look,' he continued, 'we don't have to go down the same route. Keith was great, absolutely, wild in life and on drums, but in some ways that held us back. Now we've a chance to do something completely different.'

They had my attention now. They knew it. Bill cut in. 'And we're going to negotiate a new record deal. You'll be part of that.' It sounded like a fresh start, for everyone. I wouldn't be Moonie mark II. We'd be The Who, setting off in a new direction. Bill continued with further reassurance. 'And listen, Kenney. If there is any legal stuff to sort out with your other band, I'll deal with it all. You don't have to worry about anything.'

There was only one possible answer.

From that meeting, I went straight to the Lazy Racer rehearsals. I explained what had happened, being totally honest. I said it was a very difficult decision, because I loved working with them, I loved what we were putting together, but on the other side, this was The Who and they really want me to join.

They understood. 'Kenney, you've got to.' They were very gracious. Too gracious? Too understanding? 'Hello?' I momentarily thought. 'They've got their eye on another drummer!'

In all seriousness, I was touched by their reaction. Especially when later they came to see me while The Who toured the States. We met up afterwards and had a good time. No hard feelings. I was delighted when they recruited Henry Spinetti to replace me and went on to record a couple of excellent albums.

* * *

I was officially unveiled as a member of The Who in January 1979, following relatively straightforward contract negotiations. I was asked to become a full member of the band, to which I agreed. There was no sense of the three of them, then me. No attitude of employers and employee. They wanted me to be an equal partner. We also arranged for 10 per cent of earnings to be put aside for Keith's estate, to ensure his daughter was looked after. Critical to us all.

Pete was as good as his word in terms of this being a fresh start, with the band now a five-piece, following the addition of the excellent John 'Rabbit' Bundrick on keyboards. I felt that was a positive move on Pete's behalf. Rabbit fitted in extremely well – not least because he could hold his own with Pete, myself and John Entwistle in the alcohol stakes. No mean feat. Roger was practically teetotal, but the rest of us enjoyed a drink back then. Lots of them. Early on in the new era, however, Rabbit misread the band, thinking it was okay to be knocking them back during rehearsals at Shepperton Studios. He'd seen me swigging Cokes and assumed they were topped up with brandy. Not when rehearsing – too much to learn in a short space of time. For all the infamous Who antics down the years, professionalism was at the core of the group when there was work to be done; Rabbit soon understood what was required.

I found it quite emotional being back at Shepperton, because it had been the Faces who'd put the studio on the map. When The Who heard us raving about what a fantastic facility it was they went off and purchased the place. And now there I was revisiting my old haunt, this time as part-owner, having bought a share as a stipulation in my contract.

The first major concert for the new incarnation of The Who was scheduled for 12 May in the Frejus Arenes, south of France, promoting the films *The Kids Are Alright* and *Quadrophenia* at the Cannes Film Festival.

We knew we couldn't turn up at such a big event without first having a run-through somewhere else, so we hastily arranged a gig at the Rainbow Theatre, Finsbury Park. By then I knew about two, maybe three, hours' worth of Who songs, but I was still learning, and petrified. Contractual obligations and various PR commitments to introduce the new line-up, plus recording additional material for *Quadrophenia* had eaten up the weeks since I'd joined and we'd only had about 10 days to rehearse. That really wasn't long enough, because Who songs are incredibly complex. *Was I going to remember them?*

I also had to learn how to deliver the tracks in a way that wasn't trying to ape Keith, but would still resonate with Who fans. There were some great fills that fitted in perfectly where Keith put them, but I knew his drumming. He was a chancer. Some of those fills were by accident, quickly improvised and sometimes finishing just in the nick of time to make it back to the tempo. That was one of the things that made Keith's drumming so exciting and vibrant. The best fills I kept in, where Keith had them – you couldn't improve on those. But some had to go. I kept it tight, adding jam to the mix where I thought it worked best. That wasn't Keith's style at all, he tried to spread confection over everything he touched. But I wasn't Moonie. Keith summed it up best himself, when he commented, 'I'm the best Keith Moon-style drummer in the world'. He got that right. No one ever came near him.

In truth, the fills and rolls were the least of my worries. Those I knew how to execute. They were part of me. Unlike these new arrangements. With the limited rehearsal time, it hadn't been possible to absorb them as I would normally. I found that hard. I had to get it right, obviously, so I placed notes on a music stand to my side, roughly outlining what I had to do. That meant trying to read my scribbles while playing at the same time. I gave it a go, but quickly found it too confusing and distracting. 'Fuck it, I'll wing it.' It worked out okay. The boys in the band seemed happy.

The trickiest bit was having to wear the cans for 'Won't Get Fooled Again', 'Who Are You' and 'Baba O'Riley'. You can't play those songs without listening to a click track through your headphones. Keith did exactly the same. Those three numbers require the addition of a sequencer on stage, to play the multi-channel organ tracks that Pete had originated in his studio, heavy with effects and complicated turnarounds. When the sequencer cut in, the only person who'd be keeping time would be me. With the clicks in my ears, I'd be in control of the track, maintaining the tempo while the others did their thing until, on my cue, they would come back together. For those songs, I was going to be the leader of the band, no question. I had used click tracks many times before during session work, but never live. I was terrified, and at times sent cross-eyed concentrating so hard on the back and forth speeding through my cans during those sequencer parts. Somehow I managed, thank God.

It wasn't only the music that distinguished my first Who concert from everything I'd been involved in previously. For the opening number, my focus was so complete I didn't look up, but by the end of the second song I managed to lift my head and squint out at the audience. All I could make out through the haze was a sea of faces, blokes' faces! I'd never seen so many geezers in my life. I was going to have to get used to that. Completely opposite to the Small Faces and Faces. Bit of a culture shock.

Thanks to all the years we'd known each other, I felt comfortable looking out on Pete, John and Roger, especially as they were very supportive throughout the concert, giving me nods, thumbs up and generally making me feel like an integral member of the group.

At the end of the gig I chucked my sticks high into the air. Totally relieved that I'd made it through okay, with the fans reacting positively. Entwistle came running over to me give me a hug. 'I bet you're glad that's over, aren't you!' Too fucking right I am, John.

I appreciated John's gesture, and his understanding of my emotions. We were pals, drinking buddies. I liked him a lot, he was a very normal guy with a wonderfully dry sense of humour. But you needed to concentrate hard to pick up his jokes. He spoke so quietly I learned to lip-read. No doubt whatever he was saying sounded perfectly clear in his own head, but for me, catching his words was a struggle. Before I sussed out watching his lips, I would resort to nodding a lot and saying, 'Yes, John,' whenever I guessed it appropriate. I'm sure half the time he must have been thinking, 'Why the hell is Kenney always agreeing with me?'

During the gig, to help calm my nerves, and no doubt those of a possibly sceptical crowd, Roger had come out with a good line, introducing John and Pete as the two new members of the band. I thought Roger's comment spoke volumes. The three of them, and virtually everyone in the audience, must have been acutely aware of Keith's absence, and yet Roger had made a point of welcoming me in a light-hearted manner, sending a message to the fans that we were going to be okay. Yes, it's a new line-up, not what anyone would have wished for, but we're cool with it, relaxed and comfortable on stage together, ready to continue making great music. It meant a lot.

Roger also gave an interview where he stated that he'd attended a séance not long after Keith's death, during which Moonie contacted him to say that The Who had to go on in his absence, and that I was the only possible replacement. Roger was openly stating that I'd been Keith's choice, and the rest of the band were more than happy to listen to him.

Roger was giving off positive vibes everywhere possible. It didn't last.

CHAPTER 12

KNOWING
MY LUCK

In early May 1979 I found myself sitting on a balcony in a luxurious villa in Frejus, overlooking the Mediterranean. Pete was out on a yacht, relaxing, readying himself for the concert at the Arenes in a couple of days. The rest of the band were chilling, enjoying the magnificent setting. I was on a high. The Rainbow gig had been a success and I felt more confident about performing with The Who. I knew there was better to come and was fired up about the challenge.

On top of all that, we'd landed a huge recording deal. Professionally, life was good. I'd also played my part in the contract negotiations that had taken place in New York that spring.

While enjoying a walk one morning in Central Park, Bill Curbishley and I discovered we had a lot in common, both Eastenders with similar attitudes and approaches to life. Having chatted about our backgrounds and aspirations, we took a moment on a bench to watch the horse-drawn carriages clatter by, carrying tourists through the park. Sitting there, our talk turned to business.

'Well Kenney, I'm off to see Warner Brothers at lunchtime. I'm meeting to negotiate the new deal.'

'How much are you going to ask for?'

'Well, I don't know if it will work, it's a long shot, but I'm going for five million.'

I looked at him. 'That's not enough.'

'Really? How much do you think I should look for?'

Without hesitation I replied, 'Fifteen million dollars.'

For a second, Bill's eyes widened. Then a huge smile split his face and he started to laugh. Loud and long. It was one of those laughs that consume every inch of the person. His whole body shook, as did the bench beneath me. I sat quietly, straight-faced, waiting for Bill to compose himself.

Eventually he calmed down. 'You're serious, aren't you Kenney?'

'Yeah.'

'Well, seeing as you're the new boy, I'll do that.'

I hadn't picked the number out of a hat. I knew what I was saying. Flying over on Concorde I'd read that both David Bowie and Paul Simon had just agreed big deals for a similar figure. If they could do it, so could we.

At about three o'clock that afternoon Bill called me in my hotel room. 'Kenney, are you busy? Good. Come up and see me for a few minutes, if you don't mind.' Sure.

'What's up Bill?' He looked kind of crestfallen.

'Well, it isn't good news, I'm afraid. I did as you suggested, I went for 15 million.'

Ah. That's it. 'Oh well, you don't get anywhere if you don't ask.'

'That's true Kenney. They didn't go for it. But I'll tell you what I did get.' He started to smile. 'Ten, plus an additional two million non-recoupable against royalties. For the prestige of having The Who on the label.'

Nice.

I thought about that moment as I enjoyed the late-afternoon Cote d'Azur sunshine, with a glass of wine sitting in front of me and a gentle sea breeze keeping the heat at bay. Idyllic. After all those bum deals, money worries and pass-the-parcel debts, finally I'd cracked it. A professionally negotiated contract, fair all round, hassle-free. Now we could concentrate on the music. What could possibly go wrong?

A knock on the open glass doors behind me broke my reverie. It was Bill. 'Kenney, got a moment? We have a slight problem.'

Drip.

Imperceptibly, with those five words the timber beams underpinning the structure of the band began to rot. The decay that would eventually bring collapse had begun worming its way into our foundations. Blissfully unaware of the significance of the moment, however, I cheerfully turned in my chair to face Bill. It couldn't be anything too serious.

'What's up?'

'Roger. He doesn't want you to share the money.'

'What'd you mean?'

'It's not the 10 million. That's fine. It's the additional two. He won't share that.'

'What's the reason?'

Bill looked awkward. 'He doesn't think you deserve your cut. He says you haven't earned it, because you didn't contribute to building The Who's name from day one.'

I took a few seconds to absorb what Bill was saying.

'Do Pete and John feel the same?'

'No, they don't have a problem at all with sharing the money.' That spoke volumes to me, especially when it came to John. He was always getting himself into money problems, and yet was still happy for a four-way split.

'Well Bill, he has a point. I wasn't there at the beginning. But on the other hand, he didn't help build my reputation either. And that carries weight, you know it does. He can't claim, given the circumstances, that me joining the band hasn't added value. There wouldn't be a deal on the table if I wasn't here. I'll tell you what, fine, tell Roger he can keep his money. But my name can't be used to promote The Who, or any of the albums. How does that sound? Fair?'

I stuck to my guns. I didn't feel it was acceptable to have been invited to join the band, as an equal member, and then be told, you can have this bit, but not that bit.

Later that evening, following a round of promotional engagements, Roger and I were sitting at the kitchen table. Everyone else had gone to bed. Roger leant back in his chair and looked directly at me.

'About that non-recoupable advance, I'm not giving in you know.'

'Nor am I.'

'Well, I am definitely not fucking giving in to you.' He was getting louder. 'What the hell entitles you to money earned from all the shit we went through to get to where we are today?' Roger was on his feet by then. I jumped up to confront him, while he continued to rant. 'Were you there for 'My Generation'? 'Substitute'? Even fucking 'Who Are You'? No, you fucking weren't. Or any of the others. You are not getting a penny of that two million!'

'The only reason you have a band any more is because of me!' I fired back, pointing my finger across the table at him. I was getting angrier and angrier. 'And the only reason you got a deal with Warner is because of me!' Not strictly true, but I was furious with him.

'That's bullshit!'

At the same moment, both of us realised we had to stop. Our fists were clenched. The situation could have turned nasty. Roger wheeled away. I stepped back.

As he left, he shouted over his shoulder, 'I'm not giving in!'

'Well, I'm not giving in!'

Bedtime for the schoolboys.

Next morning, we held a meeting at around 11 am. We were all there, Pete included. Just as we were settling down, Roger eased me to one side. 'Kenney, about what we were discussing last night. It's alright.'

That's all he said. Clearly something happened before the meeting, whether Bill or one of the others had had a word I don't know. What I'm certain of, however, is that he would have hated having to say that.

Roger and I had known each other for years, and I had thought I understood him, but following that incident I realised how wrong I was. Not long after, Bill mentioned to me in passing, 'You've got to understand, Roger doesn't think of you as a friend. He doesn't think he knows you very well.' Pete wouldn't have said that. Nor John. We were mates. Roger clearly thought differently.

At the time, I genuinely believed taking a stand was okay. I wasn't really bothered about the money, there was plenty to go around. More than plenty. To me, it was a matter of principle. Now I think I was wrong. I should have caved. I should have respected Roger's viewpoint. It was a valid case he made. But I didn't, and the rot slowly began to seep further in. Now I could sense it. A faint smell, but it was there. It would take years before the resultant decay brought the house crashing down. There were many good times ahead. And some bad ones.

* * *

18 August 1979, Wembley Stadium.

I walked in to my dressing room ahead of The Who's largest-ever UK concert, to find a greetings telegram, featuring a lovely drawing of two butterflies. It was stamped 'HARROW, MIDDX'. It's one of my most prized possessions, ahead of all the gold discs and awards.

'GREETINGS KENNEY JONES DRUMMER OF THE WHO WEMBLEY STADIUM WEMBLEY

GOOD LUCK FOR TONIGHT

MRS MOON AND FAMILY'

I felt very emotional when I read those words. I knew Keith's mum well. Moonie and I used to go and visit her. For her to think of doing that, less than a year after her son died. It meant the world.

The spirit of Moonie was with me that night.

* * *

16 September 1979, Madison Square Garden, New York, in the middle of a run of concerts. My birthday.

As a present to myself, I packed in smoking. I'd been puffing away since I was about seven or eight, but I haven't touched a cigarette since. I'd once heard a doctor called Samuel Hutt, who later went on to have a successful country music recording career as Hank Wangford, say 'As long as you give up the habit by the age of 25, you'll be okay'. Although I missed his cut-off point by a few years, those words had been echoing around my head for a while. The 1970s were coming to an end, and somehow the time felt right.

To celebrate my special day, the boys threw me a huge party. Fantastic fun, especially when they wheeled out the massive cake, decorated with an equestrian theme, with lots of little plastic riders and horses. It looked brilliant. I cut into the cake and began handing slices around. I don't know who started it (any ideas, Pete?), but moments later cake was flying everywhere. Now, I have been involved in a good few such incidents, but never anything on this scale. The movie *Apocalypse Now* had recently been released. It had nothing on Madison Square Garden that night. Sponge carnage. Even the ever-immaculate John Entwistle didn't escape. John was one of those guys, like Tony Curtis in the movie *The Great Race*, who could walk through the biggest food fight in history and emerge totally unscathed. Not this time. Afterwards, I remember asking John if he was okay. 'I was,' he replied, 'until I wiped my face and discovered a showjumper stuck to it!'

I enjoyed a lot of laughs with John during my years with The Who. And I made a few quid out of him. The roadies used to have bets on what colour of suit and matching boots John was going to wear on stage. He never let anyone know in advance, but I could work it out by the colour of socks he brought with him to the venue. I never told the roadies that little secret, and instead just innocently placed my bet. Good luck boys.

* * *

3 December 1979. Cincinnati Riverfront Coliseum.

For us, just another big gig, three dates into our first US tour. Until we walked off stage.

At first, everything appeared normal. By the second or third song, however, we could sense something wasn't right. None of the crew were visible at the side of the stage. That never happened. Normally you'd glance over and Bill and others would be there, cheering us on, encouraging, giving the nod that everything was going well. Not this time. The wings were empty, there was no one to bounce off. It felt like we were out there on our own. An eerie sensation, lonely almost.

The crowd was acting perfectly normally though. Cheering. Singing. Rocking. A problem backstage, then? We didn't suspect for a second that an awful tragedy had already occurred.

As we closed the set, the auditorium was raucous, ringing with chants for more. Bill was there at the side, waiting for us. He said there'd been an incident, but didn't explain what. 'Get back out. But cut the encore short. One, maybe two songs. That's it.'

We played the songs, waved our towels in appreciation at the audience and strode off. Bill ushered us into the dressing room. That's where he told us: 11 people, 11 fans, dead. Crushed, he said, trying to get in. We were speechless. Devastated.

Back at the hotel, we sat alone in our rooms. The normal after-gig drink at the bar an impossibility. Bill's words had shocked us all. We needed time apart, to try and take in what had happened. We'd come to the city to play a concert, and now these poor kids were dead. Very quickly I realised that being on my own wasn't doing me any good. I had to be with the others. I was just pulling myself together to go and sit with Pete, to talk, when the door of my hotel room burst open and half a dozen journalists barged through. Somehow, they'd got hold of a pass key. 'Kenney, how do you feel about what has happened? What do you want to say to the families of the dead fans?' A hail of questions I found shocking and disturbing.

I wasn't capable of making any sort of statement, even if I'd wanted to. Which I didn't. I was still trying to come to terms with the tragedy. Thankfully, just as I was floundering, confused by the sudden invasion, the hotel security arrived and threw them out. I later learned that reporters had also been into Pete, Roger and John's rooms.

Later that night we did come together. We needed each other. We hadn't been personally involved in the incident, we hadn't experienced the horror that others had faced, but these were still our fans. That weighed heavily. Bill explained there was to be an investigation and until that was concluded we were not to pass any public comment. That was hard, of course, as we were constantly asked about it, the questions often laced with a sense that somehow we were responsible. We were the band playing that night. Parents had put their sons and daughters in our care. And we had let them down. That was the implication. Or at least that's how it felt.

We ignored the insinuations, even though they were grossly unfair and completely untrue. Compared to what the families and friends of those killed and injured were enduring, it really didn't matter what some sections of the press thought of The Who.

Sitting in that hotel room, we also spoke about whether to continue the tour. We were due to play in Buffalo, New York, the following night. Should we cancel and remain in Cincinnati, to show respect and solidarity to the city and the people caught up in the awful events? Or might we be a distraction? And would cancelling the Buffalo gig at such short notice cause additional problems, with many fans travelling long distances to attend? In the end, we chose to carry on. I think on balance it was the right decision. We were deeply moved by the events, but I am not sure us remaining in Cincinnati would have helped anyone.

In time, the facts about what happened became known. The fatal crush had come about when people in the crowd gathering in the plaza area heard our late sound check and mistakenly thought the gig was starting. It also became clear that we – the band and management – had fulfilled all our obligations. With the tragic sequence of events having been established, the bereaved mums and dads chose to write letters to reassure us that they didn't feel we were in any way to blame. What a truly extraordinary thing for them to do. Each note was an astonishing act of kindness that we found incredibly moving. How in their grief they could have found the strength to contact us, I can't imagine. We replied to every letter, expressing our deep condolences for their awful loss, and how we wished we had never played there that night. With 11 kids killed, that's exactly how we felt.

Months after the tragedy, an inquest was held in Cincinnati, at which we were quizzed individually.

I was interviewed for about two hours. The questioning started off in a very straightforward manner, gentle even. Where were you born? What was your childhood like? When did you start drumming? How did you meet the other members of the band? That sort of thing, obviously designed to put me at ease, and off guard. Then after about an hour, they casually threw in: 'Do you feel responsible for all those deaths?' 'No, not responsible, but yes, very concerned.' I sensed they were trying to trap me into accepting some sort of liability. To say that somehow we were at fault, which could have incurred implications further down the line. I felt under enormous pressure, but by sticking to the truth and answering their questions simply and honestly, I made it through.

I've never got over what happened that night. None of us have. The thought still spins around my head, 'If I had never joined The Who, those kids might still be alive.'

* * *

As the tour progressed, I remained on a steep learning curve.

When people ask me which is the best band I've been in, I answer that the Small Faces were the most creative, the Faces the most fun and The Who the most exciting. From a drummer's point of view, their music pushed you, you had to think about it.

When I joined the band, the hardest thing was not the description regularly attached to me, especially by the press, that I was the bloke stepping into Keith Moon's shoes. That never bothered me. I was comfortable in my own skin, doing what I felt was right. My role was clear in my head: contributing to keeping The Who alive, being true to the band and delivering Moonie for the fans in my own way. It would have been madness attempting to copy Keith. It's the same with all drummers. Each one has an individual style. Keith was all over the place, that's what made his playing electric; winging it, getting lost, somehow finding his way back. Just in time. I've known that feeling myself, but to play like that consistently, to try and replicate Keith in that respect, I'd have needed to be constantly stoned.

It was inevitable that when I came along The Who would subtly alter. That was understood from the start. My style was always going to keep the band tighter than previously. Pete and John were happy with that, it gave them room to explore their instruments and their playing. They both benefitted, I have no doubt.

I couldn't have approached The Who any other way. I didn't want to. Keith's style didn't come naturally to me, so I had to be true to myself while at the same time respecting everything Keith had accomplished, by happily throwing in surprises, switching to 'unnatural' when appropriate. Pete and John embraced the new sound. I soon felt I was sitting between two lead guitarists – one at the top end and one at the bottom end. We no longer had a bass player, not really, as far as I was concerned. And I mean that as a huge compliment to John. With me behind him, he could go off on his own, free to create wonderful magic, while I maintained the bass pattern. That's when I finally mastered triplets with one foot, as it was essential to keep up with John. Watching him on stage, I could tell when he was building up to one of his crazy sequences and I'd go with him on one pedal. When he heard me, he'd smile, give a nod.

It was only Roger who couldn't accept the musical path we were now on.

So no, the hardest thing wasn't Keith's shadow, it was learning the complete repertoire of The Who. That was a fucking task. We regularly played non-stop for more than three hours, running through 20-plus songs. The only time I had a moment to catch my breath was during the first half of 'Behind Blue Eyes'. There's no drumming there, thank goodness. I made the most of that.

I had oxygen on the side to help keep me going, especially in the early days. I only used it a handful of times, until I got fitter in my new role, but it was a comfort knowing it was there. When I first joined The Who I wasn't a hundred per cent fit. In the Faces I'd been very skinny, which was fine, I didn't need raw strength for those tracks. The Who songs required much greater physicality, far more exertion, to the point that I took salt tablets to counter excessive sweating. To manage the change, I had to bulk up quickly. Roger helped me with that, advising on the most effective workouts, how best to use weights, and accompanying me to the gym on occasions. I appreciated his support. He sure had a lot more practice than I did. To remain in shape in between tours I took up jogging, and bought a rowing machine for home, plus one of those bars to pull myself up. I used to be able to do sit-ups hanging upside down. Not now. Those days are a distant memory. The only bars I hang around now serve alcohol.

* * *

I found dealing with the pressures of performing in my new, high-profile, high-energy band tough enough, but lingering in the background out of sight from just about everyone else was an even harder situation. My marriage to Jan was in tatters. It had been for some time.

It's fair to say, we were equally responsible for the mess in which we found ourselves. Touring in a band, especially the Faces, offered opportunities when it came to female company and, as I've said previously, such temptations got the better of me on occasion. These were one-night stands with no emotional investment on either side: a bit of fun, great sex, both happy, then move on. Unacceptable behaviour for a married man? Yes. Affairs? No.

Jan, however, no doubt fed up with my antics, did embark on a longer-term affair, which I found difficult to deal with. Double standards? Absolutely. Nonetheless, that's how I felt.

Jan's relationship was with the well-regarded sound engineer Ron Nevison, who'd been involved with Traffic and Clapton in the 1960s, and later worked on The Who's *Quandrophenia* album and *Tommy* soundtrack (that could have caused a few awkward moments, but we remained professional). It started in 1973 I believe, a period during which Ron was working on Faces material, and I was frequently absent, touring and recording at Olympic Studios. We lived in Kingston Hill then, and Nevison was staying in the gatehouse of Mac's mansion on Fife Road, near Sheen Gate, on the other side of Richmond Park. Not far away.

My suspicions were aroused one day when Jan announced she was off shopping, at an unusual time. It didn't sound right and she seemed uncomfortable. I had a funny feeling something was up. Once she left I set off in my car to investigate.

I drove around the area until I came across her BMW parked in the next street along from Mac's. No shops anywhere near. This outing was not retail therapy. There was only one conclusion.

I knew Mac was away, but Nevison was around. I drove home, picked up Jan's spare set of keys and returned to her car. I unlocked it, took off my wedding ring and placed it on the gear stick. Not surprisingly, when she arrived back we had a huge row. I told her it was all over. 'Bollocks to you and to this!' Of course, it's never that straightforward. I'd always imagined I'd be married for life. One incident, as I thought of it then, wouldn't necessarily change that.

I didn't storm out; we kept our frosty distance, agreeing we would talk. Then a few days later I was driving back from Hampstead where I'd been speaking to Jan's mother, who was trying to counsel me on patching things up. We'd gone over and over what had happened, and by the time I came away I was hopping mad, fierce, angry at the situation in which I found myself. In that frame of mind, I foolishly decided to confront Nevison.

When he opened the door of the gatehouse, he knew exactly why I was there. I told him we needed to talk and he invited me in. Upstairs in the living room we had it out.

'What can I do Kenney? I'm really, really sorry. I never meant for it to happen. It was just one of those things.'

I listened to him, and being the soft touch that I can be, I said, 'Fine. Well, you're a prick, but what's done is done. Just don't meet her again, okay. I mean it.'

Having said my piece, it was time to leave. Ron followed me down the steep stairs. At the foot, I turned to speak to him again, catching him by surprise, and I swear I saw him trying to hide a condescending smile. Did I imagine it? Had he been smirking behind my back? Who knows. It's a long time ago. All that matters is that for that split second, in my mind he was laughing at me. I saw red.

I felt my arm pulling straight back. I swung at him as hard as I could. I sensed every East End mate of mine behind me in that punch, giving me strength. Bang. Down he went. Crumpled.

'Fuck you!' I shouted, and walked out. Driving home, I had trouble changing gears. My hand hurt. Poor me.

Next day I had a call from Mac. 'What the hell did you do to Ron Nevison?'

'I smashed him. Why?'

'Well, he's gone to Cornwall for a week. To hide his black eye!' That gave me considerable satisfaction and a bit of a chuckle, even though I knew I really shouldn't have done it.

That was around spring 1973, I think. At the time of the incident, our first son, Dylan, would have been almost a year old. He was my main reason for attempting to repair the marriage. The punch had also unexpectedly brought some peace to the turmoil that was raging in my head. We struggled on, trying to make things work, but that period of relative domestic calm didn't last.

In early February 1974, while in Sydney with the Faces, I received a telephone call from Jan. She'd had enough, she said. She was leaving me. She didn't explain why, which left me wondering. It didn't really matter. I'd wanted to remain together if possible, but now that lifelong marriage I had hoped for was over. And I was on the other side of the world, helpless to do anything about it. Upset and in shock, I took some time to pull myself together before heading down to the bar. I needed company and I knew the boys would be there. I told them what had happened and as I did, I felt a weight lift from my shoulders. I had no choice but to accept what Jan had said. And having done so, I thought, fuck it.

The tour closed at Budokan Hall, Tokyo, on 20 February, and a few days later I arrived back at Heathrow unsure where I was going to be living. By then I had reconciled myself to the fact that a new phase of my life was about to begin. It came as a surprise, therefore, to find Jan waiting at Arrivals. She'd had a change of heart she explained (or a rejection?). Could we try again?

Fast forward to winter 1978. We were still together but at breaking point, despite another beautiful son, Jesse, having been born the previous May. We'd given it our best, but failed, both having damaged the relationship beyond repair. Unhappy parents, regularly at each other's throats, does not create a positive environment in which to bring up children. Time to go our separate ways. In my head, certainly.

It was then that I received that call from Bill Curbishley.

When I joined The Who I parked the difficulties in my relationship and immersed myself in music, which helped bury my problems. I couldn't deal with any aggro. That might sound selfish, hiding my head in the sand for my own sake, but I felt all my concentration had to be focussed on learning the new songs. No distractions. I was elated to be in the band, and I wanted it to be a success. If the price of that was to give the impression that Jan and I were getting along, so be it. I knew the truth: there was no way back. It was only a matter of time, but in the short term I needed an easy life if I was to make The Who work. To be fair, initially Jan was supportive, more settled and more predictable. She gave me space, which made life easier for us both.

Until April 1980, during our second US tour.

Jan, along with the other wives and girlfriends, flew out to California for a few days' holiday, but when it was time to leave, with the band ready to move on to the next concert, in Salt Lake City, Jan refused.

This was not how The Who operated. Vacation time was carefully planned; families and partners were welcome, but when it was time to hit the road again, to get back to work, that's what had to happen. The band was a professional unit, focussed on the job. Jan's refusal to co-operate put me in a difficult situation. Suddenly I was the source of disruption on tour. It was the last thing I wanted.

I tried to explain how I felt to Jan, but she wouldn't listen. 'I don't care what the rest of the girls are doing, I will not be sent home like a naughty schoolgirl.' She remained on tour for another few days, to make her point. Screw the band.

For me, we'd taken a step back to the pre-Who world, in which I was married to Jan the time bomb, ready to explode at any moment. It was too much.

Worse was to come during one of the gigs following our departure from California.

Early in the set I noticed Jan with Jesse Ed Davis standing at the side of the stage. It was great to see Jesse again, but I thought, *Shit. This could be awkward*. With the Faces it would have been no problem, it happened all the time. That's what Jesse would have been thinking. Everyone was allowed in the wings during Faces gigs. Looking across while we played then, I'd likely see wives, girlfriends, family, friends, Joe Bloggs and Uncle Tom Cobley. But in The Who, no. It was different. The band rule was no one other than crew at the side of the stage.

At the end of the gig, as I walked off, Bill Curbishley draped his arm around me. Not that unusual, but somehow it felt different. Almost as though he was comforting me. He remained like that, all the way to the dressing room. Then, as I was towelling down, I noticed Jan wasn't around. Bill explained she'd gone back to the hotel.

'What's up?'

'Come over here a moment Ken, let me have a little word.' Quietly he told me what had happened. 'You probably saw Jan and Jesse during the show. Well, when I realised where they were, I went over and politely asked them to move back a bit, out of sight. I explained it was strict Who policy. Maybe right at the end, I said, but not now. Jesse was cool about it, of course, he understood. Not Jan, I'm afraid. She turned to me, Ken, and said, "Don't you fucking tell me what to do." Then she threw her drink over me. If she'd been a bloke I'd have thumped her.'

'Oh fucking hell Bill, that's all I need.'

'Listen Ken, don't worry about it. It's fine by me.'

'It's not fine Bill. I can't cope with this shit anymore.' I appreciated the fact Bill was willing to take it on the chin, but I couldn't. I felt embarrassed for him and myself. I was still the new boy and again she was making trouble. This wasn't the Faces, where pissing around was part of the culture: no one would make a fun T-shirt out of this. This was The Who and I had to respect their standards. Even more than that, it was a widely known band rule, and that made it my rule. She must have realised that. I couldn't live with it any longer. The final detonation of the time bomb had occurred.

Bill was great. He tried to reassure me that everything was going to be okay. But I knew it wasn't. When I got back to the hotel I told Jan that this really was it. We were finished.

Roger and his wife Heather came down to my room the next morning. They'd obviously heard what had happened between Jan and I, and wanted to talk me out if it. Roger was being genuine, trying to help.

'Kenney, you're a family man. You've got lovely kids, don't you think that's worth another go? The band really don't care if Jan was on the side of the stage, it's not important. Don't end your marriage over an insignificant incident.'

What he was saying was coming for the heart, and I appreciated his concern. It was good of him. But he didn't know the whole story. Pete and John knew more, but not Roger. I tried to explain some of the history. How the atmosphere at home was no good for Dylan or Jesse and that they would be much better off if Jan and I separated. I don't know if he understood.

I spoke to Jan before she left. I wanted to say goodbye, and make sure she realised I meant goodbye. I explained that finally I was leaving. I'd compromised in the past, sometimes to my own benefit, but now I was adamant. Most of the time I can be pretty easy-going, willing to let things slide, but when I feel I've been pushed too far, and it doesn't often happen (it can take a while), I dig my heels in. I won't be moved on what I think is right for me and those I love.

Our marriage ended there.

Later I talked to Bill Curbishley's and his wife Jackie about my feelings. I told them my marriage was definitely over. They were great, sympathetic, understanding, but also clear-headed. To them, not knowing the full background, it appeared a rash decision. At one point, Bill said to me, 'Ken, you need to be careful here. Consider what you're doing. You have two kids. If you go through with this, however hard you try to make it work, there will be pain. And think about you and Jan. Jackie there, she's my wife, right, and she represents a part of my life, who I am. It's the same with you two. It's a lot to lose.'

That made me think, take a moment's pause. But deep down I knew there was no turning back. Bill was spot on. Jan did represent a part of my life, but my old life.

'I appreciate what you are saying, both of you. I really do, but my mind is made up. I'm sad, incredibly sad, especially about Dylan and Jesse, but I'm convinced it's the right thing to do. For everyone involved. I'm okay about it. It's been weighing me down and I'm upset that it's come to this, but I also feel like I can now finally come up for some fresh air. I can't live the lie any longer. We've been suffocating each other too long. I need space to breathe.'

Both Bill and Jackie nodded, they understood. Then jokingly I added, 'Knowing my luck, though, I'll probably meet someone on this tour'.

* * *

A couple of weeks later we were in Toronto. The first half of the tour was coming to an end. Two gigs there, one in Montreal, then back to England for six weeks, before reconvening. As the only clear night was after the first Toronto concert, we arranged a party to celebrate the end of that segment of the tour. As now a free man in my mind, I was looking forward to it.

The event was in a club close to the hotel. I walked there with Bill and Jackie. As we entered, I clocked this gorgeous blonde girl striding out. *Wow, she's lovely.* I asked where she was going.

'Home.'

'No you're are not! Please join us at our table.' 'I stuck out my hand and introduced myself. 'Hi. I'm Kenney Jones. And you are?' We shook.

'Jayne, Jayne Andrew.'

She came back inside, and I acted like an ass. I wasn't exactly looking for love at the time, so having settled Jayne at our table, I proceeded to abandon her for the first half of the evening, up and down like a yo-yo, saying hello to everyone, having a drink, and only occasionally checking back with my guest. Surprisingly, Jayne remained, chatting away to Bill and Jackie like they were old friends. Eventually it struck me. Kenney, you're being a right idiot. Every time I was back at the table, I'd been finding myself more and more attracted to Jayne and interested in what she had to say. I decided to hang around in the hope that she would forgive my rudeness and allow me to get to know her better.

We connected like nothing I had ever experienced before.

It turned out she was a model who had been invited to the party by her agency, but as she hardly knew anyone, she'd decided to head home early. If I'd arrived 30 seconds later, my life from there on would have been totally different and, I have no doubt, far less happy.

* * *

The tour kicked off again in San Diego on 18 June, from where we moved to LA for two nights at the Forum followed by five at the Sports Arena. I asked Jayne to join me. In Canada, I'd been offered a glimpse of a golden future. I didn't want it to slip away.

At the first of the Forum gigs, after completing the final encore, I was walking down the stairs from the stage, sweating buckets, and there was Rod Stewart, his arms wide to give me a hug. He was there to support me being in The Who. I was touched. I wasn't expecting him. He'd attended the concert, and come backstage to pass on his congratulations, and invite Jayne and me and a bunch of others back to his place for a party. Just what I needed. I'm not sure the same could be said for Rod's wife Alana, who was seven months pregnant at the time. An impromptu party? Probably not what she was longing for.

During the same run of gigs, Roger Taylor and Brian May from Queen also came along. They and the rest of the band were staying in our hotel, the infamous Chateau Marmont, and we had a drink together the following day by the pool. Roger kept saying to me how great he thought the concert had been, and how well I'd done. 'Kenney, I really mean that. I would tell you if I didn't think you'd been good enough for The Who.' Once again, just what I needed.

As we sat there basking in the Californian sun Jayne could hardly believe her eyes. Up until that point in her life she knew no musicians, never having had any involvement in the music scene whatsoever. Naturally, however, she knew of Queen, but only as four guys in flamboyant costumes. Now here was Freddie Mercury, in small, tight trunks diving into the same pool in which she'd recently been swimming. 'Surreal,' was her assessment.

Jayne moved over to England that year and we rented a house together in Trevor Square, Knightsbridge. She had a lot to put up with, right from the beginning.

Not long after I joined The Who, an eclectic bunch of friends and acquaintances had come together to form an occasional drinking group, the Percy Boys. It comprised me, Justin de Ville-neuve (Twiggy's manager), Tommy Nutter (Savile Row tailor), David Essex (singer), Brian Harris (photographer), Johnny Gold (owner of Tramp nightclub) and Peter Blake (artist). Different ages, walks of life, perspectives, but all great fun. We would meet in various restaurants to start the evening off – Langan's Brasserie in Mayfair was a favourite – and we very rarely had to pay for our meals. When the time came, the waiters would go over to Peter and ask him to draw something on a napkin. That would cover the bill.

From dinner, it would be on to a pub and then, inevitably, Tramp, where we would end the evening on the dance floor. Now that I was living nearby, I'd often be the first drop-off for the taxi, very late and very drunk. The boys would prop me up against the door, ring the bell and leg it. When Jayne answered, I'd fall in, full of giggles and charm. I thought. It didn't take long for Jayne to grow tired of this, and when it happened once too often, she opened the door, let me fall halfway in, and left me there all night, my feet sticking out into the pavement.

Thirty-seven years later, Jayne and I are still together and very happy, blessed with four wonderful children, two girls and two boys, to add to my Dylan and Jesse – Casey, Jay, Cody and Erin. I am also a granddad five times over, to three granddaughters, Dylan's Daisy-mae and Jesse's Bonnie and Kaya, and two grandsons, my elder daughter Casey's Zac and Fin. They have brought enormous joy and happiness to my life.

I am incredibly proud of all my family, and everything they have achieved.

CHAPTER 13

TESTING TIMES

The end was not precipitated by any repeat of the angry exchange in Frejus – there was no explosive argument to mark the moment. Instead, the corrosive drip, drip, drip continued to eat away at the timbers supporting the band, leaving them slowly crumbling, ready to collapse at any moment.

Roger was susceptible to the whispers he was hearing within his circle of friends. 'Oh Roger, it's not like the old days, is it?' 'It's not like having Keith back.' Of course it fucking wasn't. Roger heard what he wanted to hear.

Small, seemingly inconsequential moments contributed to the decay in our relationship. Walking into the dressing room at one of the early gigs, I discovered a girl I knew from Faces days sitting chatting to Roger. When she saw me, she jumped up for a hug, 'Kenney, lovely to see you'. Then she turned to Roger, 'About time you had a sex symbol in the band.' It was a stupid thing to say, and it didn't appear to go down well with Roger. As far as he seemed to be concerned, The Who could only ever have one pin-up. And it wasn't me.

Drip.

I wasn't blameless in the growing rift between Roger and myself. During 1982, around the time I was getting divorced, everyone in the band was asked to contribute 20 grand for Who sound engineer Bob Pridden's pension fund, myself included. I should have said, 'Yes, of course, no problem'. I should have understood that I was being treated as an equal partner, which brought responsibilities as well as benefits. And I liked Bob. But I'm sorry to say, I refused. I felt I couldn't release the money then, as it formed part of my assets and given the divorce situation, there could have been legal implications attached to writing a large cheque at that stage.

By not doing so, I handed Roger another opportunity to stick the knife in.

Drip.

It was a very difficult situation, but I accept that my assessment of the appropriate course of action was wrong. I should have had the balls to hand over the money and deal with any fallout that followed. I didn't, and I regret that. Roger was quite rightly annoyed, but at the same time he didn't make any attempt to understand my situation or my reasons. He could quite justifiably have disagreed with my decision while at the same time trying to see things from my perspective, however much that perspective was bollocks. He never bothered. We all make a wrong call, and the reasons are important. If I'd refused out of spite or nastiness, fair enough, drag me over the coals. But I was in a bad position, feeling vulnerable, and I think – hope – that makes a difference. Not an excuse, but a reason. However flawed.

Such incidents certainly weakened my position, but what really fed Roger's resentment, allowing it eventually to become untenable, was the fact that whenever we played together, in the studio or live on stage, every time he turned around, it felt like he wanted to see Moonie. Instead, he saw me. He and Keith never really got along that well, but they got on at not getting along.

They made it work. And now, it seemed to me, after Keith's death they had become the best of friends.

The collapse came in early 1983. First, Pete drove down to my place in Leigh, Surrey, which I'd bought a couple of years previously. He wanted to talk. I suspected I knew the subject. 'I can't do this anymore,' he said to me. 'I can't be with The Who. I think it's finished. I'm going to speak to Roger and John.'

On the one hand, Pete's announcement wasn't a complete surprise. The clue had been there in the fact that our 1982 tour was billed as a 'farewell'. On the other hand, however, the intention then had been to morph into a studio band with possible one-off appearances from time to time, as Pete had stated clearly he couldn't face another full-on tour. John hated the idea, but okay, it might work. In one respect it had to. Warner was expecting a third album, to follow *Face Dances* and *It's Hard*. The financial implications of failing to produce that could be significant. In that regard, Pete's candid assessment of the likely future did come as a shock. I urged him to reconsider.

Shortly after the visit, my views became largely redundant. I received a call from Bill Curbishley. It proved to be very different from the one in 1978.

Apparently, Pete and John had grown weary of listening to Roger banging on. His complaining had been ringing in their ears for a while. Back in 1981, an exasperated Townshend came to see me, saying he was thinking of trying to find a way to bring in a different singer. I told him he couldn't do that. Roger was such a charismatic frontman, one of the best, with such a distinctive voice, that there could no Who without him.

Deep down, Pete understood that. The two of them were intertwined, feeding off each other. That's how The Who worked. In the process of creating their songs, Roger often laid down his vocals after Pete had produced the demo, a demo that usually included Pete's own take on the whole arrangement, including the words. Roger would then work with that, re-framing Pete's interpretation into his own unique style, which worked brilliantly.

It was a more structured approach to what I'd seen before. The likes of Steve Marriott or Rod Stewart, for instance, would come into the studio when we were set to record and play around with the lyrics, jamming vocally, until they found what they were looking for. Roger could have done the same, I'm sure, but that wasn't how he and Pete liked to operate, because they were so musically connected. Intertwined.

Inevitably, Pete and John eventually capitulated. Roger wanted me out and they gave up resisting. The Who is thicker than water. I understood. I'd like to have heard directly from either of them on how they viewed the situation, but it never happened. That hurt. Bill made it absolutely clear, however, that neither Pete nor John had any problem with me whatsoever. Only Roger.

With Pete and John having agreed to throw in the towel, I was left bruised by Bill's call, absolutely, but the knockout punch never landed. Instead, The Who stuttered on as was, in an uneasy limbo as contractual arrangements, TV commitments, photo shoots and PR events were fulfilled, with the fans left in the dark as to what was happening behind the scenes. Throughout this period, I acted professionally, undertaking all my obligations, while considering myself free to begin redirecting my musical gaze in a different direction.

Finally, Pete took the decision to quit the band, as he'd indicated he would when we spoke in Leigh. He'd been thinking seriously about branching off into a full solo career for a while and decided the time had come. He informed Roger in May, and confirmed it at a band meeting in June, at which I was present. On 16 December his departure was official, with Bill Curbishley negotiating us out of the Warner deal.

The Who was over. Only, it wasn't.

* * *

In the summer of 1985 Bob Geldof contacted Pete, asking him to re-form for a one-off charity concert at Wembley Stadium – Live Aid. Pete agreed and made the calls. We were back in action.

Unfortunately, around the same time I'd learned that Roger had been talking up how unhappy he'd been with me in the band. I had tried to speak to him about it but he wouldn't return my calls. My frustration boiled over. I'd had enough of the things he'd been saying and felt I must stand up for myself.

As I was leaving the Speakeasy Club one evening with my great mate Mark Singer, I overheard that Roger was in the restaurant with friends. That spelt trouble. With more than a couple of drinks inside me, I went back down to have it out. I wanted to know what he felt was so wrong with me. I approached him as he was sitting at the table and had a right go, 'Thanks for fucking calling me back! I've had the decency to call you, and you don't have the courtesy to return the call.' He was embarrassed but, thank God, didn't react. Immediately feeling foolish, I walked out.

I tried to call and apologise. I knew I was out of order, but I was unable to make contact until we met at the Live Aid rehearsal. I told him I'd been attempting to get in touch and that I was sorry for my behaviour, it was spur of the moment and I shouldn't have done it. Roger just looked at me and said, 'Don't worry. It's fine. It's cool.' I knew what he was really saying: 'Fuck you Kenney. If you think this concert is a way back into the band, forget it.' I'd played right into his hands.

My manner of transport on the day of the Live Aid concert may not have helped our relations. A helicopter. Big deal, rock bands regularly fly to gigs in helicopters. This time, however, I was piloting myself. Too flash? Maybe. But I loved it.

A couple of years previously, enjoying a dinner party at John Lodge's, the Moody Blues bass player, I'd met a guy called Ged Hughes. I was lucky to remember our encounter. Dinner at John's house always involved multiple bottles of wine and very little memory the following day. Fortunately, however, I did recall my conversation with Ged. He was a successful businessman, supplying fruit and veg to supermarkets, and as we chatted he mentioned he flew helicopters, sharing one with DJ and TV presenter Noel Edmonds.

'That sounds great,' I said. 'I've always wanted to fly a helicopter.'

'No problem. I'll come over and pick you up. You can have a go.'

Two days later he flew over to Leigh, landing in the garden. I strapped in, we took off and he said, 'There, you take over'.

This was not quite a first for me. I'd flown one previously, very briefly. Ironically with Roger. Back in the very early days of my time in The Who, while rehearsing at Shepperton, Roger suggested we go for a ride one afternoon in his helicopter. Great. I was impressed, I thought Roger meant he would be flying, but no, he had his own pilot.

Shortly after take-off, the pilot asked if I would like to man the controls. Yes, please. I loved the sensation, the sense of freedom. You break all ties with the earth, like cutting the umbilical cord. Over land I had no problem at all, but when I flew across a nearby reservoir – wow! – that was a shock, a totally different sensation. Your perspective changes immediately and it's suddenly very hard to gauge the horizon, which turns the world into an alien environment until you adjust. Nevertheless, disconcerting as that moment had been, I wanted more. It was the same when I first rode a horse. The necessary hand, eye and feet co-ordination felt second nature. The pilot commented on it. Roger was thrilled.

I got my licence in 1984. It was bloody difficult, but I loved the challenge. Other than maths, very briefly, core school subjects had always been beyond me because I didn't want to learn. I wasn't interested, and because of that I made no attempt to work with my dyslexia. Studying for that licence, however, I was determined to succeed because I enjoyed what I was doing. Nothing was going to stand in my way; my dyslexia would just have to be a partner in this. I see those three months of hard graft, intensive study and numerous flying hours at Fairoaks Airport, Chobham, Surrey, under the guidance of Ken Summers, as my academic qualification.

I learned in a Bell 47, the MASH helicopter. Once you fly one of those, you can fly anything, because in the Bell 47 you have a manual throttle at the end of the collective (the lever that changes the pitch of the rotors). That makes flying a helicopter a lot harder. While your left hand is engaged in managing the throttle and pitch, your right hand steers using the cyclic, which resembles a joystick positioned between your legs. Adjusting the gauges on the dashboard and operating the radio then requires a deft juggling act. Left hand off the collective and on to the cyclic; right hand reaching out to do everything else required. This manoeuvre can barely last a few seconds before the RPMs begin to drop. Your left hand then has to reclaim the collective and throttle to bring the engine's revs back up, and your right returns to steering. Take-off really requires two feet to operate what are known as the yaw pedals, and four hands, if only you had them, acting in a co-ordinated blur during those crucial seconds – stirring the soup it's called, an apt description. Impossible as it initially seems, you learn. It's exhilarating and scary when you first take control. You can't quite believe you've done it but, much like driving a car, in time you programme yourself to perform the tasks automatically.

More modern helicopters are easier, for two reasons. First, the pilot's seat has been switched to the starboard side, the right. Secondly, there's now an automatic throttle on the collective to adjust the RPM. This buys valuable seconds. No longer does your left hand have to be so tied up with maintaining the revs. Darting back and forth between the collective and cyclic is a thing of the past. Instead, now your right hand can remain on the cyclic to steer, because with the change to a starboard seat your left can reach the dash to deal with the gauges and radio, and critically you have time to do so. It's a much better system, but the Bell 47 will always hold a special place in my heart. David Essex and I owned one between us for a while, before I converted to a 206 Jet Ranger and finally a Squirrel. Both wonderful aircraft, but you never forget your first love.

On a whim, I asked John Entwistle one day, just before Live Aid, if he fancied coming for a ride in my helicopter as part of a documentary that was being filmed. I'd thought he might hate the idea. All a bit too showy and potentially dangerous. Really not his scene at all. John had never even learned to drive. In many ways, we were very different. I enjoy being in control, whereas he couldn't give a damn and was perfectly happy to let others take the front seat. He was like that on stage, quietly going about his business as Roger and Pete took all the attention.

John surprised me when he readily agreed to my suggestion, replying in typical John fashion. He talked like he walked, slow and deliberate.

'Come for a ride in the helicopter, John?'

'Oooh, I don't really know ... Yes, yes alright then. I'm a very trusting sort of person, Kenney.'

At the end of the flight, when I asked him if he'd been scared, he just shrugged. 'It had its ups and downs.'

On the day of the Live Aid concert, everyone's first appointment at Wembley Stadium was 9 am to attend the official opening with Princess Diana and Prince Charles. I flew from Leigh to Battersea Heliport, thankfully landing perfectly in front of the on-looking pilots. From Battersea, we were to be taken by a massive helicopter to Wembley. I was in 'Live Aid 2', and the pilot, having seen me arrive, asked if I wanted to co-pilot. Absolutely. I wasn't qualified to captain one of those big beasts, but I was definitely up for the chance to be co-pilot, which would also mean I could add the flight to my log book. Those things take off with the nose dipped, then reverse in the air to gain translational lift before soaring into the sky. Fabulous. All helicopters basically fly the same, but the size of that monster was very different from what I was used to. For safety, the pilot was on it with me the whole time, dual control giving him the option to take over if necessary. I'm glad to say there was no need, as I landed smoothly on the cricket green next to the stadium, where my taxi driver mate Ronnie was waiting with my Rolls. We all piled in and drove to Wembley Stadium. It's important to arrive in style!

After the official opening and return transport to Battersea, I flew home to watch the concert on television with Jayne, until it was time to fly back to Wembley, about an hour and a half before our slot. As I walked into the stadium to perform that evening, a strange sensation hit me. Everything that I had worked so hard to achieve, all the skills and experience I had gained over the years, seemed to come together in that moment. I'd flown myself to perhaps the biggest gig the world had ever known, and would shortly be playing in front of 70,000 people live and almost two billion on television, in one of the greatest bands of all time. It's just about the only occasion I ever remember thinking, indulgently, not bad for a little Herbert from Stepney. That, and parking in my old school playground, of course. Of similar magnitude.

I was lucky to be at Live Aid. Nine months previously, driving back home to Surrey from a birthday dinner for Bill Wyman at Tramp nightclub in central London, Jayne and I were involved in a nasty accident. Jayne was driving while I was in my usual state after such occasions, dozing in the passenger seat, when another driver jumped a light and broadsided us, sending our car spinning 50 yards up the road before crashing into a high kerb. I found myself upside down in the footwell, unable to open my door. Next to me, Jayne was non-responsive and covered with blood. I thought the worst. I managed to clamber into the back seat, kick my way out, and scramble around to Jayne's side, where, after a frantic few moments, I succeeded in prising the door open and pulling her free. I could see she was breathing, thank God. The ambulance arrived quickly and Jayne was taken to hospital, where she made a full recovery after being wonder-fully well looked after.

At the hospital, they asked if I required treatment. No, I'm okay, I insisted. It wasn't until I woke up the following morning at a friend's house in Putney that I realised how wrong I was. Just being in Putney should have been a clue. I'd been given a lift there by the police, completely forgetting that I had a house of my own in Trevor Square that I could have stayed in. I guess I'd taken more of a knock to my old loaf than I'd realised. Waking up that morning, however, it wasn't my head that was causing the problems. I'd knackered my back, left shoulder, arm and hand, with the ligaments and tendons all messed up. The extent of my injuries meant I required a lumbar puncture – resulting in the worst headaches I've ever experienced – and six months of rehab, five days a week, during which I was strapped into a neck harness and left hanging for half an hour every day, to take the pressure off my spine.

I honestly thought there was a possibility I'd never drum again. Three or four months after the accident I was set to play on a Bill Wyman album, *Willie and The Poor Boys*. I attended one session and pulled out. I couldn't do it.

The fact that on 13 July I found myself walking into Wembley was proof that the torture of rehab had paid dividends. I owe those physios considerable thanks.

I found performing at Live Aid exhilarating. I was proud to contribute to such an important cause, and happy to be back with The Who, once again fully involved in band decisions, such as over which tracks we should play – 'My Generation', 'Pinball Wizard', 'Love Reign O'er Me', 'Won't Get Fooled Again'. A technical hitch meant the satellite went down during our opener, 'My Generation' – appropriately as Roger was about to sing 'Why don't you all fade away' – so only the Wembley crowd saw the first two songs. But really none of that mattered. The experience was unbeatable. I'd love to have had more of it. It was clear, however, that this was a one-off. I doubted very much I'd be playing with the boys again.

I was wrong.

In February 1988 we came together at the Royal Albert Hall for the British Phonographic Industry (BPI) shindig, at which The Who received the award for Outstanding Contribution to

Music. As with our previous performance, this did not go without a hitch. The ceremony was broadcast live on BBC1 and inevitably it overran, resulting in poor Rick Astley being bumped from picking up his gong for Best British Single, so that we had time to take to the stage. We managed a couple of songs before 'Substitute' was quietly faded out in favour of the immovable object that was the *Nine O'Clock News*.

A final, and perhaps fitting end, to my Who career.

* * *

Looking back now on my time with the band, my overriding emotion is disappointment.

I am totally comfortable with my contribution to The Who. I played very well, I know I did, especially towards the end, after I'd kicked the booze in favour of Perrier (it was the 1980s) and immersed myself in the music. That would have been around the start of 1982. I didn't give up drinking (my teetotal days ran for a couple of years) because I was reaching for a bottle every morning. I didn't feel I was slipping down a path toward alcoholism. It was more that I was drinking too much, although no more than Pete and John, and I felt it was clouding my judgement and hindering my performances. I was even putting on a bit of weight. There was a lot going on in my life then, tensions with Roger, the divorce, and I realised I was getting smashed to mask those concerns. That was no good. Drink was getting in my way, rather than helping. I woke up one day and decided I had to get a grip. To perform at my peak, alcohol had to take a run and jump.

During that final tour, which kicked off in Washington DC on 22 September 1982, I became increasingly confident and comfortable in my own skin. I felt able to introduce more of my own style because by then I understood fully what made Who songs so special. Live on stage I was at my happiest. Playing my arse off, watching Pete swinging his arms in giant circles, thrashing his guitar, Roger leaping across the stage, twirling his mic like a crazed major in a marching band, and John the Ox standing stock still, his fingers producing magic. It was the only place I wanted to be. Then it all went tits up.

The biggest problem we had, I believe, was not stepping into the new world that Pete had spoken about when he recruited me. It just never quite happened and that made me uncomfortable. Instead, we kept playing the same type of stuff but with less impressive material. Part of the reason for that, I'm still convinced, was Pete's reluctance to put forward his best songs for The Who.

It's not that the tracks we recorded were rotten, they just weren't quite up to the high calibre expected of Who songs. We could have embraced a fresh approach to the music, while remaining true to the core values that made The Who, The Who – street-wise, electric energy, anthems, fire and brimstone. In place of that, however, we ended up Who-Lite, a diet version of what the band had once been, similar looking but with a synthetic taste.

I contributed to that, to an extent, when I replaced the traditional big tom-toms that Moonie and I had been weaned on with the new-style smaller concerts toms that had become all the rage. It was the modern sound, and they were great, but perhaps a step too far away from Who traditions. I know they drove Roger nuts.

We did record some good tracks. 'You Better You Bet' from *Face Dances* is a great song, combining the need for impeccable timing with lots of fills. And from *It's Hard* I enjoyed 'Athena',

'Cry If You Want' and also 'Eminence Front', although its slight disco feel prevents it from being a classic.

We also allowed ourselves to become distracted with non-music related issues. Not Roger, he remained focussed, but certainly in the early days Pete, John and myself were drinking too much, and they were taking too many drugs, plus throughout that period we had personal problems, divorces and relationship breakdowns. None of that helped.

One area of The Who that did impress me throughout was the professional way in which they viewed the band as a business, as well as a rock group.

While the business side couldn't touch the music in terms of adrenalin and excitement, I found it fascinating. We'd hold board meetings with the lawyers and accountants, at which we discussed possible investments. It was always interesting, but one that really captured my imagination was a company that made life-size, high-definition holograms. I remember one of Keith Moon. Massive, with incredible detail. He was drumming and it freaked me out. I felt as though he was actually in the room, with dirt under his fingernails, the lot. Amazing.

It's a good way to run a band. You are in it together, looking to build on your joint successes for financial stability. The Faces had been a million miles away from that. The money we made was split equally five ways, with songwriting royalties accounted for separately, and that was it. The Small Faces set-up was similar. We could have taken more control of our finances in those two bands, but we were never on top of it, and I wasn't experienced enough to know how to go about setting up any type of investment strategy. Instead, we just drifted along, never making the most of what we had. Not like The Who. For the 1982 tour we did a deal with Schlitz beer. In exchange for a significant amount of money, their logo was on the tickets and they could use Who songs in TV adverts. Hundreds of thousands of fans saw us on that tour; millions heard the songs on television.

* * *

Roger, Pete, John and myself never played together again after the BPI Awards. We never will. On 27 June 2002, John Entwistle died of a heart attack in the Hard Rock Hotel, Las Vegas.

I was in shock when I heard the news, but despite my upset I did have a quiet smile to myself when I learned the details. He'd had a drink with Pete and Roger in the hotel bar, and then, following an earlier hit of cocaine, John's weak heart gave in as he lay in bed next to a stripper. His death summed up much of his life, perhaps as he would have wanted it.

John's funeral was held at the village church in Stow-on-the-Wold, Gloucestershire. Beforehand we all met in a local pub, where we were invited to go up to John's huge mansion, Quarwood, to see him in his open coffin. I declined. Six years previously my lovely dad had died. Like John, my father also had an open coffin, but the person lying there had looked nothing like the man who was my dad. I hadn't needed to see him that way to say goodbye, and the same applied to John. My memories of both are so positive and vibrant, and that's how they should be left.

* * *

The Who could never re-form properly, not without John, but Pete, Roger and myself did play together on one further occasion. For a very important cause that's close to my heart.

In 1983, as part of obtaining my helicopter licence, I was required by the Civil Aviation Authority to have a full medical.

Mine was being conducted by a Dr Trump, which put me in a good mood from the off. I was sitting in his office as he checked through my notes.

'So Mr Jones, I see here you are a musician?'

'Yes, that's right.'

'A drummer, I understand.'

'Correct.'

'And what band do you play in?'

'The Who.'

'Ah, right. First thing for today then, a full hearing test.'

We ran through all the normal procedures – heart, eyesight, reflexes, all that – and I passed with flying colours, as I made sure to comment on to Dr Trump. I'm sure it was the first time he'd heard that one at a CCA medical. At the end, while filling out the forms, he kept glancing up at me.

'One last thing Mr Jones. Something completely separate. Does the left-hand side of your neck give you any pain? Any trouble swallowing? Anything like that?'

'No. Why?'

'Oh, just precautionary.' He started gently prodding my neck. 'Does that hurt?'

'No,' I said, slightly worried.

'Just one moment please.' Dr Trump pressed the intercom on his desk and called in a nurse.

'Can you spot anything unusual about Mr Jones's neck?'

'Yes, doctor. That side's bigger than the other.'

Fuck. What's going on?

'Now, I'm sure there is nothing to worry about. I'm a doctor whose whole family has been plagued by thyroid problems. I always end up focussing in on that, no matter what. I'm sure it will be fine, but I am going to give you a note to take to your doctor. For him to have a look.'

I left Dr Trump's surgery and went immediately to Wimpole Street, where my doctor, Adrian Whiteson, later co-founder of the Teenage Cancer Trust with Roger Daltrey, had his practice. By this point I was very worried and so walked straight past reception, making for the consulting room. The receptionist jumped up from her desk as I opened Dr Whiteson's door. 'Mr Jones! You can't barge in there.'

There was a woman talking to Dr Whiteson. She looked perfectly healthy to me. I called back over my shoulder to the advancing receptionist: 'Never mind her. She's probably only got a cold! Look at this.' I pointed at my neck. 'It's serious!'

Dr Whiteson stood up. 'Hold on Kenney. Just a minute please. Take a seat downstairs and I'll see you in a few minutes.'

Quarter of an hour later he called me in. 'Kenney, really. You can't just burst in like that.'

'I'm sorry. But check this out. My neck's exploding!' He laughed. We'd known each other for years through my regular check-ups for insurance purposes, and always got on well.

Dr Whiteson examined my neck and immediately sent me down the road for a scan, followed by an appointment with a specialist, a Mr John Chalstrey.

Sitting in Mr Chalstrey's Harley Street waiting room, I convinced myself this was all a waste of time. I didn't feel the least bit unwell, and anyway, if this was really was serious, wouldn't Adrian Whiteson have fixed me up with a doctor, rather than a 'Mister'?

I was shown into Mr Chalstrey's room, where he was sitting writing at a huge desk. I took a seat and after a moment he put down his pen and looked straight at me.

'I'm afraid it's not good news, Mr Jones.'

'What is it?'

'I'm sorry to say you have an adenoma.'

'Thank God for that. I thought it was cancer.'

He carried on looking at me, not saying a word. Eventually I broke the silence. 'So, what is an adenoma?'

'Cancer. It's growing in the left side of your thyroid.'

Slap. I'd been hit in the face. Cancer. Cancer. Cancer. The room suddenly felt as though it was filling with water, quickly rising over my head. I'm drowning. So why was he just sitting there talking? I couldn't hear a word he was saying. Help me.

Slowly the water subsided. I dragged myself back to reality.

'So, what's the score?'

'Well, we don't know if it's benign or malignant. We'll only discover that once we have it out. It's the size of a small egg.'

I couldn't believe it. As he spoke I felt nothing. Shock I guess.

'We need to sort this out as soon as possible.'

I wasn't thinking straight. 'I've got a holiday booked in Florida in a couple of weeks. Can it wait until I'm back?'

'Let me tell you. If you were my son, I'd have you in tomorrow.'

That pulled me up. 'You can adopt me.'

Within the week, I was booked into the London Clinic. I still couldn't believe there was a problem. I was feeling one hundred per cent fit.

On the day of the operation Mr Chalstrey came to explain what was going to happen, about the pre-meds, the anaesthetic and the procedure he would be performing.

'I'll be making the incision along a crease in your neck.'

'But I don't have a crease in my neck.'

'You will have soon.'

Then he told me I would need to sign some forms.

'What for?'

'Well, once we have you open, we need your permission to take out anything we think necessary, if we discover the cancer has spread beyond the thyroid. For example, into your vocal chords. It's unlikely, but we have to be able to deal with every eventuality.'

That's when it fully hit me. The seriousness of the situation. I don't know why. Maybe it was the thought that the cancer could have spread everywhere. All through my body. I was terrified, shaking like a leaf. They administered the pre-meds, but I swear to God they didn't work. I had never felt less relaxed.

As they were pushing me to the theatre on the trolley, I was grateful for the complicated array of pipes and plumbing I could see high up in the roof. It took my mind off the situation. That's all I can remember, until waking up after it was all over. Maybe the pre-meds worked after all.

Back in my room, as I slowly came around, still very woozy, I focussed on two figures at the foot of the bed ... Jayne ... and Jan. Apparently I said, 'I plead diplomatic immunity'. And fell straight back asleep.

A few hours later, after Jayne and Jan had gone, I had a visit from Bill Curbishley. It was good to see him.

'Hey Kenney, how are you doing? You've been in the wars, I see.'

'Yeah, but I'm alright. Apart from needing a pee.' The drip in my arm had been running too fast, the painkillers shrinking my bladder, which stopped me peeing. I'd tried and failed a few times and blamed it on the nurses who had to accompany me. I can never have a wee when I'm being watched. They adjusted the drip and by the time Bill arrived I was desperate.

The nurses helped me up, supporting me to the loo as I held on to the fluid bags attached to the drips. Bill was watching all this and started to crack up. 'Kenney, you look like an old-fashioned night watchman with two lamps.' That made me laugh.

Earlier, Mr Chalstrey had been in to report that the operation had gone well (he did a brilliant job – you can hardly see the scar), and that they'd removed the lump and performed a quick test, which showed signs of malignancy. Further tests would be required to confirm. 'It looks as though we caught it just in time. It doesn't appear to have spread.'

Three weeks later the full results came through, confirming it was malign, early stages. I'd been lucky, thanks to Dr Trump.

Mr Chalstrey explained that the other half of my thyroid would take over, which would be fine for a while, but it was impossible to know for how long. Eventually I might have to take thyroxine tablets to replicate my thyroid function.

Ten or so years later I found myself becoming unusually tired and visited my GP, who after tests advised that she felt the time had come to start me on thyroxine medication, but that it was a one-way trip. Once I started, I'd be on it for life. There was no real decision to make. I needed it, I recognised the fact. I couldn't be exhausted all the time.

It has made the world of difference, after we worked out the correct dosage. Initially my GP started me on 100 mcg, but at that level I felt like I was back in the Small Faces, wired on uppers. She reduced the dosage to 50 mcg. Much better. That's what I'm on now.

Since then I've been monitored regularly through blood tests, initially every three months, then six and now yearly, to make sure the tablets are doing their thing and there's no indication of the cancer returning.

Then in 2013, the nurse who was looking after me suggested we also do a PSA test for prostate cancer. I wanted to say, 'No thanks, there's no need'. For years I'd undergone those health checks with Dr Whiteson, which had included my prostate, and he had always been very clear in spelling out the symptoms I should be aware of. That's how I knew I was clear. I wasn't pissing over the bloke next to me in pub toilets, I wasn't waking regularly during the night desperate to go. Not often anyway. Yes, sometimes I had to get up once, twice, maybe three times, and yes, that had been going on for a few years, but I put it down to drinking too much wine before I went to bed. Surely that's why I was a little dehydrated, resulting in those little spurts, coming on me more often than I would have liked? That's all it was. I was fine. I was deluding myself. I'd wanted to say no, to avoid unnecessary stress, but 'yes' came out. Thank God.

The results revealed my PSA levels were higher than they should be, at 6.7. A second test within a week set alarm bells ringing. In that short period, the level had risen to 6.8. I needed further tests. I went into Royal Surrey County Hospital to see Professor Stephen Langley, a urologist specialist and now a good friend. Oddly, I wasn't scared. If it did transpire I had cancer, I'd focussed my concerns on the possibility of my prostate having to be removed, and all the resultant problems that can bring; potential erectile dysfunction being the most glaring. That was obviously a worry, but overall this seemed less frightening than my first cancer. I felt that having beaten that one, all the time I'd had since was a bonus. With that attitude, I could face anything.

This was a problem to be dealt with, and I was taking action. I hate anything hanging over me. Provided I can do something to sort out whatever the issue is, I'm okay. It doesn't get to me. It's only when things drag on, slip out of my control, that I feel myself being sucked under.

Biopsies, blood tests and an MRI scan confirmed the cancer, but again it hadn't spread. The nurse who suggested taking that PSA test probably saved my life.

Professor Langley explained the options, and how I was a candidate for brachytherapy, involving the injecting of small radioactive titanium seeds into the prostate, which destroys the cancer over a period of 8-10 months. The seeds weaken as time goes on, but they remain in there for life. You need a card if you are travelling, in case you set off the security alarm at airports. It sounded like something out of a spy movie. That's what I went for. In my circumstances it seemed to me a no-brainer. The tests also uncovered an additional problem, a blockage in my urethra (the tube that takes urine from the bladder) caused by my enlarged prostate. That had to be dealt with first, through what's known as a TURP operation, using a laser to clear the prostate tissue that was causing the blockage. That had been the reason for my pee slowing down. Nothing to do with those late-night drinks. Or the cancer.

During this period, as I was processing a flood of information, making critical decisions, I was hit by an even greater blow. Mum died.

Her sister, Aunt Floss and Floss's daughter Madelaine were with me when it happened, in the Royal London Hospital, a short walk away from Mum's beloved Havering Street and the community she adored. All the previous day, Mum had been delirious, so we'd all decided to stay with her. In the morning, around nine o'clock, with the three of us by her bed, holding her hands, she took her last breath, knowing, I hope, how loved she was.

Driving back the short distance from the hospital to Havering Street with Floss and Madelaine I turned on the radio. 'Crazy' by

Patsy Cline was playing. Mum's favourite. We burst into tears. Mum was sending us a message, we all thought it. That she was okay. Happy now with Dad.

In January 2014 I had the cancer operation, which was a success. The side-effects were tough, though. Especially not being able to sleep. I found myself having to get up regularly every night, with an extremely uncomfortable sensation of feeling I needed to pee, but not managing anything. I'd stand there and nothing would happen. By the morning I'd be exhausted, which is very debilitating. I ended up sleeping in a room on my own, watching a lot of television in the middle of the night, catching cat naps during the day whenever possible.

Once the swelling had reduced, I was able to pee normally, like that little boy in Brussels. Great. Running taps were a nightmare though. They would have me sprinting to the loo in a second. Filling the car with petrol also almost caught me out on a couple of occasions. That noise. I'd be intending on a full tank, but only manage a fiver's worth before dashing across the forecourt in search of the toilet. I learned to take a bottle with me in the car, just in case.

The recovery process takes a year of discomfort and a year of healing. It's only recently, after the third year, that I have properly felt myself again.

While I was recovering, Jayne and I decided we wanted to raise awareness of prostate cancer with a concert at Hurtwood Park, our polo club in Surrey. We've organised others since, and generated a fair few bob for the cause. Initially we thought we would keep it relatively low-key, just me and my band, The Jones Gang. As the date drew nearer, however, we decided it would be fun to invite some friends along to each play a couple of numbers. Jayne sent out about 12 emails and virtually everyone said they would love to participate. We ended up with an astonishing line-up, sort of by accident.

Accompanied by our fantastic house band – Geoff Dunn (drums), Dave Bronze (bass), Jim Cregan (guitar), Josh Phillips (keyboards) and John Thirkell (horn) – we had Mike Rutherford (without Genesis or his Mechanics) and John Lodge (without The Moody Blues), and an amazing string of solo acts: Nik Kershaw, Alvin Stardust, Judie Tzuke and John Parr, plus Jamie Johnson, a finalist on that season's *The Voice*. Poignantly, Steve Marriott's daughter Mollie also sang, beautifully. Following Mollie, my band performed a Small Faces selection, before Mick Hucknall joined us on stage, belting out some Faces numbers. Mick then teamed up with Jeff Beck for a set including the Beatles' 'A Day in the Life'. Comedian Vic Reeves acted as compere throughout the evening.

Then came the finale.

Jayne had emailed Bill Curbishley to see if Pete and Roger would be interested in taking part. Bill was immediately keen and said he would check with the other two. They were up for it, with me on drums (as Pete said, 'Kenney knows all the songs!'), plus support from the house band. We were on.

Bob Pridden came down to help the house band rehearse, then on the night, bang on time, Pete and Roger turned up, had a drink, posed for photos, and the three of us walked on to the stage, with Dave Bronze standing in for John. The fantastic Rock Chicks (Susie Webb and Zoe Nichols), aka the Fabbagirls, who had kicked off the whole evening with their Abba covers, provided backing vocals. Roger and Pete were in sparkling form, rocking through 'I Can't Explain', 'Substitute', 'The Kids Are Alright', 'Pinball Wizard' and '5:15'. Finally, everyone joined us for a rendition of 'It's Only Rock and Roll', and I was transported to The Wick in the 1970s, with Ronnie and Mick.

It was good to be back together with Roger and Pete. Whatever had happened in the past, whatever had been said, we were three friends on stage, making great music into the night.

The only person who appeared at the event who we hadn't approached ourselves was Alvin Stardust. He contacted Jayne when he heard about the concert, saying he'd love to be involved. We were delighted and Alvin was clearly very keen, regularly calling the polo club office to make sure we hadn't forgotten about him. Of course we hadn't, but by then the event had taken off like we had never envisaged and there was a hell of a lot to organise. Jayne assured Alvin he was firmly on the bill and not to worry.

Alvin's passion for our fundraiser surprised us, but we thought no more of it until we were clearing out the clubhouse bar in preparation for the rehearsals and Jayne noticed a single in its sleeve propped up on one of the beams, Alvin's version of 'Pretend' from 1981. Neither of us had any idea how it got there. 'That explains it! It's a sign! Stardust at Hurtwood is clearly meant to be,' we laughed.

Alvin went down a storm on the night, singing 'Pretend' (naturally) and 'Johnny B. Goode'. The crowd loved him. As did we, his showmanship and enthusiasm were infectious. He seemed so full of life and energy.

Then a couple of months after the concert, we learned that Alvin himself was battling prostate cancer and had been for more than a year. He was determined to keep his illness private and, of course, we respected those wishes.

By the end of October, Alvin was gone.

'Pretend you're happy when you're blue,' Alvin sang that night at Hurtwood. I couldn't follow his advice when I heard the news of his death.

* * *

I'm going to finish this chapter with a plea. Prostate cancer is a killer. One bloke in eight will get it, but if you catch it early, then it is very treatable. I'm living proof. Everyone should be aware of it, young and old, fathers and sons, brothers and sisters, husbands and wives. It shouldn't be taboo. It's an illness, that's all. We can talk about it. It can be dealt with.

Boys, get yourselves tested, especially if you are over 50, even if you're not exhibiting symptoms of feeling the need to pee more often than normal, but not a lot happening when you get there. Don't leave it too late. Your options for treatment reduce, the further advanced the cancer is.

One simple call could save your life.

CHAPTER 14

BAND OF BROTHERS

The first Small Faces album on Immediate was released in the US, with a slightly amended track listing, under the title *There Are But Four Small Faces*.

I wish that were true today.

Steve went first. I was in New York when I heard. It was the second occasion a death had been announced to me in that city. In October 1975, a friend called my hotel room to inform me that one of my favourite drummers, Al Jackson Jr from Booker T & the MGs, had been shot and killed. 'No,' I said, laughing, 'you're confused. That's an old story. His wife shot him a few months back. That's what you're talking about.' It wasn't. There had been another shooting, this time by an apparent intruder at his house. Al Jackson was shot five times in the back. The case remains unsolved.

On the morning of 20 April 1991 I received a call from the press. God knows how they found me, as I was registered under a pseudonym.

'What do you think about the death of Steve Marriott?'

'What you talking about? Don't play jokes. It's not funny.'

'Oh. You don't know. Steve Marriott died this morning. In a fire at his home.'

It wasn't until later that I heard more about it. It seems they found him in a cupboard. The theory goes that Steve fell asleep with a lit cigarette, the blaze took hold, and when he woke smoke was everywhere. Then in the confusion of escaping he mistakenly opened the cupboard door, at which point it was too late. Steve collapsed. It's unbearable to think about.

In the band, I was probably closest to Ronnie Lane – we met first – but almost side-by-side with Ronnie was Steve. We were different characters, he was an even bigger Herbert than me, but we got on. We all got on. There weren't any cliques and we rarely argued until right at the end.

The last time I saw Steve was in 1980, at a birthday party Jayne threw for me at Stringfellows. Both Ronnie and Steve were there. Early in the evening, Steve came over to me. He was laughing. 'Alright Ken. How you doin'? Lend us a few bob.' That was typical Steve, acknowledging my good fortune in joining The Who with a joke. At least I assumed it was a joke. He wasn't looking great, a little heavy, hair thinning. That's not how I remember Steve Marriott.

He was a scallywag, the Dodger always mucking around. A slight screw loose, but no more. Most of the time he was smart and articulate. And boy could he sing, play the guitar and write songs. On stage, no one could touch Steve. I loved watching him, that swagger and cockiness justified because he was that good. That's how I remember Steve. That, and his beaming smile and dirty laugh. Over the years, we enjoyed a lot of both.

It was at Steve's funeral that I discovered he had a six-year-old daughter, Mollie, who I'd previously known nothing about. Steve and Mollie's mother, Manon Pearcey, had been childhood sweethearts and then got back together again years later. Finding out about Mollie brightened an otherwise sad day. It felt as though

Steve had left a parting gift. Mollie and I have since become very close, she calls me Uncle Dad. Mollie has a wonderful, soulful voice, and is now releasing her own material. Her father would have been very proud of her.

Manon is now married to Joe Brown, which is lovely. I know how heartbroken Joe was when his wife Vicki died. Mollie now has a genuinely wonderful stepfather, a stepsister in singer Sam Brown and a stepbrother, together with two half-sisters and a half-brother, Steve's other children. It's a strong support network for Mollie, which I am delighted about. I am very fond of her.

In 1996, the Small Faces were honoured with the Ivor Novello award for Outstanding Contribution to Music. Mac flew over from his home in Austin, Texas, Ronnie's brother Stan stood in for him, and Woody collected the award on behalf of Steve. Afterwards I spoke to Steve's mother. For me, her few words capture the essence of Steve better than anything else I've heard.

'Steve would have hated to grow old.'

* * *

We didn't realise it until years later, but I first met Ronnie Lane long before I knew who he was, long before the fateful meeting in the British Prince pub. We were in the Army Cadets together, at a training camp in Aldershot, Hampshire.

This would have been around 1960, when I was 12. Military uniforms were a common sight then, as young men were still being called up for National Service, although the numbers were declining. As a kid, I looked up to those soldiers, desperate to be just like them. That's why I joined the Cadets, the Royal Green Jackets, 32nd Company, Rifle Brigade, the fastest marching unit in the army at 188 paces to the minute. I'm not sure I contributed much to that record – the rifles they gave us, .303 Lee-Enfields, were bigger than me. I felt very grown up carrying one, but it was awfully heavy for a little boy. The company was known as 'The Mugs', in other words, the ones who were always first to engage the enemy. That's where the speed marching came from: 'Can't wait to go to war, let's march there quickly.' I was very proud to be part of that.

At the barracks in Aldershot, all the equipment was pre-war, including big rotary machine guns on tripods, which became scorching hot when fired. As part of the training, proper soldiers would show us what to do with the guns and then give us a go. Before firing you're supposed to dig your heels into the ground and pull back against the weight. No one mentioned that to me. I took my turn, settled down, finger on the trigger, and pulled. Next thing I knew I was being dragged down a hill. Bullets spraying everywhere. Blanks, thank goodness. The older lads thought it was hilarious. As did I. I wanted another go straight away.

It was only after Ronnie and I got to know each other that we joined the dots and realised we'd been at the same camp. I was telling the story of a training exercise involving crossing a mine-field, and one of the boys in my group leaping over a five-bar gate straight on to a mine. These weren't real, of course, but when 'detonated' they set off a big plume of smoke. The boy in question got such a shock he jumped a mile in the air, leaving his boots behind. As I was telling my tale, Ronnie was leaning forward in his chair, nodding vigorously. 'Yes, yes, yes, that's right! That was me!'

I could hardly believe it. Especially when it then emerged that not only had Ronnie been the Flying Cadet, he was also my partner in crime in a prank that got us both into trouble. It turned out the colonel didn't see the funny side of us slipping that adder into his bath.

Those early shared experiences, although unrecognised at the time, were a significant factor in the strong bond that developed between Ronnie and myself. All four of us were great mates, but I always felt a special kinship with Ronnie.

I only pieced together the clues to Ronnie's illness after he was diagnosed, not long before I joined The Who.

Ronnie and I used to carry his mother in her wheelchair to and from the lifts in the block of flats where she lived. I was always happy to help whenever I was around, never thinking too much about what was wrong with Mrs Lane. Multiple sclerosis, I later learned. It may not be hereditary, but if it's in your close family's genes your chance of developing the disease significantly increases.

Ronnie was forgetful, even in the early days of the band. We'd have left a gig and be half way down the motorway, heading home, when he'd suddenly announce. 'Oh, we've got to go back. I've left me bass in the room.'

His memory might have been poor, but his speech and movement were generally fine in those days. Except occasionally, when he would slur his words or trip up for no apparent reason, often when he was tired. We naturally accused him of secretly hitting the bottle, which he would deny, growing quite angry if we went on too much. That anger was born of frustration, I now think. This was the early stages of the disease, I'm certain, although none of us, Ronnie included, recognised it as such.

It was during the recording sessions for Pete Townshend's album *Rough Mix*, released in 1977, that Ronnie's illness first began to have an impact on his bass playing, when he felt a numbness in his hands. Within a year or two he'd been officially diagnosed and, Ronnie being Ronnie, he set out to look for alternative methods to counter the debilitating effects of MS. He tried hyperbaric oxygen treatment – breathing pure oxygen in a pressurised tank – and flew to the States for a series of snake venom injections. Did any of it provide his sought-after respite? I doubt it.

In 1983, Ronnie asked Eric Clapton – a friend of Ronnie's and a regular visitor to Fishpool Farm – to help organise and play at a concert to raise awareness of MS and generate funds for research. Eric immediately agreed and approached Glyn Johns to produce the show. From there it quickly snowballed. I became involved, as did Charlie Watts, Ray Cooper, Jimmy Page, Jeff Beck, Chris Stainton, Steve Winwood, Andy Fairweather Low, Bill Wyman, Fernando Saunders, Paul Rodgers and others. In September, we put on two gigs at the Royal Albert Hall in London, the first in aid of Action into Research for Multiple Sclerosis (ARMS), the organisation Ronnie was supporting in the UK following his attempts to find new remedies, and the second a benefit concert for the Prince's Trust charity.

Charlie, Bill and myself were in the first unit on stage, with Eric, Andy and Steve, playing a selection of their songs and covers, followed by Jeff Beck's unit, then Jimmy Page. Jimmy hadn't played a major gig since Led Zeppelin's 1980 European tour, just before the band split up following John Bonham's death in the September of that year. Since then, Jimmy had become something of a recluse, certainly within the music world, which probably accounted for his nervousness at the ARMS gig, which he clearly took steps to overcome. Frankly, he was pretty much out of it, at one point playing his two-necked guitar with one hand on the upper neck, the other on the lower strings. Despite that slight mishap, Jimmy Page was Jimmy Page, brilliant on stage. I thought Jimmy was the bravest of all the guys involved in the ARMS concerts, because he was really putting himself on the line.

Rehearsals for the London shows had taken place at Glyn John's home studio in Warnham, West Sussex. There was a togetherness and purpose amongst all the musicians – we were taking it seriously but at the same time having a laugh, enjoying each other's company. That atmosphere extended to the pub up the road.

We were sitting there having a few beers by the window one afternoon when Jimmy joined us.

'What do you want to drink, Jimmy?'

'Eh ... give me a minute, I've forgotten something.'

With that he turned around and went back to his car, which was parked right outside the pub. What the hell's he doing? Peering through the window, we could see Jimmy sitting in the driver's seat, with his head down on his lap. At that moment, he must have accidently leaned forward a fraction, just enough for the top of his head to hit the horn. He got the fright of his life, shot bolt upright, and there he was staring at us, his face covered in a white, sparkling powder. Ah, that explains it.

By the time of the concert Ronnie was largely wheelchair-bound, unable to play any instrument. Seeing him in that condition was devastating. The madcap years of the Small Faces, with all the laughter and the nonsense were now a distant memory, but this was still Ronnie, physically weakened but just as strong in spirit. Backstage he listened to the music, loving it, nodding in appreciation, his boyish, cheeky grin just the same as always. Then at the end of the concert, he showed us all the real meaning of guts and determination. Following a rousing rendition of Eric Clapton's 'Layla', he walked out to join everyone and sing the closing number, 'Goodnight Irene'.

It had been intended as a one-off gig, but with the reaction being so positive, both from the public and all the musicians involved, and the fact that tens of thousands of pounds had been raised for a cause now dear to all our hearts, the decision was taken to reconvene for a short, intense US tour.

We opened in Dallas on 28 November. No one was being paid for their time, save for expenses. For me, that wasn't possible. For tax reasons, I wasn't allowed to work in America because The Who tour of the previous year had finished in late December, within 12 months of the ARMS concerts. That didn't worry me in the least, I was happy to do it buckshee, but I was very touched when, after it was all over, the guys clubbed together and bought Peter Blake's portrait of me as a gift, the one that appears on the *Face Dances* album. A classy gesture and I was grateful.

After two gigs in Dallas, we moved on to San Francisco for three nights, then two in LA and closed with two concerts at Madison Square Garden in New York, 8 and 9 December. Short and intense indeed. The only way to make that schedule possible was to hire a chartered jet, a customised Boeing 707. This was not exactly a regular plane. It had a room in the back containing a huge bed with a giant seatbelt over the top. That made me laugh. Plus a bar and separate areas where you could chill out in private. It was also a plane I knew well. The Who had used it for their tour, with the same crew.

The captain was a young guy, who we got to know quite well, as he and his crew mates would come along to the gigs. He used to write poetry which he read to us during the flights. A captive audience, if ever there was one.

Over the course of those two weeks I chatted with him on many topics, including my interest in flying. He'd clearly been paying attention. Approaching New York for those final two concerts, he offered me the opportunity to take the co-pilot's seat and fly the plane down the Hudson River. He explained it would be perfectly safe, he could take over at any time if necessary, but otherwise, I'd be flying. What an incredible thrill to be in control of such an aircraft, looking down on the Statue of Liberty. I got a huge kick out of that.

Some of the guys had to come in and out of the tour because of long-standing previous engagements, but essentially the line-up in the US was much the same as the Royal Albert Hall. Unfortunately, however, Steve Winwood had to pull out entirely due to prior commitments. Joe Cocker took his place.

Joe was a lovely guy and wonderful to play with. I've never felt so comfortable on stage as I did with Joe. I wanted to stay there for as long as possible. Everyone felt the same. It wasn't only that he was such a fantastic singer, he had an ability to make you feel sky-high when you were with him. He'd be smiling, pleasant, calm, happy – magical almost – complimenting you all the time with smiles and gestures. It's a wonderful gift that not many people possess.

On stage wasn't the only time Joe made you feel sky-high. On our plane he smoked one after another of what we called Jazz Woodbines: huge cigar-like joints, as thick as your thumb and twice as long, stuffed full of weed. He'd sit there quite happily, chatting away, blowing smoke all over whoever was next to him. I enjoyed the experience on a couple of occasions, arriving at those gigs stoned out of my head even though I hadn't had a single puff.

With the addition of Joe Cocker to the line-up, our US finale altered slightly from the Royal Albert Hall, in spectacular fashion. There couldn't have been a more appropriate song than 'With a Little Help from My Friends'. Eric Clapton, Jeff Beck, Jimmy Page on guitars, Bill Wyman on bass, myself, Charlie Watts, Ray Cooper and Simon Phillips all on drums, and everyone else backing vocals. And best of all, Joe's voice. As Ronnie said, 'To think that my having something so negative could result in something so positive.'

The nights, however, belonged to Ronnie, walking out for 'Goodnight Irene' to thunderous applause. The final concert at Madison Square Garden was hugely emotional. Ronnie and I hugged, smiled at each other and nodded in recognition of what we'd achieved. And not just on that tour. There was a bond connecting us that would never be broken.

ARMS was a happy tour. There were no egos, just a lot of fun and a lot of shopping – especially in San Francisco, where I came away with a number of snazzy new sports jackets and Eric Clapton with some comfy shoes and a new belt. Perhaps our wildest days were behind us. Incredibly, punctuality became a badge of honour. I'd never seen anything like it on tour. If the airport transport bus was leaving at nine o'clock sharp, everyone would be there at 8.59. Well, not quite everyone.

In LA, we were on the coach waiting to leave the hotel, but there was no sign of Jimmy Page. We waited and waited and eventually he turned up, dishevelled, debauched and hungover, with a bird on each arm. Thank God for Jimmy.

The tour was a big deal in the States, President Reagan even sent Ronnie a personal video message of congratulations afterwards, and we generated a lot of coverage, publicity and money for a very good cause. It's such a shame then, that the aftermath left a horribly bitter taste in the mouth.

The intention had been to use the money raised from the tour to set up a US equivalent of the ARMS UK organisation to fund MS research in the States. Ronnie played a leading role in this, even moving to Houston to support the new organisation. In late 1984 he hired a Houston-based attorney, Mae Nacol, to run ARMS America. From there everything went downhill, and it took a terrible toll on Ronnie. The Texas State University received a chunk of the millions raised, but the rest seemed to disappear in fees, salaries, expenses and God knows what else. I have no idea what happened, I'm not sure anyone really does, but a year or so later the Texas Attorney General's Office stepped in amidst allegations of mismanagement of funds, leading to the closure of ARMS America. Ronnie became embroiled in all this, even, I understand, facing a lawsuit for libel and defamation of character from Nacol. Eventually, out-of-court settlements ended the fiasco, leaving Ronnie embarrassed that he'd let his friends down. Not a single person thought that, but he took it hard.

When ARMS American collapsed, Ronnie and his wife Susan quickly relocated to Austin, Texas, and then later to Trinidad, a town in the Rocky Mountains of Colorado. By this stage he was struggling financially, unable any longer to make a living out of the one thing he loved the most, his music. All the boys contributed to his medical bills, with Rod and Woody taking the lead in that, while I fought hard to wrestle back royalties owed to the Small Faces, eventually achieving a degree of success and some income for Ronnie.

In 1994, Mac also moved to Austin, and I'm sure he hoped to see more of his old friend, to help him out, but it was shortly after Mac's arrival that Ronnie and Susan moved to Colorado. Mac, however, did manage to keep in touch to some extent, and would call me up with reports of Ronnie's deteriorating health. That's when I started to call Ronnie at least once a week. It was heartbreaking. He was virtually paralysed and couldn't breathe properly.

I could hear him straining, and so I'd talk away, answering questions as if he had asked me something. I'd tell a joke and Susan would come on to say Ronnie was laughing. I could picture his smile. Then he would try and talk, but he could barely say a word. Horrible. I'd come off the phone and cry. One of my best mates, once so full of life, now so diminished.

I knew it was coming, I tried to steel myself for the moment, but when Mac called to say Ronnie had gone, I found I wasn't prepared at all.

The boss of A&M Records, Derek Green, asked if I would give a eulogy for Ronnie at a Nordoff-Robbins Music Therapy fundraising event that Derek was organising. I really don't enjoy public speaking, I'm very shy, but of course I said I would. I was honoured. Clapton was there, Wyman, Woody, Elvis Costello, George Michael – a star-studded line-up.

I didn't write anything down, deciding instead to speak from my heart, to try and explain a few things about Ronnie, what I felt about him. Ronnie had given the world so much joy through his music, but more than that, I said, in my opinion he was one of the bravest men I had ever met. Suffering from such a devastating disease, Ronnie could have just thought, 'Fuck this, I'm off, I can't take it,' but instead he battled on, campaigning on behalf of fellow MS sufferers while dealing privately with his own pain. That's how I saw him. A man who never gave up. I don't know how he found the strength. I could hardly speak towards the end, but as I began to struggle, Eric Clapton gave me a thumbs up and mouthed, 'You're doing great'. That helped me make it through.

Afterwards, Woody came over, dumbfounded. 'I have never heard you sound so profound, Kenney.'

'What's that mean?'

Ronnie was very popular, a good man, funny, with a dry sense of humour and held in high regard by the music world. After the eulogy I spoke to many of the people in that room and they all recognised Ronnie's huge talent as a singer, bass player and songwriter. He'd have found that strange. He always felt inferior.

'Compared to all these famous people,' he would have said, 'I'm just a normal bloke.'

* * *

Mac and I bonded in the early days when Steve and Ronnie would elbow us out when they were in their songwriting mode. Fine, we'll go to the pub. You know where to find us.

Mac was very funny, and smart, but also probably the most serious member of the band. He'd take things to heart, let them get to him, then moan about it.

Perhaps the issue that put Mac's back up most was money. Mainly because he spent it like mad. On himself.

He met his first wife, Sandy Sarjeant, on the set of *Ready Steady Go!*. She was a dancer on the show and when Mac saw her, back in November 1966, he fell instantly in love. They married quietly a year or so later and were happy together for a while, but Mac can't have been an easy person to live with. Whenever I went over to their place for a visit, I could be sure what was on the menu for dinner. Beans on toast. That's all they ever had in because Mac would have spent their money on records. Then he'd be up all night listening to them, spending the next day in bed. Steve was similar in that regard.

When Sandy and Mac divorced, none of us were surprised.

Mac was a great one for falling head over heels. When at the end of 1972 Ronnie Lane left his first wife, Sue, for Katie McInnerney, Sue moved to Canada and Mac became besotted. He flew over to see her. They had a fling, and then she gave Mac the elbow, leaving him upset and unhappy in love. Again.

A few years later, however, he did meet the love of his life. Keith Moon's ex-wife Kim. They married in 1978 and moved to California, then Austin. Their happy marriage lasted 28 years, until on the morning of 2 August 2006, as Kim was driving to work, she took a second to check her phone messages, ran a red light and smashed into a truck. She died instantly.

Kim's death threw Mac completely. He told me that it was impossible for him to get over it. He was right, he never did.

Mac's death came out of the blue. I'm still struggling to deal with it. Weeks before he'd been in my house, talking about getting the Faces back together. He was his normal self. Having a moan. Having a laugh. Being funny.

It was the morning of 3 December 2014. A Wednesday. I was in the car, all set for a very happy day. First I was dropping off my daughter Erin at college, and from there I was off to the local hospital to see my elder daughter Casey's newborn, my first grandson. Just before I dropped off Erin, the phone rang. Mac's son, Lee. 'I've got some bad news, Kenney. Dad died last night, in the early morning.'

Seconds before I'd been full of the joys of spring, elated at having a grandson, and suddenly, Bang. Mac was gone. I didn't know what to do. I didn't know if I could drive. Erin was very concerned for me. She'd heard Lee's call and seen my body slump. I made it to the hospital to meet a wonderful little boy, Zac, with tears in my eyes. Happiness and despair. They are never very far apart.

Later I worked out that my grandson had been born at exactly the same moment Mac passed away. I sometimes feel like some of Mac's spirit is in little Zac – he can be a gorgeous tearaway.

* * *

I'm always thinking about our time together in the Small Faces – it never leaves me. Not because I live in the past or wallow in nostalgia. It never leaves me because it affects my everyday life.

For many years I've been on a quest, the only one of us to do so, trying to recover our royalties, correct the wrongs of the past and reclaim our music. Steve died too young, Ronnie's illness made his involvement impossible, and Mac gave up years ago. I won't let it go. I'm a little terrier. Someone once told me that the paper trail in situations like this is always too complicated to follow, and that's why they get away with it. 'Fuck the paper trail.' It's our legacy. Steve, Ronnie, Mac, me.

It's complex and ongoing, but the key elements are as follows.

A critical issue is that we never signed away our rights, the control of the songs and the recordings. We agreed standard contracts with Don Arden, in which we received a peppercorn royalty, while the copyright in our recordings sat for a limited period – our agreement lasted for three years plus a possible two-year extension – with Arden's company, Contemporary Records (or possibly Decca, that was never absolutely clear). It was messy, certainly. Control of the songs then passed through a string of corporate hands, but we always had a strong claim to regain the rights, because we'd never given them away completely – only during the time when the Arden contracts were in force. When I joined The Who, they had gone through something similar, but because the band stayed together, they worked through the problems, rode them out. If you don't stick together, you kind of give up and if you join another band, you can forget your past. We were guilty of that.

It was only when the concept of 'sleeping on your rights' was explained to me in the 1970s that I started to take action. If you don't do anything with your rights, if you don't take some action, you can lose them. Eventually they lapse. Fuck that. There was no way we were going to allow that to happen. We brought in lawyers, even though we knew we weren't going to get anywhere. That didn't really matter. The point was to remove any possibility of being accused of sleeping on our rights. We were creating our own paper trail.

Around 1992/93 I explained all this to my then accountant, John Cousins, and he fixed up a meeting with Terry Shand, owner of Castle Communications, who by then controlled the copyright to our back catalogue. They acquired it from NEMS, which in turn had been bought in 1972 by a company part-owned by Pat Meehan Jr, son of Don Arden's right-hand man. So for a while, the little guy we took around with us for fun in the early days of the Small Faces ended up controlling our songs.

Initially I told John I had no intention of talking to Terry Shand. I felt he was screwing us by holding the copyright and paying a pittance, to keep it all legal. Why should I go to him? In time, however, I changed my mind. A meeting was the only way to move the situation forward, to our benefit.

Throughout the morning at Castle's office I remained stern and stand-offish. Perhaps to break the ice, it was suggested we go to lunch. I wasn't at all happy about that, lunching with the enemy. However, I knew it was the right thing to do, to keep the discussion going, so off we went, to a French restaurant near Chessington Zoo, one I used to go to years ago. A good omen?

We were making small talk at the restaurant when Terry Shand turned to me and said, 'What's your wish list?' 'I wish you'd give me back the fucking catalogue.' At that point it all kicked off, very heated, me standing up and jabbing my finger at Terry. John Cousins had to restrain me.

Terry then said something that surprised me, he explained he hadn't realised how bad our situation was, and that as he was now looking to sell the company he wanted to put it right. Okay. Good. We started talking, there in the restaurant and back at the office. Eventually lawyers were talking to lawyers, accountants to accountants and it was becoming complicated. Then Terry made another good move. He called me as I was cutting the grass on one of the fields at the polo club.

'Kenney, this is crazy. We should get together and sort this out ourselves.'

'Let's start right now.' We began negotiating. He made an offer, I countered. On it went, up to £250,000. Once I'd achieved that, I knew I could double it.

Throughout this period, I'd been keeping Mac informed, and spoke to him about Terry's offer. Quarter of a million, plus a new royalty of 15 per cent. Mac was dead keen on accepting. He'd never seen that much money before, he said. I was convinced we could go further, we hadn't even involved auditors yet. I urged Mac to hold off, to see what I could do.

Then my dad was taken ill, diagnosed with leukaemia. He died a few days after being admitted to hospital.

I was with Dad right at the end. We had all been in to see him the day before – my kids, Mum, Jayne, everyone important to him. As we were preparing to head home I suddenly felt this strong sense that I shouldn't leave him. It's not like me at all to stay overnight anywhere if I can avoid it. I like my own bed and I certainly don't like hospitals, but that night I couldn't bear the thought of Dad being on his own. I had to be with him.

I sat in an armchair beside his bed. I made myself comfortable, the nurse gave me a blanket and I settled down for the night. Now and again, I woke up to Dad asking for a sip of water. I held the glass to his lips. 'I'm here Dad, whenever you need me. Right next to you.'

That kept on throughout the night until around four or five in the morning. I remember it was still dark outside when Dad started to talk, as though he was speaking to someone, but not me. I don't know if he was awake or dreaming or somewhere in between, but he was definitely talking. I didn't disturb him, until after a few minutes he called out.

'Kenney, Kenney, I need to go to the loo.'

Dad was a big man, but I managed to sit him up at the side of the bed, ready to get him on his feet. Although he was very weak, he could still walk, with help.

I was standing in front of him when he looked up at me, our eyes connected, and he put his arms around my neck. Then he collapsed, as if he was falling right through me. I could barely hold him up.

'Dad, Dad, I've got you. I've got you.'

I managed to cradle him in my arms and gently lower him on to the floor, at which point I immediately called the nurse. Dad was finding it hard to breathe. I knew what was happening. 'Dad, Dad, don't go. Please don't leave me.' He was fighting so hard to stay alive, to please me. But he couldn't hold on any longer. Quietly, he slipped away.

Under those circumstances, I couldn't face any further business negotiations. Even though I felt we were settling too early, I agreed to Mac's request. We accepted the deal on the table. Terry Shand had done the decent thing, eventually. I appreciated that and we've become friends.

That situation lasted for a year, until Castle was indeed sold to a North American company, and then again to Sanctuary Records. They had a good group there, Johnny Chandler and his team were passionate about the project and began to reinvigorate the catalogue through re-mastered albums, reissues, all that. Good ideas and a decent marketing budget meant we began receiving royalties. Not only that, but as a result of one of the other key points I'd negotiated, we had joint creative control. That meant they were required to call me and Mac, and through us, Ronnie, to approve all their plans. It felt like we had our music back again. At least in part. In 2007, Sanctuary was bought by Universal, and it's now under the Universal label that Johnny Chandler and I continue to work on new and exciting ideas for the catalogue.

I've enjoyed an unexpected bonus from being so heavily involved in breathing new life into the Small Faces music. I've eventually become a fan.

For a long time after we split I couldn't listen to the records. Not because they brought back bad memories, it's that I couldn't bear the thought of listening to a series of mistakes. When I was playing, all I could hear were my imperfections as timekeeper. In those days, you didn't have click tracks in headphones or anything like that to help you. You had 'feel' and 'emotion'. Those are the most important elements, but at the time I was paranoid. I kept thinking there were certain little things I could have done better. Now, I wouldn't change a thing. Those slight imperfections make the music real.

Looking at our performances and listening to our records now, I think, 'Okay, I get it'. I'm not really aware of me, as the individual I was then, instead I hear a drummer with swing and a strong beat, playing on great songs with a great band. I'm pleased to have finally arrived at that point.

There are many other additional complications in relation to our rights and control.

Way back, one of the things we did get right, thanks to Andrew Oldham's advice when we signed with Immediate, was to set up the music publishing company Avakak. Our music rights were assigned to this company in March 1967, in an amendment to our original Immediate contract. The four of us were equal stakeholders, with Andrew and his partner Tony Calder also holding shares, which they gave up when Immediate folded. All those shares combined amounted to around 70 per cent of the company. Then when the Small Faces finished we sort of forgot about Avakak. The cheques weren't coming in (they should have been) and I was distracted by earning a bit more money with the Faces. I kept thinking I'd get around to sorting it out, but never quite did at the time. However, for the past 25 years or so, I've been investigating various avenues to reclaim our company. It's a tangled situation.

Following a series of corporate acquisitions over the years, EMI ended up with what I believe is our slice of Avakak. Uncovering that Avakak paper trail proved to be a long, laborious process. Back in the 1990s, I received assistance in the task from the Performing Rights Society, and a guy called Chris France, who was helping me chase our missing royalties. Having tracked down those Avakak shares, and therefore rights in the Small Faces catalogue, we attempted to show they should sit with us alone. At the time, however, it wasn't possible to make our case and we had to park the claim. That is still very much in my mind, however, and I am continuing to pursue those rights, even though EMI's music and publishing arms have since been sold separately. I'm not giving up.

Chasing down our rights can be a tortuous business, but I will never stop. Ronnie, Steve and Mac deserve nothing less.

There will always be but four Small Faces.

CHAPTER 15

A STORK'S TALE

An unexpected consequence of the ARMS concerts was reconnecting with Paul Rodgers, of Free and Bad Company.

By the time of the rehearsals for the Royal Albert Hall gigs, The Who had all but collapsed, and I was looking for a fresh musical challenge. I'd known Paul for years, Free had supported the Faces on one of our US tours, but it was during that ARMS period that we properly spent time together.

Shortly after the US tour, our paths crossed again at Tramp nightclub.

'Ah, Kenney, just the man I want to talk to.'

'What's up, Paul?'

'Fancy having a play together?'

'Sure.'

From there, we progressed slowly. Initially only jamming together intermittently over a number of years, having fun, whenever our busy diaries allowed. Eventually, around the tail-end of 1988, it reached a point when we realised we weren't just enjoying ourselves, we were loving it. Time to take this to the next stage.

We decided to form a band, but what the hell were we going to call ourselves? We went back and forth with possibilities, until out of the blue it came to me. I called up Paul. 'I think I've got it – The Law.' A short, punchy word, that would look great on an album sleeve.

Following Paul's positive reaction, I continued. 'I've also got this song title that's been buzzing around and around my head, 'Laying Down the Law'. What'd ya think?'

'Great. Leave it with me.'

By the next day, Paul had written the skeleton of a song, which we then worked on together. It ended up reaching the top of the rock charts in the US.

Our primary purpose in forming The Law was to enjoy ourselves, free from the usual band pressures, so we decided to work alongside a series of top-class musicians to produce our eponymous album, people such as Dave Gilmour, Chris Rea, Bryan Adams and Def Leppard's Phil Collen. We didn't rush anything, if one of our collaborators wasn't available, fine, we'll wait. Those were the origins and the ethos behind the band. Fun, not stress. The resultant album, released in 1991, was great, timeless, every song commercially sound and great quality. No fillers – that's always been very important to me.

We'd done what we wanted to do: create a successful band, have a number-one single and enjoy the process. That had been the intention behind the project from the start and that's what we stuck to. One album. Done. Move on to the next thing, which in my case wasn't music-related.

* * *

I didn't find polo; it found me. It's a wonderful sport – football on horseback, a fabulous combination.

Bryan Morrison, who I am very sad to say died in 2008 having collapsed into a coma at a polo match a couple of years earlier, was a music publisher who over the course of his career in the 1960s and '70s represented bands such as The Pretty Things, Pink Floyd and the Bee Gees, and later Wham! and George Michael in the 1980s. In the mid 1970s, he also managed a fashion designer, Bill Gibb. That's how I first met Bryan, at the champagne reception to celebrate the opening of Bill's new Bond Street shop.

Bryan introduced himself as a fan of the Small Faces, and as we chatted our conversation turned to horses. I expressed my enthusiasm, telling Bryan that I had always had two hobbies in life. One was drumming and the other riding. One I earn money from, I said, the other has kept me sane. I explained I'd been riding for years, and more recently had tried hunting and, through that, showjumping.

Bobby Stone, the lovely woman who owned those stables that Steve Marriott had taken us to all those years ago, and who went on to be head of the Pony Club, introduced me to both activities. Through Bobby I rode with a hunt in Essex, and after she'd seen me tackle the hedges and ditches, she suggested I come along to her indoor school and try my hand at some jumping. Sure. Once I'd tamed Bobby's fences (hers was a crash course, literally for me at the beginning) word soon spread that I could handle a horse. The equestrian world is relatively small, and as Bobby was good friends with some big-time showjumpers, I began to receive invitations to events. In between band commitments, I participated in as many as I could, which in time led to appearances at the International Showjumping Championships, then staged annually at London's Olympia exhibition centre in the run-up to Christmas.

That was a few years in the future. Back at the drinks reception, Bryan suggested I join him at the Old Berks Hunt near the village of Bucklebury in Berkshire. A fantastic experience. I found countryside riding exhilarating, but most of all I loved sharing a tipple or two with Bryan. Tex Ritter once sang about spurs that jingle jangle jingled. With Bryan and I, it was hipflasks. You could hear us coming a mile off.

Bryan also mentioned that he had recently taken up polo, at Ham Polo Club, around the corner from Kingston Hill where I was living. He invited me to come along, but I declined. What's the point, that's a posh game, they'll never let the likes of me in there. I'm from the East End. 'Don't worry,' Bryan countered, 'so am I.' Alright then, fuck it. I'm up for it.

By chance, on the day I took up Bryan's invitation in March 1976, Ginger Baker, Cream's drummer, was also at Ham, learning to ride and play. A crazy coincidence, as crazy as Ginger himself. As I was being instructed in the various techniques of the sport, from time to time I'd hear a wild cry in the distance, and turning in my saddle I'd see Ginger, either on his arse, or madly chasing after his horse, polo stick in hand, the tassels of his Wild Bill Hickok jacket flowing behind him. It was lovely to see Ginger again. We had a good old natter, once he'd caught his breath and soothed his bruised bum from all those falls.

I took to polo naturally. The co-ordination of a drummer, like when flying helicopters, worked well with what turned out to be a good eye for the ball. I hit it 17 times in a row on that first Ham visit. That was something of a surprise. I'd never really been very sporty when I was younger. I liked playing football as a kid, usually over at Shadwell Park, but my career ended abruptly following one match in which I thought I was doing great, everyone shouting and cheering me on as I slotted the ball home. Into my own goal.

I enjoyed my introduction to polo, but knew it was unrealistic to take it much further. I didn't have the time to look after the four polo ponies that would have been required. Showjumping more than adequately satisfied my equestrian appetite during that period of my life.

Many years later, in the mid-1980s, I bumped into Bryan and his wife Greta in Tramp. Where else? We had continued socialising over the years, with Bryan regularly on at me to try polo again. I'd explained my situation, but he persisted. Now with The Who behind me, things were different, even more so when Bryan explained that he had recently bought some land and was in the process of establishing his own club, which went on to become The Royal County of Berkshire Polo Club, near Windsor. Bryan invited me over to take a look at the fields already laid, and said he'd be delighted if I would agree to becoming an honourary member. I told him I'd think about it seriously, at which point Greta leaned across the table towards me.

'Kenney, you really have to do it this time. You have the talent, but soon you'll be too old. This is the moment. Take it.'

I'm so pleased I followed Greta's advice. Although it had been something like 15 years since I'd held a polo mallet, once again I took to the game like a duck to water. Over that summer season I was at Bryan's club virtually every day, playing for the team there.

Since then, polo has featured very prominently, and very happily, in my life and that of my family. Two of my sons, Jay and Cody, have played professionally, Cody still does – summers here and winters in New Zealand. I took part in many tournaments over the years, reaching a one-goal handicap, which is pretty good, given that only a handful of players every attain a three-goal or better rating (the scale starts at minus two, and goes up to 10 – there are only a dozen or so players in the world with that handicap).

Polo seems to attract drummers. Stewart Copeland of the Police also played, and along with Mike Rutherford in the late 1980s and into the '90s we teamed up for matches for Cartier around the UK and at Palm Beach and Santa Barbara in the States. We tried to enlist Roger Taylor of Queen, introducing him to the sport at a match at the Kirtlington Park Club in Oxfordshire. He seemed keen, initially, until one of the players unfortunately took a tumble and broke an arm. 'Not bloody likely,' was Roger's succinct response to our offer.

Throughout those years of playing, it never crossed my mind to own a polo ground. I was enjoying the competition and camaraderie, that was more than enough. But, as with the game itself, although I wasn't looking for a club, a club found me.

Jayne and I had recently moved into a new house, tucked away in rural Surrey with our family – Casey and Jay then. Our mail box was located at the bottom of our front path, and standing there with Jayne one morning, I opened an envelope containing a nice fat royalty cheque, just as Jayne was reading a letter from the estate agent who had helped with the house purchase. Apparently, the land adjacent to our property, 181 acres, was about to go on the market. Were we interested?

It was set-aside land, wild, covered in bindweed, ragwort, nettles and docks, brambles and gorse. Completely overgrown. Of course we're interested.

There go the royalties.

Our thinking at the time was to view the purchase as a longer-term investment. I liked the idea of owning the land next to us, and perhaps, down the line, I could think about development. That appealed, but beyond those vague notions there wasn't a plan. Until I was showing a mate around.

'You know what Kenney, this would make a cracking golf course.'

Interesting.

We drew up plans. Submitted them. Rejected. To be fair, the clubhouse we were proposing was dreadful.

A better idea began to form. By then Jayne and I had already organised a charity polo event to raise funds for a local children's playground. The day had been a great success. Actress Stefanie Powers lent some very welcome showbiz glamour to the match, and around 750 people attended. A seed had been sown. We could take this further, much further. I went back to the planners and admitted that I really didn't know why on earth I'd suggested a golf course, given that I didn't even play the game. Polo was my sport. That attracted their attention. Time to turn on a bit of charm. I confessed that I agreed with their comments on the original club-house plan, it had been an inappropriate design, but I was now thinking of something different. More in keeping with the area.

I explained I'd recently saved a 400-year-old barn that had once stood in the local area, with the original beams now in storage, painstakingly numbered and preserved. I then went on to outline my vision of re-erecting that barn on the site, refurbished with a modern bar and restaurant, revitalising a piece of Surrey history that would otherwise have been lost.

My only problem was that I couldn't decide the best location. At that point, one of the planning officers pointed to a spot on the plans. 'We would put it here.'

Gotcha.

With planning approved, we set to work. The enterprise took two years to complete.

First, we had to kill off all the weeds in the fields, then remove the topsoil to gain access to the flint beneath. That was extracted by a large digger, which I drove myself. I found that exciting and fulfilling, handling a full-size Tonka truck. I'm just a big kid at heart. What the machine couldn't dig out, we removed by hand. Local farmers provided invaluable assistance throughout this period. With the six fields now flat and clear, the topsoil was replaced, the grass sown and a thousand tonnes of sand spread over each field. That's a twice-a-year job, at the start and end of each season, to ensure good drainage and the best possible playing surface. Over the years we have deposited hundreds of thousands of tonnes of sand at Hurtwood Park. I sometimes think there must be more there than on Southend beach. It all cost a fortune. A lot of the money I've earned is in those polo fields.

Right from the beginning, once I'd decided on creating a polo club, I'd been able to envisage it exactly. That's how my mind works. I saw the position of the playing fields, the car park and the sweep of the road, constructed from rubble that was once Dorking Hospital. I had also imagined the clubhouse, exactly where the planning committee suggested. Their assessment had been spot on, given the topography of the site and position of surrounding residences. Myself and my great friend Colin Woods, an airline pilot and part-time architect, worked on the plans for the interior together. As with the layout of the grounds in general, I had the barn clear in my head. I knew precisely how I wanted it to look, and Colin had the skills to translate that on to the page. His coaching was also invaluable in helping me develop, at least temporarily, the most essential attribute when dealing with planning applications. Patience. Not something that comes naturally.

The barn was the last addition. Hurtwood Park Polo Club opened in 1994 with a temporary marquee clubhouse, the permanent structure completed three years later.

It was great fun erecting that barn. Digging out trenches for the foundations with the giant Tonka truck, which by then I'd become very proficient in handling, then carefully reconstructing the outer shell, just as it had originally looked. Walking up and down those fields carrying all the materials I lost a considerable amount of weight, and loved every moment.

I'm a practical person, I like achieving things, being outside and active, exploring. We came across long-lost apple trees and rediscovered ancient woodland. I found myself magically back in Kent, hop-picking and scrumping. Wonderful. I never wanted to go to sleep. During those years, the fields were my home.

When it was all finally completed, I remember walking around the perimeter, taking in everything we had achieved. My mind strayed back to that day at the Ruskin Arms, the day we were supposed to be rehearsing. If the weather hadn't been hot, if Marriott hadn't suggested bunking off, I might never have discovered my love of horses, and the polo ground might never have been built.

Prince Charles and his sons have played at Hurtwood Park many times. He has a lovely dry sense of humour and excellent comic timing. We were in a match together and our team won, meaning someone had to go up and accept the trophy.

Prince Charles said, 'Kenney, Kenney, are, are you going to get the cup?'

'No Sir, I think you should. You are our guest here.'

'No, no. You pick it up Kenney.'

One of our other team mates, Martin Brown, offered to do the deed, but Prince Charles was having none of it. 'This is your club Kenney, I think you should be awarded the cup.'

This kept going around and around, and before you knew it we were having a friendly argument. 'You pick it up.' 'No, you're the one.' Eventually I said, 'Sir, I really think it should be you, as honoured guest of the club.'

Prince Charles then looked at me, slowly raised his eyebrows, and smiled. 'Bad luck Kenney.' As heir to the throne, he has the last word. We fell about laughing. And, of course, I picked up the cup.

On a separate occasion, I happened to mention to Prince Charles that I'd heard he was a massive fan of the 1950's radio comedy, *The Goon Show*. When I first learned of Prince Charles's love of that programme, it made me smile. It still does. I am just two months older and I like to imagine us as two young boys, each sitting at home, tuning in the radio to catch up on the latest antics of Neddie Seagoon, Eccles and Bluebottle. Two lads laughing at the same sketches, one in Buckingham Palace, the other in London's East End. The prince and the pauper. I also understood that he had a large private collection of recordings.

'Yes, that's correct Kenney. I do.'

'Fantastic,' I said. 'I'd love a copy Sir, if possible.'

Up went the eyebrows again. 'Would you?' No copy for me, then.

Not everything went quite as Prince Charles might have wished at Hurtwood. Polo is a dirty, sweaty game. A few moments tidying up to make yourself halfway decent before the presentations is essential. I was over by my horsebox, parked next to Prince Charles's, towelling down and thought I'd better have a quick pee before the start of the formalities. My son Jay, who would have been about 12 at the time, was sitting on the fence opposite, looking down the line of boxes.

As club owner, it was customary for me to accompany Prince Charles as he walked across the polo field, with the crowds milling around, on his way to the prize-giving. I didn't want to miss him, so I called out to Jay, 'Has Prince Charles left yet?'

From directly behind me I heard, 'No, Prince Charles is right here.' I was so startled, I turned around mid-wee, very nearly splashing the toes of Prince Charles's boots. He and his security guys dissolved into fits of laughter.

Prince Charles gave up polo a few years ago, having been a great supporter of our club, for which we have always been very grateful. We still occasionally meet, at charity events and the like, and whenever we do, he smiles and says, 'Ah, Kenney. Are you still playing the drums?' And I reply, with a smile, 'Yes, I am Sir. Are you still playing the cello?' I used to laugh with him about a television interview I remember watching. He was a young man then, playing the cello. Sitting next to him was his younger brother, when ping, one of Prince Charles's strings snapped, hitting Prince Andrew smack in the eye.

* * *

On 27 July 2001, Hurtwood Park hosted a very special occasion. That morning, after 21 happy years together and four wonderful children, and following the legalities at the local register office, Jayne and I had our marriage blessed at St Nicolas Church in the Surrey village of Cranleigh. We were joined by 200 guests and a grinning Cheshire Cat, carved into a pillar in the church and reputedly Lewis Carroll's inspiration for the character in *Alice in Wonderland*. After the ceremony, our families, including our four kids, my mum Violet and Jayne's parents Stuart and Joan, plus my boys Dylan and Jesse, together with all the guests, congregated in our clubhouse for a champagne reception followed by a three-course meal in huge marquee. Jam roly-poly was on the menu. I couldn't have been happier.

It was a very special day for us both. As I said at the time, 'This marriage has been a long time coming, but we have finally got it right.' The comedian Jim Davidson took on best man responsibilities, jokingly spending most of the morning trying to talk me out of going through with it, and guests included Mike Rutherford and his wife Angie, Oliver Tobias (who read from the *Song of Solomon*) and his wife Arabella, John and Kirsten Lodge, Paul and Stacey Young, Zak Starkey, Stefanie Powers, David Essex, Bill Curbishley, Bryan and Greta Morrison, cousin Roy and a coach full of family and mates from the East End. So many different aspects of my life in one place. Friends old and new, music and polo, Stepney and Surrey, Canada and Britain. And Jayne, stunning. A perfect day.

It seemed impossible that 21 years had passed since I picked Jayne up at Heathrow airport, to start our lives together. That didn't exactly go according to plan, the picking her up bit I mean, not the sharing our lives. That's been everything I could have hoped for.

My intention had been to go low-key, to forget the rock star image and be standing at Arrivals with my Volkswagen Golf outside, just plain old Kenney Jones. Admittedly, wearing pink cowboy boots.

The best laid plans, and all that. The night before I had been at Tramp nightclub (naturally), where I was being very sensible. My intention was to drive the Golf to Heathrow that evening, and stay overnight in the airport hotel, to be on location to meet Jayne early the next day. I left the club around midnight, and was driving west down Piccadilly when, Smack, my front left wheel crunched into an open manhole, mangling the suspension. I managed to limp the car around the corner, ironically into Half Moon Street, where I abandoned it with a note outlining what had happened and jumped in a cab to the airport.

At reception, I explained I needed a car first thing in the morning, to pick up Jayne. No problem at all, Sir. It will be waiting for you. Great. At the crack of dawn next day sure enough, there was my car. A nice under-stated, non-ostentatious, simple ... Rolls-Royce. The guy at reception had recognised me and assumed that's what I would want.

Not exactly the low-key welcome I'd been planning. Nor were the next few hours. Having dropped off Jayne's bags, I asked her what she fancied doing on her first day in England.

'I don't know. It's your country, not mine.'

'Right. Eh, I know. Polo.'

'What the hell's polo?'

'You'll see. Come on.'

We drove to Windsor Great Park where the Dunhill International, now the Cartier, was underway. A full house. Tickets only. Ah.

That wasn't going to stop us. A few minutes later, following a leg-up for Jayne and a bit of scrambling from me, we were over the fence and in, and quickly being followed by paparazzi, keen to snap The Who's new drummer. Good job Kenney. Nice and low-key again.

We eventually shook them off, and wandering around the event we came across Bryan Morrison's corporate tent, where we were duly invited into to join his party. Champagne, chukkas and canapés. Welcome to England, Jayne.

* * *

Buying that land and creating Hurtwood Park Polo Club has been wonderfully positive for me. My confidence in business has grown and I feel I've created something of a legacy. Our dream for the club has always been to foster an atmosphere of openness and accessibility to the sport. Hurtwood has never been an elitist club, that's just not our style. It's a family business and that ethos runs through everything we do. Right from the beginning, we've viewed polo as an inclusive sport, encouraging young kids and novices to give it a go, while at the same time creating facilities – our playing fields were recently awarded a High Goal certificate, the top grade – that attract the world's best players.

It hasn't all been plain sailing, however. Over recent years I've experienced some frustrations as I've been looking to find ways of securing Hurtwood's financial future through further development. So far, the plans have been knocked back. It's a maddening situation, as far as I am concerned. It's the waiting, the hanging around for the decisions, that gets to me. And then not being able to do anything much about it when the rejections come through.

As I mentioned in relation to my prostate cancer, if I have a problem or a situation that must be dealt with, such as the club's future direction in this case, I want it solved immediately. Get the problem out of the way, move on to the next stage. If that doesn't happen, it can drive me nuts. I find it very hard to compartmentalise. I can't put whatever is happening to one side and blithely carry on as if everything is rosy. 'Hello, lovely to meet you. How are you? Me? I'm fine.' I can't play that game.

It means I can be a bit of an arse at times, I know that. It's just that I hate waiting, for good or bad. I want whatever is going to happen, to happen now. That's what I've always been like. The banjo. The first drum kit. I was spoilt by my parents with love, and I'm impatient. There's a Queen song that makes me laugh every time I hear it. They are singing about me: 'I want it all, and I want it now.'

As I was building the polo club during the 1990s, I used to hear a lot of snide remarks suggesting I'd given up music in favour of horses. It used to infuriate me. Can't I do both?

The answer is, yes.

Throughout that period, I'd always been making music, primarily at small charity gigs at the club with different groups of musicians. Then around 2000, I was asked to support a local school in some fundraising. I put a band together, including Roxy Music guitarist Phil Manzanera and Boz Burrell (he still didn't look anything like Mac!), who had most recently been playing bass with Bad Company. A one-off, and a lot of fun.

Over the following year or so I received several similar requests, which I happily agreed to whenever possible, playing with a variety of line-ups. For one of these events, we were short of a singer. I asked Boz if he knew anyone, and he suggested a guy who'd been in Bad Company, Robert Hart, who he swore was a better singer than Paul Rodgers. High praise. I decided to go along and see Robert in action. Boz was spot on, Robert Hart was great.

Robert agreed to play at that charity do, along with my old mate Gary Grainger, a member of the band I almost formed with Rod Stewart and who went on to co-write 'Hot Legs'. There was a good vibe around the gig, we were hitting it off. That got me thinking. Could this go further? We spoke about it and agreed to give it a go. 'And if becomes a hassle,' we all agreed, 'we'll ditch it.'

We enlisted another old pal, Rick Wills from Foreigner and briefly the 1970s incarnation of the Small Faces, and by the autumn of 2002 we were in the studio, recording some material, including a song that Robert and I worked on together that caused quite a stir. Mentioned in Parliament. Banned by the BBC. Just like the old days.

The song was called 'Mr Brown', not actually written about the then Chancellor of the Exchequer Gordon Brown, but as the lyrics seemed to fit, the song was quickly adopted by the media and portrayed as exactly that. A modern-day protest song taking a swipe at stealth taxation. So I was told.

'Mr Brown, you're robbing me. You're unattached emotionally. Is there a colour to the sky in your world? You give with one hand and take with the other.'

Powerful stuff. Which couldn't be played on the BBC. Too political. So I was told.

I had a lot of fun being interviewed about the track, happily playing up the protest-song angle. Why let the truth get in the way of a good tale? Then in a further bizarre twist, the lyrics were quoted back to Gordon Brown during the parliamentary debate after his Budget speech, which I suspect did not please him. I was glad to have all my taxes in good order, in case he decided to set the Revenue on me.

The following year, around March, we made our live debut in Guildford for a fun night of Small Faces, Rod, Faces, Who and Foreigner covers, under the name ... Big Face. That couldn't last.

By summer we were The Jones Gang, the core of which was Robert, Rick and myself. Robert and I started writing songs together, which resulted in the 2005 album, *Any Day Now*, and single 'Angel' in September. I thought we would struggle for airplay, particularly in the States, but I was wrong. 'Angel' proved to be a hit, reaching number one in the US. It was great to be back in the limelight. Clearly, when Americans adopt you, they adopt you for life. That felt good. Not bad for a bloke whose only interest, apparently, is horses.

Music continues to play the biggest role in my life, outside of family. The Jones Gang thrives, with a fluid line-up that suits everyone who is involved. We perform at charity events and one-off gigs across the country. The challenge is finding the time in between all the other projects I'm juggling, including playing in other bands, more at the social end of the spectrum, plus working on the concept and script for an animated film of *Ogdens' Nut*

Gone Flake, charting Happiness Stan's adventures as he searches for the other half of the moon, and re-interpreting that album with a classical score for concert performances. Then there's always the possibility, if the time proves right for everyone, of the Faces playing and touring as we're constantly being asked, plus perhaps a new Jones Gang album, organising more concerts at Hurtwood Park, continuing to look after the Small Faces back catalogue, chasing down those royalties, and ... and ... and ...

* * *

My earliest memory is of a dream I had aged three.

I'm in a basket, carried by a stork, soaring over London chimney pots. Now we are swooping along the Thames, I can see the docks, the ships, the men unloading. Looking ahead, there's Buckingham Palace. That's where we are going, that's my destiny. So why is the stork slowing down? Circling above these houses. It's tired. Confused. Come on lazy, not much further. Keep going. Just along the river. The big building. The one with the flag on top. But no, the circles are descending, I smell coffee, see a paper mill belching out thick smoke. We're landing. My basket is gently settled on to a doorstep. I look up. I can see the house number, 34.

Since then, I've been looking for that bird. I used to say that if I ever found it, I'd wring its bleedin' neck. I never meant that. If one day I do track down the stork, I'll be thanking it with all my heart. Without it, I would never have embarked on this adventure. And it's far from over. There's plenty more to come.

Time to get on with the next chapter of my life.

ACKNOWLEDGEMENTS

I have sat down on many occasions over the years intending to write this book, but it never seemed to be quite the right moment. Now, though, as I approach my seventieth birthday, I realised the time had finally arrived to give an account of my life in and around the music business. So far, of course!

It has been an emotional journey. One filled with laughter and tears as I remembered those who are no longer with us, both in the world of music and in my personal life, and those who have made my life complete. Of those I have lost, my mum and dad deserve the biggest mention. Without them I would not be who I am. And then of course there is Ronnie, Steve and Mac – 'my brothers in arms'. We created something very special. Aunt Floss, the last survivor of Mum's generation of Wards, you also deserve a very special mention, and my heartfelt thanks, for always keeping an eye out for me.

As the decades have passed, I have been fortunate to meet some exceptional people through music. I'd like to take this opportunity to thank them: my great friend Mark Singer, who has supported me so well; Rod Cousens, for his keen enthusiasm and unwavering support; Rod and Woody, for being there throughout all these years and for your long-standing friendships; the boys in The Jones Gang – Robert Hart, Rick Wills, Pat Davey, Josh Phillips, Jim Stapley, Johnson Jay, Dave (Bucket) Colwell, Mark Read and Nick Cook – we have had such fun!

I would also like to thank Val Weedon, who has been there since the beginning. A big hug and kiss to you, Val, for your support over all the years. Val and Pauline Corcoran ran the Small Faces Fan Club and looked after us incredibly well. Pauline sadly passed away in 2016, but Val continues with her hard work and enthusiasm on behalf of our band's loyal fanbase. Thanks also to John Fisher for his meticulous work in charting my whereabouts over the last 50 years or so, David Wilson for all his detail and research for this book, Maggie Hanbury, my literary agent, and Mark Taylor, who keeps my finances in order – or tries to!

Special thanks to Professor Stephen Langley, for guiding me through my prostate cancer treatment and saving my life.

A big thank you to all the team at Blink Publishing and Thomas Dunne Books, for believing in this story.

Of course, mention must also be made of some other very important people who have joined me on my journey and made my life better: Bill Wyman, Allan Love, John Lodge, Mike and Angie Rutherford, Jimmy and Pauline Tarbuck, Bill Curbishley, Bill Harrison (gone, but certainty not forgotten), Grahame Goudie (what would I or my drums do if you weren't there for us?), Jim Davidson, Steve and Gillie Lamprell. The list is endless, and if I have forgotten anyone, I am sorry. It's a lovely problem to worry about. I count myself extremely lucky to have such a wonderful and extensive group of friends.

My cousin Roy, who is more of a brother to me, has been there forever. I love him to bits. And my wife Jayne, who has been my rock for 38 years now. We have raised six children (Dylan, Jesse, Casey, Jay, Cody and Erin) together, along with the introduction of my grandchildren, Daisy-mae, Kaya, Bonnie, Zac, Fin – and a new one due any time.

I hope you enjoy reading my story as much as I enjoyed writing it.

INDEX

(In subentries, the initials KJ refer to Kenney Jones; JED to Jesse Ed Davis; RL to Ronnie Lane; RD to Roger Daltrey; SM to Steve Marriott; SFs to Small Faces; RS to Rod Stewart; PT to Pete Townshend; JW to Jimmy Winston; RW to Ronnie Wood)